The Unenviable

Stories of Psychological Trauma and Hardship among Immigrants and their Families

David G. Mirich, Ph.D.

SAKURA PUBLISHING
Hermitage, Pennsylvania
USA

The Unenviable

Stories of Psychological Trauma and
Hardship among Immigrants and their
Families

David G. Mirich, Ph.D.

The Unenviable: Stories of Psychological Trauma and Hardship among Immigrants and their Families Copyright © 2014 by David Mirich All rights reserved. Published in the United States by Sakura Publishing in 2014. No part of this publication may be reproduced, distributed, or transmitted in any form or by any means, including photocopying, recording, or other electronic or mechanical methods, without the prior written permission of the publisher, except in the case of brief quotations embodied in critical reviews and certain other noncommercial uses permitted by copyright law. For permission requests, write to the publisher, addressed "Attention: Permissions Coordinator," at the address below.

Sakura Publishing
PO BOX 1681
Hermitage, PA 16148
www.sakura-publishing.com

Ordering Information:
Quantity sales: Special discounts are available on quantity purchases by corporations, associations, and others. For details, contact the publisher at the address above. Orders by U.S. trade bookstores and wholesalers. Please contact Sakura Publishing: Tel: (330) 360-5131; or visit www.sakura-publishing.com.

Edit by Derek Vasconi | Cover Art by Cecilia RL & Rania Meng

First Edition
Printed in the United States of America

ISBN-13: 978-0-9911807-4-5
ISBN-10: 0991180747

FOREWORD

Immigration, and what to do with the very large number of people residing in the U.S. and arriving to the U.S. every day with undocumented status, has commanded considerable attention for decades, and increasingly has been the subject of breaking stories in the news. At the time *The Unenviable* was written, President Obama announced that comprehensive immigration reform remained a top priority for the year.

We are at the cutting edge of major changes as many states already have enacted precedent-setting legislation. On the horizon: the Dream Act, high-skilled visas, driver's licenses for undocumented drivers, slowing down deportations, providing a mechanism of legalization for undocumented immigrants that does not lead to citizenship, and DACA (Deferred Action for Childhood Arrivals). There also have been recent changes in U.S. asylum laws.

Working in the field of immigration demands an awareness of and sensitivity to diversity and cultural competence. It is essential that the needs of undocumented immigrants and family members affected by their possible removal, asylum seekers, and victims of spousal abuse and domestic violence be adequately met, and that they not encounter untoward barriers to access needed services. And, consistent with the tenets of cultural and diversity-based competence, it is imperative that those who work with these individuals receive proper training about the populations they serve, the conditions in their countries, and specific problems they face. This obligation also extends to interpreters as their assistance often is required because of a language barrier.

I had the pleasure of meeting David Mirich recently, about a year ago. Ours was a "virtual" meeting, as we interacted through the listserv of the Hispanic Neuropsychological Society. It was in the context of discussing some immigration-related themes that he introduced himself to me. We had much in common, both of us working closely with undocumented persons, and we were quick to forge a friendship. I was impressed not only with his expertise and wisdom, but perhaps even more by his passion and drive to work with individuals facing an array of immigration difficulties, and his compassion and zeal to put this book out for them and make their plight known to others. I felt honored when he asked me to write this brief foreword.

So, how is this book different? David provides a refreshing approach that delves into the lives of many undocumented individuals, and poignantly tells their stories, reflecting on their hardships, dreams, and hopes.

You will learn about 11-year-old Daniel's terrible nightmares and fear that his father might be killed if he returns to Mexico. After all, a friend of his father's had been killed in Mexico not long ago. In his sadness, Daniel came to harbor a sense of hopelessness reflected by his not showering or changing clothes, and simply not caring about anything.

Lourdes, for her young age (only 17), was responsible for her nine-month-old baby and cared for her disabled sister who spent her time between a wheelchair and bed. Lourdes worked and attended school. Despite her outward strength, Lourdes was being torn apart inside. She was an American citizen not facing deportation to Mexico. Yet, she could see no alternative but to accompany her mother and sister if they were removed. And she worried very much about what would happen to all of them and was terrified about the possibility of being victims of violence. Moreover, how would her sister's many medical needs be tended to?

Javier, a 30-year-old man, told the story as the tears flowed of how he had been abused by his wife, the woman he loved and believed loved him too. The abuse began insidiously. She started coming home late and was intoxicated regularly. The late outings progressed to entire weekends. Soon enough she became insulting and demeaning towards him. The insults escalated into violence and she pushed, hit, slapped, and kicked Javier, and threatened to have him deported if he didn't let her have her way. Despite her threatening to kill him with a knife, Javier stayed in the relationship and put up with the abuse, fearful of what might happen if he didn't, and hoping that she'd change. She did not, however, change. In fact, things got worse, and one day Javier came home to an empty apartment. She was gone and had taken all their things. Adding insult to injury, she continued to call Javier and told him he owed her money and demanded that he pay for things she bought.

Nadia, who is more than 30 years old, became aware of her interest in women when she was 18 years old living in Eastern Europe. Amidst rumors that she was lesbian, the Dean of Students ordered her to stay away from the young woman she had fallen in love with, and her father beat her upon finding out. The relationship ended tragically when Nadia's lover's brother stabbed his sister to death. In the end, it was Nadia who was arrested while the brother, who murdered his own sister, became a hero. Nadia brought shame to her family in a culture that ostracizes lesbians. An empty shell and freak of nature, Nadia was spat on and yelled at and treated like an abomination. Things got so bad for Nadia that she knew she had to leave and sought refuge in the U.S. Far from finding immediate relief in the U.S., however, Nadia twice attempted to take her own life. Nadia continued to have nightmares and was terrified at the aspect of being deported.

The title of the book, *The Unenviable*, conveys a picture of a class of human beings that is unwanted, undesirable.

The stories about Daniel, Lourdes, Javier, and Nadia, to name a few that are in this book, are touching. The reader is left with the following conundrum: what will it take to make the unenviable, the undesirable, enviable and desirable?

Read the book and find out.

- Roy Aranda, Psy.D., J.D.

Dr. Roy Aranda is both a neuropsychologist and an attorney and has been a widely recognized as an expert in these areas. He has made presentations in the fields of psychology and law across the country and internationally as well. He has written for a wide variety of publications and as received many honors for his work. He is a bilingual Spanish speaker and has worked extensively in performing evaluations with individuals with cases involving immigration status, as well as in the forensic arena with violent offenders and sex offenders.

Table Of Contents

DISCLAIMER

The narratives in this book came directly from psychological evaluations performed on individuals seeking legal residency in the United States. They are rewritten in the first person, and all names and even places have been changed to protect the privacy of the individuals evaluated.

Preface

I have long wanted to share these stories of immigrants to the United States as a way to help Americans to better understand the lives of these nameless people we refer to as "undocumented workers," "illegal aliens," or even, "illegals." These particular stories are somewhat out of the ordinary however; as they are derived from psychological evaluations I performed for immigration legal cases. It is the purview of the psychological profession that its practitioners deal with the dark shadows and experiences inherent in the human personality. As such, the narratives in this book are significantly compelling and even shocking in the depths of suffering these individuals have endured; including severe abuse, cruelty, and persecution. These cases are highly complex matters and often involve the lives and well-being of American-born citizens.

I am neither an advocate for my clients, nor have I involved myself politically in voicing my personal views concerning immigration policy. I consider myself to be an unbiased professional who performs a comprehensive psychological evaluation on clients referred to me. I don't accept all referrals, as many times I do not find that a case has any compelling features. Additionally, I find that immigration attorneys most typically refer to me the "winnable" cases. I then comment on my findings in my reports and in court testimony as an expert witness. I have proven over the years that my work is solid and my judgment sound.

That being said, I find my work in this area has tremendous personal resonance. My own grandparents struggled with immigration status long after their arrival in this country, though the historical circumstances and context are somewhat different. Years ago I set out to document their lives and through visiting Montenegro, the country of their birth in Eastern Europe. This experience gave me a unique understanding of immigrants and the reasons that lead to illegal immigration. Additionally, like the people in the stories that follow, my own family history has been marked by individuals with significant psychological challenges. I too have suffered abuse and neglect as a child which I documented in the book "Losing my Mind: Dark Secrets of a Wounded Healer."

My aim in writing this book is to illuminate for the reader the intricacies of the immigration system which affects the lives of us all. These stories are part of American history and the tapestry of daily life. This is not only because immigration is central to the story of the United States, but because immigration policy is an ongoing piece of the American political and cultural landscape. While the particular individuals and nationalities change over time, their stories and motivations for migrating remain the same. In the introduction I will attempt to explain some important distinctions as to how things work in the immigration process so that the reader can better understand the system, as well as my role in it. However, I am not a legal expert and can only give my bird's-eye viewpoint from having worked in the field for more than 14 years.

Introduction

This book contains several dramatic human stories derived from psychological evaluations used to discern "extreme hardship" or "exceptional and extremely unusual hardship" for immigration cases. Rewritten and reorganized into linear, first person narratives, the evaluations become miniature memoirs that depict the lives of ordinary people who hope to attain security, safety, and stability in the United States. The narratives begin with an account of the patients' childhood experiences and family life. Then, they trace the circumstances that led to how they entered the United States illegally or, for US citizens and legal residents, when their immigrant loved ones entered their lives. The stories then follow the trajectory of their lives up to the point in which the development of their legal cases prompted the need for a psychological evaluation. Each narrative begins with my impressions and initial dialogue with the patient and ends with concluding remarks on the case and known outcomes.

Legally, the stories fall into two broad categories. The first is of undocumented immigrants seeking legal residency based on the hardship they would experience if they were to be deported or "removed." The second is of Americans who have become reliant on undocumented immigrants and who face significant adversity if their loved ones are deported or removed. The evaluations are part of larger court cases to determine if sufficient evidence exists to allow an immigrant to stay in the United States. In many cases, my assessments constitute the most important evidence the court will hear regarding the hardships associated with "removal."

The United States Congress has written laws that determine the complex parameters within which an applicant for legal permanent residency can qualify to remain in the United States. One form of relief often used in immigration court is called "cancellation of removal" or "suspension of deportation." Undocumented immigrants must meet elaborate criteria to become lawful residents. First, they must have already resided in the country for seven (suspension of deportation) or ten (cancellation of removal) years. This requirement often complicates many of these narratives, as the lives of illegal immigrants have become embedded with American citizens and legal residents. This makes the threat of deportation quite harrowing and complicated for themselves and their families.[1]

---

[1] The legal counting of the years is subject to a little-known law called the "stop-time rule," which stops counting time for the immigrant the moment he or she is served with immigration court papers or, alternatively, the moment he or she commits a deportable offense, like shop-lifting or domestic violence, or working with a fake ID. This is important because immigration court cases sometimes drag on for years. But by legal magic (the stop-time rule) those years don't count toward eligibility for suspension or cancellation despite the fact that the person is actually right here in the US, often working and raising a family of citizen

Second, they must be of good moral character. This means they must adhere to the laws of the country; in particular, they must not have committed deportable offenses, of which there are far too many to list here. Immigrants or their loved ones must be very aware of statutory time limits for filing their cases, and it is critical for them to be guided by a skilled immigration attorney in order to navigate these complexities.

My assessments are concerned primarily with the third criteria; that of determining "extreme hardship" for "suspension of deportation" or "exceptional and extremely unusual hardship" for "cancellation of removal" applications. Such applications are based on the psychological profiles of individuals affected by the deportation or removal of an undocumented immigrant. In suspension cases the hardship of the immigrant may also be considered, but not in cancellation cases. In cancellation cases only the hardship of the immediate family who are deemed "qualifying family members" (and who must also be citizens or lawful permanent residents) is weighed. It is worth noting that suspension cases ended in 1997. Then Congress changed the hardship standard from "extreme hardship" to "exceptional and extremely unusual hardship." After 1997 the cases became much more difficult for the immigrant, which was what Congress intended at that time.

---

children. Explaining such legal "mumbo-jumbo" to poor, uneducated immigrants is nearly impossible. They must take it on faith.

In another context, the "extreme hardship" standard is still regularly applied. This is the "waiver" context. Waivers are complex legal applications used regularly in my cases for persons "adjusting status" through a family member. A very common waiver we use is found at Immigration and Nationality Act (INA) Section 212(h). We call it an I-601 waiver because immigration form I-601 is used to apply for it. Within the legal definition of an I-601 waiver, "extreme hardship" means that deportation or removal would seriously jeopardize the well-being of a spouse, fiancée, parent, or child under 21 years of age, who is a citizen or a legal permanent resident of the United States. A provisional waiver allows Mexican immigrants to voluntarily go to Ciudad Juarez, across the border from El Paso, Texas, in order to apply for a visa for legal reentry into the United States; reentry still requires proof of extreme hardship. Waivers are applied in many contexts, both in the US and abroad.

Other more complex laws provide temporary or permanent residency to immigrants, documented or otherwise, who face persecution or torture if they are deported to their native country, such as in asylum cases. Another kind of case involves immigrants who were victims of crimes committed by a citizen or a legal permanent resident of the United States, such as domestic violence. Here a U-Visa may be granted or in some cases the victim can self-petition under the Violence Against Women

Act (VAWA). It should be noted that men also qualify for protection under VAWA.

Federal immigration judges and other authorities within the Department of Justice and the Department of Homeland Security daily make decisions that have a profound effect on the lives of "illegal" immigrants. Considerations to determine extreme hardship include exposure to crimes, financial, medical, and in a relatively small number of cases, psychological factors. The psychological evaluations discern and elucidate the problems and issues that affect a person's ability to function in the world in a stable manner. The immigration judge's concern is whether the immigrant's or U.S. citizen or resident's mental or physical health might deteriorate even further if they or their loved one is deported. Hence, the evaluations apprise the court of psychological hardships and may influence the formulation of the decision to deport or to extend legal temporary or permanent residency.

The psychological evaluations that I perform characteristically document long-standing or pre-existing issues with depression, post-traumatic stress, learning disorders, health problems, or other afflictions. For immigrants, they may require the continuation of a type of quality medical, psychological, or special educational service that is not available to them in their home country. For the U.S. citizen or legal resident who is dependent on a loved one that happens to be an undocumented immigrant, deportation might place them under undue stress because their lives will become seriously disrupted in the absence of the immigrant spouse or relative.

Sadly, the emotional hardship due to the separation of family members is considered a "normal" consequence of not following the rules of legal immigration. Loss of employment, the forced relocation of a family, and the loss of the family home because the undocumented resident is forcibly returned to the country of origin, whether "voluntary" or not, do not usually constitute "extreme hardship" or "exceptional and extremely unusual hardship" without a lot more proof. Serious mental health issues that U.S. citizens or residents suffer, such as the resultant depression due to being separated from a family member, also do not usually qualify as adequate hardship. However, a pre-existing history of depression or some other mental health disorder, along with the resurgence of chronic symptoms, may sometimes be considered adequate hardship, depending on the facts of the individual case, which is where my work becomes essential.

The reports that I provide to the immigration court reveal the history of trauma, violence, abuse, and the subsequent emotional and mental struggles that stem from these experiences. Typically, as an expert witness, my testimony in court concerns the mental health history and condition of U.S. citizen or resident patients and how they might be affected if their undocumented spouse is deported. Alicia and Gino are examples of such cases. In the case of 63-year-old Andrea, the need for in-home medical care, handled by her spouse, is a consideration as well. Refugio, an elderly Mayan, is highly dependent on his young son who faced deportation. Unfortunately, in many cases the fear of deportation can push someone with a history of mental health struggles to the brink of a psychological breakdown that follow a predictable course and often results in a bad outcome. The stories of Karina and Maria are examples of this type of situation. Additionally, the potential impact on a U.S.-born child of such disorders as depression or anxiety that may result from being separated from a parent may be considered adequate hardship, as in the cases of Daniel, Lourdes, and Sara.

Quite incredibly, the separation of parents and small children is not routinely considered adequate hardship. An example is that of Maria, mentioned above, whose child requires frequent medical attention. Her husband returned to his country of origin on a lengthy "voluntary deportation" to await the outcome of his case and is no longer is able to support the family financially. Conversely, a judge may choose to suspend deportation or cancel removal due to the potential impact on U.S.-born children resulting from the deportation or removal of a parent who came here illegally.

Cases of abuse and cruelty to an immigrant by a citizen or permanent legal resident of the United States is a category of hardship that makes one eligible for a temporary U-Visa. The immigrant may be the victim in a qualifying crime and have aided the prosecution in some way.[2] The law allows for relief in such cases, as the U.S. legislature has correctly determined that it is not right for a U.S. citizen or resident to mistreat and abuse an immigrant, regardless of their residency status. As an example; Angela's employer ignored requests to be paid for work performed, in violation of the Fair Labor Standards Act, and then reported Angela to Homeland Security to have her deported in order to avoid paying her wages.

An undocumented, foreign-born spouse who has suffered victimization at the hands of an abusive and cruel American citizen or resident that threatens to have the spouse or former spouse deported presents a compelling case. Although the threat might rarely be carried out, it provides a powerful lever for coercion, and even extortion. For men, this can mean that they work for the benefit of a controlling wife, as in the case of Javier and Fernando, both from Mexico. A'mer, a Syrian, was threatened with the loss of his Green Card if he did not pay his short-term wife $10,000. In the story of Nalin, from India, his in-laws, also from India, controlled his movements and extorted all of his earnings from employment.

Immigrants are subject to various forms of cruelty and abuse, such as in the cases of Delia, Raquel, and Seo-Yeon. Delia, and Raquel suffered

---

[2] The prosecutor must certify the U-visa application.

constant humiliation and emotional abuse, and Seo-Yeon suffered sexual abuse and rape during her short marriage to an older American man. These women are protected by the VAWA, which included a provision that allows those being abused by their American or legal resident spouses to apply to have their resident status changed. Please note that the cases covered in this book involve a more subtle discernment of abuse than the outright physical battering that tends to be documented by police reports.

A special category of narratives illustrates the abuse suffered by "mail-order brides" from Eastern Europe; Dina, Ilie, and Tatiana. These women found themselves with men who were isolative, abusive and alcoholic–after it was too late. U.S. citizens or resident men can sign up with an International Marriage Organization (IMO) and pay these for-profit businesses for the opportunity to choose a bride that they can bring to the United States–hence the term, "mail-order brides." Men browse agency listings and pictures and choose from among hundreds of women. For their part, women enter into these marriages because they wish to gain the American Dream of freedom and opportunity for themselves and their children or future children.

The United States has always been a place where people sought to escape political or religious persecution, in groups and as individuals. By the late twentieth century, political asylum became a human rights issue, as being forced to return to the country of origin could place the life of the immigrant in imminent danger. These concerns were recognized internationally through the auspices of the United Nations, which established its own laws and guidelines. In the United States, Congress codified methods to allow individuals threatened with harm related to their race, ethnicity, religion, political viewpoint, or social identity to apply for temporary visas or permanent residency, even if they arrived in the United States illegally.

Although these narratives include complete personal histories, the legal system is typically not concerned whatsoever about the undocumented immigrant or anything concerning any hardship caused by deportation or removal. Usually it is only in the cases of applicants seeking asylum that the court wants to know about the details of their lives. In political asylum cases, many times the immigrant has developed psychological problems, such as post-traumatic stress disorder from the experiences of persecution or violence including torture. The stories of Bijal, a Sikh from India; Leon, from Rwanda; and Nicolae, a Romanian, are examples of these kinds of experiences. A lesbian, gay, bisexual or transgendered (LGBT) sexual orientation is a cause for persecution in some countries as reflected in the narratives of Abraham, from Guatemala, and Nadia, from a former Soviet Republic, as well as 20-year-old Andres who arrived in the United States with his immigrant parents at the age of five.

Marco, a hermaphrodite, escaped persecution in El Salvador for his unique sexual situation.

Asylum cases in this book include several Central American immigrants who suffered from political or gang violence, often since childhood. Oftentimes gang violence arose as the political turmoil subsided leaving no safe opportunities to return to the native country. Abelino, Alejandro, and Dario are examples of Central American refugees who faced extortion upon return to their country. Another example is Esteban, a soldier in the Mexican Army for eight years who faced certain death for refusing to join a cartel after the military no longer required his service.

Many of the narratives concern how well a child would fare in the parents' native country, contributing to a sense of impending calamity. As a bilingual teacher who spent time in the public schools in various countries, I saw firsthand the daunting issues facing families returning to their home country. For instance, if the child does not know how to speak, read or write in the parent(s)' native language, such a child may not be able to receive an adequate education in the parents' home country. Effective schooling in a different language will be all but impossible for them. Most children do not attend school beyond the sixth grade in these Third World countries as they are needed by the family to work. They have fees to pay and uniforms and supplies to buy. They encounter an impossible competition with the hierarchy of parents who have long been part of the fabric of the neighborhood school and who have secured for their own children the few available benefits.

Children also face other sociocultural and sociopolitical problems. Once in their parents' country of origin, these American children are seen as foreigners. They are referred to as "Americans" who speak the native language poorly. They dress differently, think differently and simply don't fit in. These young Americans are ill-prepared for the cultural shock of such a forced relocation, let alone the prevailing issues of poverty, gangs and violence. The kidnapping of such people who once lived in the United States is not unheard of because they are thought to have some money. When the American-born children inevitably return one day to the United States upon their eighteenth birthday, their English skills will have fossilized, and they will be ill-equipped to compete with others their age that completed their education in the U.S. and formed longstanding social and occupational contacts. These problems are a special concern for older children, as young children are assumed by the court to be able to "adapt" if they were to be forced to accompany their parents to their country of origin. Sadly, this very obvious form of hardship is seldom considered sufficient in and of itself.

If a child is receiving Special Education services in the United States, a judge may take such circumstances into consideration. I have evaluated many U.S.-born special-needs children of illegal immigrants who require special educational, physical or mental health support. The special needs of their children are often the only reason that undocumented workers even have a chance of remaining here in the United States. One of Delia's children, a legal resident, requires mental health services unavailable in the small town where she was born in Mexico. Many other stories could be included in this book if space and time allowed. The narratives are not proportionally representative of the evaluations that I conduct. For instance, only a relatively small number of mail-order bride evaluations exist in my caseload. The wives or husbands who are citizens or legal residents and whose spouse is or may be deported constitute the lion's share of cases referred to me. Most stories in this book are of young people in their twenties and thirties, and in my experience this basically describes the typical age group seeking legal residency. The stories that follow are derived from among the most compelling of the hundreds of psychological evaluations that I have conducted back to the year 2000.

This introduction provides an outline of the various forms of "hardship" endured by my patients. Beyond the legal framework, the narratives contained in this book recount the unique circumstances of individuals suffering from extensive psychological trauma. The stories are presented in a linear, stream of consciousness style in order to convey the intense emotional nature of these sagas. The "voice" in each story may not sound uniquely different to the reader, as the primary goal is to provide a clear account of the experiences of violence and abuse. Yet, the narratives do not end with such horrors. Most often, immigration to the United States has positive consequences. This is true for the American citizens whose lives become intertwined with an undocumented immigrant, as well as for the undocumented immigrant who finds relief from the past through a new life in the United States. In this way, these narratives present much like oral histories that tell us something about immigration as well as psychology in contemporary American culture. What they all have in common is powerful drama and human courage to restore mental health in their lives.

The immigrants who come to me for a psychological evaluation are always referred by a private attorney. For individuals seeking political asylum or in cases of an extreme hardship waiver, mental health issues can best be validated through a psychological evaluation. In addition to a clinical interview, a mental status exam, and other specific instruments are often employed. Personality inventories, such as the Minnesota Multiphasic Personality Inventory-2nd Edition (MMPI-2) and the Millon Clinical Multiphasic Inventory Third Edition (MCMI-III), are typically used. The Beck Depression Inventory (BDI) and the Trauma Symptom Inventory (TSI) are often employed as means to substantiate the client's complaints of psychological distress.

Additionally, I often administer an IQ test and other cognitive instruments in the cases of potential neuropsychological disorders, including traumatic brain injury, learning disorders, and dementia, as they relate to the legal case and the referral question. I have been trained in best-practices and in the area of the assessment of the linguistically and culturally diverse. I have developed college curriculum in bilingual assessment, theory, research and practice, and have instructed at the university level. I follow the American Psychological Association standards and guidelines in this area and am well-versed in the selection and use of appropriate instruments and interpretation of the data and results.

When available, previous psychiatric and medical records are examined in order to confirm the individual's statements about their psychological history or condition. In some cases, interviews with relatives or friends provide insight into the psychological condition of the person seeking legal residency for themselves or a family member. On occasion, I might even require a potential client to submit to a polygraph examination in order to verify certain claims the individual has made. I do not accept cases in which I have any doubt as to the veracity of the character of the person seeking my services.

Hardship if Undocumented Family Member is Deported

DANIEL

Daniel is quite small for his age, far too small. His thin, almost frail looking build resembled that of a much younger child, not the ten-year-old boy that he was. There was a dense cloud of sadness hanging over this child, dimming his bright, inquisitive eyes.

Daniel didn't speak much. He hardly spoke at all, actually. His mother told me that Daniel had always been quiet in comparison to other children, but had almost stopped talking altogether once he learned that his father could be deported to Mexico and the family separated. I turned to look at Daniel and asked him, "Is this true?" He simply stared at the floor. He was in bad shape.

It wasn't hard to spot the clinical depression that was taking over this child's life—and at such a young age it was quite rare to see it at this level. Daniel was slow and lethargic in his movements to the point where even his words and understanding were impossibly slow. "He didn't used to be like this" his mother told me.

"Oh, I bet," was the first thing that came out of my mouth.

I knew from experience that this kind of depression demanded an outlet for every single one

19

*of his dark feelings. I knew the quiet, frail child
sitting in front of me was unlikely to be this silent
and passive all of the time—he must have some kind
of a release for all of the heavy misery that he
carried inside.*

*Daniel's mother told me that Daniel had become
progressively more irritable and even violent with
everyone in the family (aha! There it was). She told
me of how Daniel gets into fits of anger where he
will yell at everyone and even throw things around
the house. "He says he wants to die," she told me
somewhat hesitantly; "he says it all the time."*

*Daniel became increasingly tenser in his chair
as his mother described his behaviors. She had put
him in the hot seat and there was nothing he could
do about it. He knew he couldn't throw a fit of rage
in here, outside of the safety of his home. Daniel
looked tremendously uncomfortable. He bit his lip
and braced himself as his mother and I spoke. He
knew that soon it would be his time to speak.*

My name is Daniel and I'm only 11 years old. I
don't know what I'm supposed to say about my life;
I haven't been around all that long.

I am afraid of sleeping. I've had constant
nightmares ever since I can remember and lately
they've become much worse. I wake up in the
middle of the night drenched in sweat, my hands

aching from balling them into fists, my fingernails digging into my palms.

I wake up startled and afraid—I often don't know where I am and I can't help but scream in terror. Everything is dark around me at those times. My mom says she sees me hold my head and cry in my sleep. She tells me that she wants to wake me up, but she knows I'm panicked and terrified when I first open my eyes. She tells me that she doesn't want to make me feel that way so she just holds me and cries too. She doesn't know how to help me.

I've never been able to make friends. I don't understand other kids—not even my own brothers and sisters. I look at the other kids at school and they don't seem to have any problems. They play and joke around and seem so different than me. I never feel like playing; I don't think I've even tried to make a joke this week. I'm always so tired and angry at everything—it's all pointless to me. It bothers me that other kids are so happy and don't seem to have a care in the world. I've never felt that way, much less nowadays. I wish I was like the kids in the movies and escape my waking life by dreaming of spaceships and adventures, but I don't even get to do that—instead I get nightmares every night.

Even though I don't care too much about school, I still do okay. I turn in most of my homework on time and I don't get failing grades. School is pretty easy. My parents are always pushing me to do better though, and I resent that–the pressure. It's not that I don't understand what I'm being taught; it's just that I don't care. I don't care about anything.

It's weird to feel so different from even your own siblings. It makes me think that there's something wrong with me. I don't even know how to show people that I love them. I see my sisters hugging and kissing my parents, but I can't even bring myself to do that. I feel so far away from them, so far from everyone else.

Things began to get bad for me in the fourth grade. I just got angrier and angrier to the point where I couldn't stand people. I couldn't stand my teacher trying to explain the class and I couldn't stand the classmates around me. I was so tired of feeing small in every way, so different and less than everyone else. I could tell I was getting close to something exploding inside me. Something not good.

My teachers weren't happy with the way I was in class, so they began to call my parents in to speak to them and I got in trouble when they came home from those meetings. I think my parents wanted to help me, but they didn't know how. They tried talking to me, offering me rewards, yelling at me, punishing me… but nothing worked. I was even surprised myself. I didn't know what was wrong with me; I'd get so frustrated with everyone and especially with myself that I would burst out crying. I felt so desperate.

Then things got really bad when my dad's legal case began and I was told he might have to go back to Mexico. I didn't know how to even begin understanding that; I still don't know how to understand that. What does that mean? My dad goes to Mexico and we never see him again? They send him down there and we have to go too? I know there are lots of bad people down there, drugs lords and thugs... I see it on the television. What if we get killed? My dad's friend was killed in Mexico not long ago—I heard my parents talking one night; they thought I was asleep. I guess some bad guys asked my dad's friend for money, but he didn't have any. They kept coming at him asking for money, but since he didn't have anything to give them one day the bad guys showed up and shot him.

We don't have any money either. What's gonna happen to us?

Something clicked inside me and I lost it. I began to take it out on other kids at school and I would get into fights for no reason. Small and skinny as I am, I was so angry I beat most of them up. Their parents would later call my parents and I would get in a lot of trouble. I felt like the bad apple in the family, and yet I couldn't stop myself. I didn't know how else to deal with things. I wanted others to stop laughing and playing; I wanted them to feel as bad as I was so someone could understand and help me.

My parents didn't know what to do with me and I didn't know what to tell them. They spoke with the school counselor and I began counseling sessions there once a week. She then referred me to another counselor lady outside of school, and also to a guy called Dr. Berger. He put me on some medicine that he said was gonna help me feel better. Prozac, it's called.

It's been about four months since then and I'm still going to counseling. It took me a while to get comfortable with it, but it's helped. I still get angry, but not as much, and I haven't fought with other kids in a long time. I just mostly feel sad. I'm quiet and I just want to be left alone in my room. I have a lot to think about, so that's how I spend my time—thinking.

The counselor lady seems to care and she has good things to say sometimes, but I still feel like no one understands me. I can't stop thinking about what will happen to us if the judge says my dad can't stay. I'm scared. I don't want my dad to go to Mexico and get shot like his friends or the people in the news. I don't want any of us to have to live there—I don't even speak Spanish that well. I know I don't have friends and I never feel like doing much here, but at least I feel safe and we are all together.

I feel like those little dogs that get taken away from their mother after they're born; no one asked them if it was okay because they're animals. No one ever asked us if this was okay. Why does some stranger get to come and take my dad away?

My mom says I don't care about being a boy. She complains because I don't want to shower and I don't bother to change my clothes. I just don't care. Maybe I don't feel like a boy anymore; maybe I feel like one of those little dogs that are gonna get separated from their mom and dad no matter what they want.

The counselor lady tried to talk to me about me telling people that I want to die. She said my parents were very sad and worried about that because they loved me and wanted me around, so I tried to stop saying it. But I just haven't stopped feeling that way, though. If my dad has to go... I just really don't wanna be around anymore.

I heard my parents talk about where we could live if the judge says my father has to go to Mexico, and they couldn't come up with anything. Then my dad said it would be safer and better for us to stay here if he has to go. That way we would have a place to live and go to school and I could keep going to counseling and the doctor.

I don't know how we would live here while my dad is in Mexico; my mom doesn't work—she's got her hands full with all of us. I heard my dad say that he wouldn't know how to keep us safe or even feed us if we followed him to Mexico, but he also didn't know how we would make it here on our own. It's too much for them, all of this. It's definitely too much for me.

...

Daniel is by far one of the most severe cases of childhood Major Depression I've seen in some time. By now, his social development has been stunted and his psychiatric issues have reached a critical level. He is not even an adolescent yet; if his condition cannot be effectively treated and the acuteness of his symptoms reduced, I would expect things to get completely out of hand for Daniel and his parents.

Here's the thing about Daniel: it's very clear to me that he has suffered from severe dysthymia for many years—a low-grade, long-term form of depression. His father's legal situation only made matters worse. In fact, it was the very event that pushed Daniel over the edge and into his very own abyss of depressive symptoms and suicidal ideation.

Mental health problems in children typically don't simply go away with time; they only become worse and multiply as the children grow up. This is most certainly the case for Daniel, who unfortunately is in a Catch 22-type situation. Luckily for Daniel, his parents understand that it is vital for Daniel to receive professional mental health treatment for the long-term, and therefore it is imperative that he remain here in the United States. Unfortunately, this will do him very little good if his father's legal case (the very thing that pushed him over the edge) goes sour and his father is forced to return to Mexico. If the family were to follow Daniel's father to Mexico, he would not only lack the mental health services he critically requires, but this impoverished and violent environment would severely damage his already precarious condition.

Although Daniel's mental health struggles speak for themselves and ratifies the need for his family unit to remain stable, his case is yet to arrive at a resolution. Unfortunately for Daniel's father, his case was postponed and his next hearing won't take place for another year. The entire family is allowed to remain in the United States during this time, but their legal status remains unchanged for the time being.

I referred Daniel to a different counselor in the hopes that he could make a more meaningful (and hence, more helpful) connection during therapy. I also recommended to his parents that they take him for a medication update, as it appeared that his current dosage of Prozac was minimally effective. Daniel's parents felt so incredibly helpless regarding their son's situation that they were willing to follow through on any and all advice offered to them. The next year is a blessing for Daniel in that his family life will remain stable, although still quite tense.

I find it difficult to offer a prognosis for this child when life as he knows it (and that which he obsesses about) is still so very precariously hanging in the balance. Therapy and the right medical treatment could serve to stabilize and strengthen Daniel, and I hope that he progresses in leaps and bounds. He is only 11 years old.

Note: One year has gone by and the judge once again postponed any final decisions on this case for another six months. I have not seen Daniel yet, but I've been informed that he has continued with his mental health treatment and appears to be doing better. I only hope it's true.

ALICIA

Alicia was the boisterous kind, somewhat of a rare sight in my office. She was short and thin, with a vivacious look in her eyes and an exceptionally animated chatter. She and her husband contrasted one another almost perfectly. He trailed into the office right behind her, polite but reserved and wary in his demeanor. Something about his manner conveyed that he was no longer amused by Alicia's quirky behaviors.

It was extremely difficult at first to see past Alicia's lively and colorful presentation and I suspected that was exactly what she intended. Any attempt to approach the situation at hand was met directly by one of Alicia's jokes and friendly dismissals. Her reluctance to open up and speak of her inner states was evident and notable. I chipped away slowly for quite a while before she was ready to trust me and tell me her story.

Alicia's gregarious demeanor quickly dissolved and she began to exhibit anxiety symptoms almost automatically. Her left leg began to shake uncontrollably as her hand travelled towards her face while she chewed on her fingernails.

"I'm just not normal," she said, shaking all the while and tugging on the skin of her neck. "He thinks I'm crazy," pointing at her husband.

"We're all kind of 'crazy' in our own way," I told her, "We're all different."

After that statement she relaxed somewhat, hope and ease coming through very clearly through her eyes, almost as if saying; "Perhaps this time I won't be judged."

She looked at me for a short, silent moment and then gave a somewhat different smile. It wasn't the outgoing, energetic and sociable smile I saw when Alicia first walked in the office, but more of a calmer and accepting one. She had made peace with where she was at the moment and what was about to take place. Yet her leg continued to shake as she leaned back into her chair and gave a deep sigh.

"I'm really not okay. I know there's something wrong in my head, with my brain. I do think I'm going crazy sometimes," she told me as she gently played with her thumbs, her gaze fixed on her hands and her lips pressed into a straight line.

"Well, if there's ever a good place to be 'crazy' that would be here and now," I told her jokingly. She laughed and dried a tear from her right eye before it got a chance to roll down her cheek.

"Okay, doctor," she said, and with that we began.

My name is Alicia and I'm 34 years old. I was born in the United States, but my family returned to live in Mexico when I was barely a few months old. I grew up in a large village nearby Mazatlan with my six siblings. I was the second-oldest.

My father worked as a migrant field-worker in the United States and we only saw him for a month or two every year. I guess at first my mother and my oldest brother were able to travel and visit him regularly (that's how I was born in the United States), but as the family grew, our resources became scant. Over time my father became a ghost to us and when he would came home to visit he felt like a stranger.

My father sent my mom $200 every month to support the family. I don't know if that's all he had or if he didn't care to send more, but it just wasn't enough to go around. Oftentimes we didn't have shoes or proper clothes to wear and we'd spend weeks eating nothing but tortillas and beans. My mother took odd jobs as a seamstress whenever she could, just so she could buy some extra rice or eggs. I usually felt so dizzy and nauseated from hunger that I could barely keep myself awake.

I didn't do well in school. I was often sleepy and hungry, which made learning very difficult for me, especially when teachers tried to make an example out of me for not knowing the correct answers or nodding off during the lesson. I was the

31

laughingstock of the class and kids liked to pick on me for my old clothes and my ratty shoes. There was nothing I could do; I wanted to eat, I wanted to wear clean clothes and shoes without holes… I just didn't know how.

Shoes… I hated shoes. If I wasn't being made fun of because of my old shoes I was getting hit with one at home. My mom had to handle all seven of us on her own, so she had little patience and used very rough means of discipline to keep us in line. We tried to avoid her and her punishment, but we were kids nonetheless and we would get in trouble for one thing or another. I remember it like it was yesterday; getting hit in the back of the head by a flying shoe, getting spanked with my dad's old rubber sandals… my mom was a tough woman. She had to be—she was alone. I just wish she hadn't been so hard on us.

Ever since I was a little girl I was very uncomfortable with dirty things and injuries, but I never thought much of it—I thought I was just being a girl, as my brothers put it. I couldn't bring myself to play with dirt and I wouldn't go anywhere near the sticks and rods and rusty buckets my brothers played with. It wasn't so much that I didn't want to play their boy games –I just couldn't help but picturing the millions of bugs living on those things and couldn't bring myself to touch them. Just the thought of them sometimes made me feel as if they were already crawling all over my body, and I would quickly begin to feel dirty and dizzy.

I called it "the Yuck." Some things just gave me "the yuck," and I couldn't get anywhere near them. I was sure I would grow out of it someday and stop thinking of things that way, but I never did. It actually got worse as I got older and now I know it is completely out of control.

At first it was just discomfort. Dirt and little cuts and scrapes made me nervous, but I could take care of it by simply walking away. As I grew up the sight of blood or injuries began to make me tremble—quite visibly. The thought of diseases and bacteria would make me cry. It happened exactly opposite of how I thought it would be; as I grew older it became more difficult to calm myself down and keep my reactions under control.

My dad brought us to the United States when I was about 15 years old. I hoped that the new environment would take care of my severe reactions to things, but it didn't. For the first time in my life I felt hopeless about these fears that plagued me. Here I was in a brand-new world, and yet very little had changed for me. Dirt and disease and blood still terrified me; "the yuck" was still very much an ever-present part of my environment.

I navigated life as best I could for the following years. I met Jeronimo when I was 17 years old and we got married when I was 20. He thought that my quirks were cute –but by then for me they were a nightmare. I played it down though; I made fun of myself and turned my reactions into a comedy show so people wouldn't reject me for being so odd. I silently thought I was going crazy and I was afraid people would leave me if they knew how sick I was becoming with all of my phobias. It was lonely—so very lonely, and I had to keep it all inside.

I picked up a new fear after Jeronimo and I moved into an apartment by ourselves, and then to a house of our own; I could not control my mind and I lived terrified with the anticipation that a stranger was going to barge through the door and hurt us. This is when Jeronimo began to see the real side of me and it wasn't so cute anymore.

I had to have the doors and windows locked at all times; it was the only way I could be in the house in peace. It drove him mad; he couldn't take the trash out without me following to lock the door behind him as soon as he had both feet in the hallway. I would try to stop myself, but I just couldn't. I'd watch him run outside to the car and I would hold onto the kitchen counter to keep me from running behind him, but I couldn't control myself. Nor could I control checking doors and windows multiple times every day to make sure everything was still locked.

It created a lot of friction between us—my inability to do certain things. Jeronimo would get so frustrated just going in the car with me somewhere because I couldn't even let him drive in peace. I always felt nervous being a passenger, and just like with my house, I absolutely had to have the doors locked and the windows rolled up at all times, otherwise I would completely freak out. I'd break into a cold sweat and I'd have to ask to pull over and let me out of the car, regardless of where we were at the time.

I didn't think my marriage would last. I never thought anyone could spend the rest of their lives with someone like me. I thought Jeronimo would get fed up with my nuisances one day and leave me, but he never did. As much as I annoyed him with the ways I needed things to be, he patiently remained by my side. We even had three children together.

Jeronimo asked me start counseling, but I was reluctant to follow through with it. I didn't think my problem was something anyone could just "talk away;" I had been trying that on my own for years. I eventually agreed to begin seeing a therapist, however, because I felt like I owed Jeronimo to at least try. I went to counseling once a week for six weeks and it made no difference. As understanding as the woman tried to be, I couldn't truly open up with her and share all of my fears and compulsions. I really tried. I guess that I never trusted anyone but me, and now it was clear that I couldn't trust myself either. After six weeks I decided that Jeronimo and I were wasting his hard-earned money and I stopped going to counseling. That was a rough day; as reluctant as I had been to go see a therapist I had a tiny hope that maybe she could help me. I understood that day that no one was ever going to be able to help me.

Aside from my fear of strangers attacking us, I developed an impossible fear of being exposed to blood or disease; it has taken over my life to the point where I can't even touch anything red. If I see anything red on the floor, a sock, juice, a Tupperware lid, I have to walk around it and get away from it quickly.

Obviously, I can't be anywhere near blood, see it, or even think about it. I can't even say the word. Ever since my kids were little I taught them to call their cuts or scrapes "reds," because I can't handle the images on my mind and the sensations the word "blood" triggers in me. My family and Jeronimo have told me time and time again that diseases cannot be transferred with dried blood and I know that, but it doesn't matter. I can't deal with it; I just can't. I won't even allow my kids to carry glasses around with them because I'm petrified that they will break and someone would get cut... and red.

There's more. Germs. For most people, germs seem to be something you keep in mind when the situation calls for it, right? When you're away from home, or when things look dirty. I wish I were that way. For me, the image of germs teeming everywhere is constantly in the back of my head no matter what I'm doing, and it drives me insane. I can't touch things or just sit anywhere, let alone shake people's hands. I carry around a big bottle of hand sanitizer and I'm constantly using it; I buy a new one twice per week. My kids roll their eyes at me, because I have to label utensils and anything I use, otherwise I can't deal with the mental pictures of germs crawling over my body as I go grab something that wasn't just mine. Most people laugh when I tell these stories; I guess I try to downplay things because I'm scared that I might be crazy. Truthfully though, it makes me sick to even think about it and even though I'm a grown woman, more often than not it even makes me cry.

Everyone has someone who makes the world right for them. Who calms their world down during hardships and even helps bear the life's shortcoming. That's Jeronimo to me. I need him here. He's rarely shocked or amused at my quirks (even when they shock me) and that makes me feel normal. He treats me like there's nothing wrong with me, and even though we both know there is, I appreciate that. I have a whole world telling me that I'm a freak; I need a place to shelter myself and rest. He is that place for me.

He is also the only reason why this family is functional. I can't even hold down a job; I can't touch things, remember? I can't even imagine being around strangers and having to touch the things they touch. People don't get it, they think I'm crazy, or just plain lazy. Jeronimo is the only one who understands the severity of it and knows I'm not exaggerating. He's seen me try to work at restaurants and other places and he's seen me come home crying every day—he knows I can't do it.

I wouldn't be able to keep my kids in line without Jeronimo—they think I'm a joke. They think of me as their "crazy mom" who they have to humor because she can't touch things or see blood. They have little respect for me, if any. What would they become without my husband there to discipline them? They would run wild. How could I support them and give them a life here if I can't even work? What would happen to all of us without Jeronimo?

Take the engine out of the car, or the steering wheel, or the wheels—and the car won't work. Without Jeronimo, we would fall apart. We're so inept without him; it's not like he's the engine or the steering wheel, he's the whole car. We would have no choice but to follow him to Mexico if he had to go; my kids would have a better life anywhere with their dad than alone in the United States with me.

But what would that reality do to me? That crude, inhospitable, unclean reality… I really just don't know.

...

Alicia suffered from one of the most severe cases of obsessive compulsive disorder I have encountered in quite a long time. Over the years, living in such misery and fear has devolved into clinical depression. Tortured her entire life by compulsions she could not understand, Alicia grew up simply thinking she was "crazy," different, and she responded by isolating herself due to uncontrollable aversions to seemingly common situations.

It is the separation from others that truly damages us; making us feel alone in the world— misunderstood, helpless and hopeless. Regardless of how hard she tried, Alicia was unable to help herself and to attenuate the inexplicable behaviors that plagued her. The same demons that trapped her in this prison of her own mind ensured that she would be unable to present herself to others as having any semblance of normalcy.

Alicia's relationship with Jeronimo has been her one tie to having a semi-normal life, and it has only been due to Jeronimo's unequaled patience with her. He has long since resigned himself to accepting Alicia's state unconditionally—he loves her deeply, and I could easily see why. She is not only exotically beautiful, but has such an effervescent and delightful personality. She certainly lights up any room she enters and everyone loves her.

But underlying that brilliant smile and jovial banter is a deep sadness and fear that her condition is incurable. She had lived untreated and unmedicated the majority of her life. Alicia had known no other adequate support system or healthy male figure other than Jeronimo, and she had built her entire adult life around him—to the point where she simply felt unequipped to deal with even basic daily living arrangements without him. This crippling state of fear and feelings of ineptitude and inadequacy has rendered Alicia incapable of holding down a job, forcing her and her children to be completely dependent on Jeronimo.

In the case of her husband's deportation, whatever little sense of peace and normalcy Alicia enjoys at the moment would inescapably fall from her grasp if she were forced to follow Jeronimo to Mexico. Not only is Mexico the land where her initial traumas took root, but the omnipresent poverty and violence of that place would compound her fears and phobias and would certainly render her non-functional. A forced relocation to her home country would trigger long-repressed traumas and present as an inescapable breeding ground to her already consuming and misunderstood compulsions. While it is true that Alicia has felt conflicted regarding availing herself to professional help. But if she is relocated to Mexico, Alicia would be denied this critical tool which otherwise would be her right as a legal permanent resident.

Alicia and her American-born children had to wait another six months from their initial hearing date before learning the judge's final decision on the matter. The infamous "hanging judge" did not allow Jeronimo to remain in the United States. His attorney however, appealed his case and continues to fight for a chance for Jeronimo and his family to return to the US. In the meantime, they reside in an exceptionally small town near Durango, Mexico, scratching to get by, and hoping that this wife and mother can hang on and pull through.

I've been told that Alicia is not doing so well. She is confined to the few walls that comprise her modest living quarters, and due to her family's economic situation she has no choice but to live with Jeronimo's family. Alicia is suffering terribly there, because at least in her own home she could feign some level of control over her phobias. Living in such close proximity with virtual strangers is a terrifying lot for her. As someone with her type of psychopathology, her relatives are nothing but "bags of germs." To make matters worse, Alicia is completely unable to leave the house and is obviously unable to find work—and would surely fall apart on the job even if she could.

My only hope is that Alicia can find a way to adapt and seek out professional help in her area regardless of the outcome of her case. Should Alicia and her family return to the United States one day, positive experiences within a supportive therapeutic environment might encourage her to continue with her treatment and find some level of relief. Of course the best-case scenario would be for her to also secure a medication evaluation in the United States and follow the recommendations of her treating physician. But these things cost money. Yet even if Alicia is never allowed to return to the United States, it is still of critical importance that

41

she somehow acquire professional help in Mexico. It is the only viable option for Alicia to survive, and she may not have much more time left.

ANDREA

Most people who have gone through what Andrea has experienced in her lifetime would exude bitterness and suspicion. Andrea was simply exhausted; it looked as if she carried every single one of her years on her back. She hadn't quite given up yet, but the look in her eyes told me she could no longer bear up under her situation and desperately needed a resolution.

Andrea had lived through a horrific childhood and has endured equally terrifying adulthood experiences. To top it off, she had contracted various diseases through the years that had deteriorated her body to its present, decrepit state. Andrea could barely walk due to muscle deterioration and pulled out a half dozen prescription medication bottles from her purse; on a daily basis she took pills for high blood pressure, heart murmurs and a variety of other ailments. "I will die soon," she told me with a resigned smile.

When I asked Andrea for the reason she had come to my office, her face lit up ever so gently while she told me, "My husband Rudolfo." For a moment it was as if I was speaking to a different person; Andrea smiled and looked away shyly while she told me how after the nightmare that her life had been, she had finally met a good man with whom she felt safe.

And just as quickly as one snuffs out a candle, her affect became somber and she began to cry. "I miss him," she told me, as she nervously tugged on her shirt and picked dog hair from her sleeves.

"Okay Andrea, let's start at the beginning," I said.

My name is Andrea. I'm 62 years old and although I was born in the United States, I am of Mexican descent. I was born in a small farm town in Texas where my dad worked as a farmer and my mom took care of us and the house.

I grew up with a lot of fear and anxiety at home; actually, one of the first things I can remember is my dad hitting my mom all the time. My parents were heavy drinkers and they would fight—they didn't care if it happened in front of us children, so I saw my dad beat up my mom quite a lot. Back then I didn't understand the ramifications of it; all I knew is that it made me scared.

The tension with my dad made my mom a very angry woman. When my mom gave you that look, you'd better know what it meant or figure it out quick—otherwise she would come for you. She wasn't like most moms either—my mom wouldn't hold back. Apparently ear pulling and spankings were beneath her; she would flat out beat us. She used pots, pans… anything that was within her reach. She even broke brooms over our heads and backs. She beat us like my dad beat her, and just as often.

Since I was the oldest daughter I was expected to help out with the house and to care for my siblings. But since my mom drank every day, I didn't just help with the housekeeping –it fully became my own responsibility. I cleaned, cooked and watched over my six siblings. I even had to get my little sisters ready for school. I grew up as if I already had kids of my own; my brothers and sisters saw me as their mom. Even though I've always been shy, this role didn't allow me to have a normal childhood like the rest of the kids. I rarely ever played with others or even had toys of my own—I was always busy cleaning or cooking, or washing clothes.

My mom forced me to drop out of school in the seventh grade. She was astoundingly old-fashioned and believed that women should not be educated, but stay home and get pregnant. I often wondered how such a conservative woman justified getting wasted every day and neglecting her children. Honestly, I don't think she really believed in much of anything—I think she just wanted me home full-time so that I could take care of everything while she kept drinking. I was really good in school, too, and I enjoyed it, and I was devastated when she forced me to drop out.

Things didn't really improve as time went by. My dad began to sexually abuse me when I was ten.

I remember being scared of going to bed at night, because this is when he would come looking for me. My sisters and I slept in one room, but he didn't care—he would still sneak in and pull me away. He scared me; he would touch me over and under my clothes and rub himself all over me before ejaculating on my thighs. He was usually drunk, but even then I knew better than to excuse him. Luckily he would pass out on the spot after he got his way with me and I was able to run back to my room.

I felt dirty, filthy. It didn't make sense in my mind why my own dad would do those things to me and I grew very angry. I didn't know how to process all that was happening and I was too ashamed to speak to anyone about it. I felt really lonely, especially because I feared I would be punished if I ever told anyone.

My dad continued to be able to rid himself of any shame over those years until he finally tried to have intercourse with me when I was 14. By then I was old enough and strong enough to resist him, and luckily I was able to do just that. I was so disgusted with him that I somehow found the courage to try and stop him—I went to tell my mom everything. She didn't believe me. In fact, she beat me for lying and threw me out of the house. I was able to stay with one of my aunts for a few days, but as soon as my mom found out she called her and ordered her to throw me out of her house too.

My mom was a crazy and violent woman. She was into black magic and I remember always seeing her trying to do evil things to other people, like putting pins through sock dolls and the like. People were seriously afraid of her, even our own family. My aunt worried about what my mom would do to her, so she told me I had to leave.

I had no place to go; I was literally out in the streets. My aunt gave me until the next day to leave and I went into her bathroom and swallowed all the medicine I found there. I couldn't bear it—there was no way out and I wanted to die.

The next thing I remember is waking up in a hospital room. When I realized I had not died I got up and threw myself out of the window. It still didn't work. I was hospitalized for several days and then unceremoniously released.

Another one of my aunts took me into her home, but first she really wanted to know why my mom wouldn't let me go back to our house. When I told her that my dad abused me she rounded up the rest of my aunts and they all went to confront my mom. This is how my relationship with my parents ended. They disowned me and my aunts finished raising me. All in all, I think I was lucky—they treated me better, taught me how to work and to give myself value.

I stayed with my aunts until I was 22. By then I had met Haro and I thought I had found someone

47

who actually loved me. I was madly in love with him. We moved in together and life was great at first, although I discovered that I had an aversion to sex. I don't know how I managed to get pregnant, but we had two kids shortly after we moved in together.

Haro went out with different women while being with me. I thought I loved him so much that I couldn't leave him, so I became blind, deaf, and stupid to his infidelities. I pretended that it wasn't happening and I continued to stay with him, faithfully. It wasn't long though, before I got infected with a plethora of sexually transmitted diseases. Any disease under the sun he brought back home and I got; I had no idea until I started getting really sick with fevers and infections. My uterus was completely compromised and I had to have a hysterectomy when I was 28.

I didn't grow up as a child—I grew up as a mother and now I had two kids of my own. I wasn't planning on having any more children, but to have my uterus entirely removed and know that I couldn't have kids made me feel less than a woman. I withdrew into myself and fantasized about the kids that I would never have. I was fighting myself from all angles; the sadness, the self-pity, the feeling of loss, rage at Haro, love for Haro… confusion. I was lost. Believe it or not, I stayed with him. Haro and I had problems, but I was too young and too naive to know when to run for my life.

Then Haro came into quite a bit of money rather suddenly. He started to buy nice cars and houses and he took me and the children on vacations around Mexico. I often wondered how he came to so much money; I knew it wasn't from a raise he got at work. I tried to put it off my mind and enjoy things, but he had become very demanding by now––he was always on edge. I had to grab the kids and leave the house the minute he barked the order, otherwise he would get angry and the situation would only get worse.

I don't know if I would rather have just remained ignorant instead of finding out the way I did. One time Haro told me to take the children and leave for about an hour. I obeyed, but I had to turn back because I forgot my wallet. I thought whatever Haro was doing was probably in the house, so I thought to enter quietly through the garage. To my surprise, when I got home I found several men removing drugs from different places in the garage. Haro was a drug dealer and he kept everything stashed in our house.

I wanted to leave him, but I realized then that I had nowhere to go and no way to support myself and my children without him. I stayed with Haro, but things only got worse.

Haro got drunk a lot and became brutally violent. One time he accused me of lying to him; he dragged me by the hair from one end of the house to the other, beat me and then played Russian roulette with me. He sat my children on the kitchen table and made them watch as an example of what would happen to them if they lied to him. I never even lied about anything, I was already too afraid of him to lie. After that I knew I had to leave; to this day my children remember that night—it changed us all.

I didn't know if I would walk out alive if I left Haro, but I needed to try. I knew something would happen to me anyway if I stayed with him, so I thought I had nothing to lose. Luckily, Haro decided that I no longer served a purpose for him and he divorced me without issue. I grabbed my kids and our clothes and we left to live with one of my sisters in Grand Junction, Colorado. I found a job in a factory and struggled to make ends meet, but at least we were safe. My children grew up and eventually left to make their own lives and I continued to live with my sister. It was the two of us now and it was peaceful.

Many years went by before I met my husband Rudolfo. He lived near my sister's house—I never really paid much attention to him. At one point he began to approach me to offer help whenever I was out working in the yard or my car. He made lots of conversation. I think he wanted to get to know me. I would talk with him in Spanish and eventually we became friends. I still felt suspicious about him though—I couldn't shake off my distrust after everything I had been through.

I guess I just didn't trust anyone and I didn't want anyone to get too close to me. He never pushed or insinuated anything; he just waited for me. Two years went by before we became romantically involved.

Rudolfo is a truly good man; he doesn't drink, or smoke... he doesn't even curse. He also seems to be a loner like me, so we've understood each other well. It might sound normal to other people, but I've always felt touched when Rudolfo asks how I'm doing and makes sure I feel safe and well—I've never had that before.

Rudolfo and I have been together for five years and they have been the healthiest and best years of my life. I always looked for someone to love me and treat me well, but somehow the opposite happened. I feel lucky to have found someone like him; he is a good man and a good husband. I've suffered from diabetes and heart murmurs for many years, but no one has cared for me the way he has. No one has even tried to make an effort to be there for me the way he has. He even ate nothing but tortillas and eggs for a month so he could save money and make sure that we could afford my treatments.

I said we are both loners and it's true, but with him I only have alone time, and I don't feel lonely anymore. I never knew there was a difference. I never knew things were meant to be so simple, effortless and just... good. We are old; we don't go out on romantic dates, or to parties or take trips, but we accompany and support each other and to me that is worth the world. I only regret that I had to live nearly all of my life before I was able to find it. And now that I've found it I don't really see the point in living without it. I thought I had encountered friendship and love in my lifetime, but it had always left me broken somehow and it chipped away at me without ever giving me a chance to learn how to fix it. I never really learned how to fix it. Rudolfo does that for me. He patches me up silently; somehow he understands and that makes me feel normal. Like there's a chance for me to live a decent life, even if it's only for the last ten years of my life.

Rudolfo was required to return to Mexico after we applied for his residency. We were told that he needed to attend his hearing in Juarez and once we were there they postponed it. The problem was that because Rudolfo walked the border he was then not allowed to return until his legal residency is approved and issued. He had to stay in Mexico indefinitely and I had to come back to the US alone.

I tried living in Mexico for a few months so we could be together, but I couldn't afford my medications any longer and I became very seriously ill. I had to go see a doctor and he told me that I had acute lung and intestinal infections. He also told me that it would be best if I returned to the United States as soon as I recovered, as I was clearly not "made to live in Mexico." He was right, I had to go back to the U.S. or I would keep getting sick.

I haven't really recovered, but it's not because of any infections. I can't bear the sadness of being without Rudolfo. I am old now, I feel old. If Rudolfo and I can't spend our last years together I don't see what's left to live for. Even though Rudolfo helped me reconnect with my siblings, I don't really want to be around them very much and my children and I don't have a good relationship. I don't have anyone else in the world.

I also will soon be destitute if Rudolfo is not allowed to come back to the United States. I can't work. My hearing is damaged and I feel a great deal of muscle pain, even though I take medicine for it—more often than not it hurts so bad I can't walk. I need help and constant medical care and I know that is not available for me in Mexico.

If Rudolfo isn't allowed back I'd have to survive on the disability income I receive, but it is barely enough to cover my medicines. I can't make ends meet here without him; I'd lose our home and everything we've struggled to have. We even went into debt to afford an attorney for his legal case and I can't keep making the payments. Sometimes I live without power and lights for a week or two because I don't have money to pay for it. The stress is more than I can bear—sometimes I feel I'd be better off if I died tonight. I don't know how I would survive here without Rudolfo and if I were to go back to Mexico, I know for a fact I wouldn't survive.

If we were in Mexico we would both have to live like he lives now, without money for food or medical care. Rudolfo lives in a shack in an extremely poor area of Juarez. It rips me apart to know that he sleeps on the floor with roaches and spiders crawling all over him, and I can't even help him. Last I saw him I noticed insect bites all over his body. I tried to send him a care package with insecticide, but he never received it. My husband is starving and he has to live like an animal—yet drug dealer Haro probably lives in a fancy house somewhere in Texas. How does this happen?

I would do away with myself if I had the chance. Rudolfo and I rely on each other; I can't handle life alone here anymore, I need him. With him my horrible life actually became good. If I don't have him, I don't have anything. I'm 62 and sick; I might as well not be here if he can't be with me to care for me like before.

. . .

I never heard back from Andrea, but her attorney called to let me know her case was dragging on and they would have another hearing in Juarez in a year. He also told me that Andrea could not handle life any longer, sold everything they had in the United States, and moved to Mexico to be with her husband.

54

I was instantly worried about her and enraged at her attorney for allowing her to do such thing. How would she survive without proper medical care? I had to remind myself that Andrea was a grown woman—and much older in fact than either one of us. I wondered how she would get by day to day in Mexico, and her attorney told me she was hoping that her disability income and the money from the sale of her possessions would bridge the gap.

Her attorney also told me that Andrea was very clear in that she would rather die with her husband in Mexico than die alone in the United States. I sighed exasperatedly. I had been hoping for a better ending for Andrea.

I often wonder what kind of life she would have had if someone would've helped her leave Haro early on—but of course meeting and being with someone like him had been subconsciously programmed into her mind as a child and seemed predestined. Andrea grew up with neglectful and violent parents and this is where she learned the basic dynamics of relationships; she grew up thinking that violence and abuse were things to be expected and accepted.

To compound this unfairness, the sexual abuse she suffered at the hands of her father for years and her mother's reaction when Andrea finally brought herself to divulge the ugly truth cemented the belief that she was worthless, and in any case helpless to change her situation for the better.

Lastly, Andrea never truly received much care and affection while growing up; although her aunts treated her well, they were busy women who did not have much time for her. When Andrea found Haro and saw that he (initially) treated her well, she could not help her situation and quickly became dependent on him. Andrea became captivated by his charm and interest he showed her, and then built her entire myopic world around it. When Haro became abusive with her, the situation became all too familiar for Andrea and her response again became that of many years prior: in her helplessness, she simply bowed down and accepted the lot in life that she had been accustomed to. She didn't feel she deserved any better.

Andrea was one of the dearest people I have met, and so undeserving of what life had thrown at her. Unless Rudolfo is allowed back into the United States, my prognosis for Andrea is quite poor. I can understand how in her mind she simply wanted to spend the last years of her life with her husband, but I worry about what might become of her if she is to remain in Mexico for long. Her medical ailments are severe, and her mental and emotional health were already spiraling downhill when I met her— but there is nothing to be done now but wait. All I can do is hope that the decision in her case will be favorable and they can return to the United States soon, for her sake.

GINO

Gino was an American-born Chicano and was tall and striking in his appearance. He walked into my office holding hands with his wife. I saw him as a pleasant, personable, and likeable young man right off the bat. He also appeared to be a well-adjusted young man, which led me to inadvertently frown as I seriously pondered if there was anything there for me to find. I often have to send such lovely people away, as the nature of this work is to uncover psychopathology. If there is none, they don't have a case to present to immigration court. I always hate having to break such news to people fighting for their lives.

Although Gino indicated that he was comfortable with his wife staying in the room with him during the interview, I asked her to wait for Gino in the waiting room. If there was anything to learn about this man, he and I were going to need our undivided attention on this matter.

Gino smiled shyly, pushed his glasses up his nose bridge, and scratched his head. "Where do we start?" he asked me, to which I inquired about his family and his life as a child. Gino kept his cool, but his smile and upbeat demeanor masked his true nature as soon as I finished my question. Guilt and shame appeared to dash across his face as he took a moment to think. He quickly responded that his

57

childhood was "normal," and noted that he grew up around many of his aunts and uncles. He then deftly tried to avoid any further questioning by changing the subject.

Every ounce of my instinct screamed at me to not allow him to lead the conversation away and lose that moment. I continued to subtly pry further into his family history. If I was ever glad to have listened to my intuition, it was on this day.

School couldn't have prepared me in a million years for a story and a character such as Gino. I understood within the first few sentences why he would not go anywhere near his past and rather kept it in a metaphorical, air-tight container shoved into the very back of his mind.

However, all the things we try hard to keep away from our awareness have a way of coming back up when we least expect them, demanding we deal with them.

For Gino, this was that day.

My name is Gino. I'm 28 years old and I was born in San Antonio, Texas. My dad left when I was a baby; I've only seen him a handful of times, whenever he decided to come around. I was told that he was a drug dealer and served many years in prison on a murder charge. I was also told that he eventually got out, but he never bothered to contact me or my brother. I heard through some friends of my uncles that my dad even died about a year ago, but no one knows for sure.

Some of my earliest memories are of my dad breaking into the house randomly and picking fights with my mom. He would usually yell and push her around, and a few times, he even punched her in the face. He never hit my brother or me, but regardless, we knew what kind of man he was. He was a screw-up. He would show up drunk and unannounced and would drag us to the desert to shoot guns. We couldn't refuse; we were afraid of him, and my mom was often at work, so there was no one there to stand up for us.

Even as a little kid, I never considered my dad as the father-figure in my life, which made me go around looking up to all the different men in my family and taking a bit of each of them with me as guidance. I remember Uncle Carlos the most; he was the one I molded myself after since he spent so much time with us. Uncle Carlos wasn't really a great guy or anything—he was kind of a screw-up himself. He would take us gambling to the dog tracks every other day, but at least he didn't hurt us or my mom. He was the best we had and I made the most of it.

My mom eventually remarried, but her new husband never felt like a father to me. In fact, my brother and I always thought he was a little twisted. He would make us eat food that had fallen on the floor only to slap us later "for eating food that had fallen on the floor." One time he made my brother and I lick the tire of his truck just because he said so, then slammed us against the truck and grounded us for a week "for licking tires." Life with him was very confusing. He would get so angry if we ever didn't do what we were told to do, yet as soon as we did whatever he asked he would punish us anyway. My mom never did a thing about it; she saw him as the discipline enforcer and let him do whatever he pleased.

My mom and stepdad worked odd shifts and long hours, so they often dropped us off with different relatives while they were away. We spent most of our time at Uncle Ricardo's house and I hated it. Uncle Ricardo was an unstable Vietnam Veteran who resorted to his belt as standard punishment for any transgression—even making noise.

His sons were even worse than Uncle Ricardo, and would simply walk up to me and punch or push me. I tried to tell Uncle Ricardo about it at first, but he would call me a sissy and threatened to beat me himself if I "didn't stop whining."

The worst of my tormentors however, was my own brother. He used to kick my ass every day until I cried. I was scared to death of being around him; he picked on me mercilessly, often to the point where I'd scream, "I wish I was dead!" He always wanted to fight and always took it out on me.

In retrospect my entire family was pretty screwed up; every one of them was a different kind of demon. My grandfather was an alcoholic, who, like my dad, abandoned the family. When my grandma remarried, the dynamics between this new man and the rest of the family destroyed all family ties and everyone along with it.

Two of my mom's sisters became meth-heads. They would go partying with their drug-addict friends and disappear for days at the time. As the years went by they both became pregnant multiple times by different men. Their kids were born with serious mental problems and many of them spend most of their time in jail these days.

My mom was sexually molested by her stepdad for years and later on by her own brother as well; Uncle Ricardo. There's talk now that Uncle Ricardo has sexually abused his own kids too, but nobody knows for sure. I've spent enough time there through the years to believe it to be true. Uncle Ricardo never sexually abused me, but it wasn't because he didn't try. From time to time he would look at me funny and try to touch me with one excuse or another, but I would run away and go find my cousins. I preferred to get beat up than stay in the same room alone with that man.

All of them messed me up and I hate them for it. Uncle Carlos was the only good person in that whole bunch of dysfunctional people, but he died in a car accident when I was ten years old. I felt alone in the world after he passed away and I often thought about suicide. I wished for a car to run me over or for someone to kill me—I thought that death would be a lot better than living any longer in my reality.

Life went about the same way until I my mom died when I was 17 years old; she went into surgery for appendicitis, but it was already too late—she died of a septic infection. I don't want to say that my mom died and I became a fuck-up, but I did. Adding my mom's death to my list of my things to bear simply broke me into a million pieces. I had already taken up smoking pot to cope with everyday life, but after my mom died I began to experiment with all sorts of drugs. You name it, I did it. I thought it would help me cope, and by cope I mean forget, but it didn't help. I think it actually made things worse, but at the time I didn't know it, and went around trying new things—desperately trying to find the ticket out of my reality.

I don't know how I managed to finish high school, but I did. I barely passed my classes, but at least I never had any conduct problems. I was too tortured at home to want to fight anyone at school. I actually considered school a momentary escape from reality and I looked forward to going there every day and feeling calm and able to breathe.

It was lonely though; other kids perceived me as different and didn't want me around. The ones that knew about my drug use ostracized me as a junkie and the rest discarded me as trash. I knew I had a fucked up family, but what hurt me the most is that no one took a chance to get to know me, they never stopped to think that I could be better –I could be more. They simply threw me in the same bag as my brother, aunts and uncles, and crossed me off as undesirable. It hurt. I really needed a friend.

I began to mix drugs with heavy drinking after graduating and although I know I held several jobs, my recollection of that time in my life is spotty. I do remember feeling very much like a homeless person, a loser. I had a roof over my head because I moved in with a girlfriend, but things didn't go well—I really was a drug-addicted loser and she dumped me as soon as she realized all of this.

I had no place to go and no money. I moved back with my stepdad for some time, but I knew he didn't want me there, which made things very awkward. I wasn't welcome to eat with him or his daughter and I had to buy my own food. I spent much of my time wandering aimlessly on the streets in order to avoid being at his house. It wasn't my house anymore—my mom had died.

I eventually found steady work in a restaurant and moved into an apartment of my own. It was dirty and falling apart, but it was mine and I could afford it. Even though I was responsible about my work schedule, I was barely hanging onto my job. I knew I was stuck in a vicious cycle; I hated where

I'd come from and I wanted a better life, yet I couldn't leave my past behind. I was dependent on drugs and alcohol to soothe me, but this prevented me from achieving anything worthwhile for myself. Anytime I tried to quit meth or pot or alcohol, however, I became an anxious, depressed, and paranoid mess and I couldn't keep it together. So I arrived at the conclusion that I needed to keep a balance between drugs and being a functional person. I struggled walking that line for a long time.

To be honest, I didn't work hard to keep my job because I was some sort of redeeming underdog, but because Andrea worked there and I simply wouldn't miss a chance to see her. We often worked the same shifts and became great friends. It wasn't long after I met her that I knew I would marry her someday; however, she had a boyfriend at the time, so I could only be her friend.

I took the friend spot in a heartbeat. I had never had a friend in my life, much less one like Andrea. She was so bright and alive that it was contagious—she made me want to do better, become happy just like she was.

Eventually Andrea became pregnant by her boyfriend and he left her a few months later. She was alone and scared and I could relate to that perfectly. I offered to take care of her and her baby and I promised I would never leave her. She accepted. I couldn't believe my luck! Was I about to have one good thing in my life for once? I was so happy and in love I thought I would burst.

Unfortunately we didn't ride off into the sunset or live happily ever after like they do in the movies. My drug addiction made for a very rocky relationship and we didn't survive it. Like everyone else, she left me and I began to date other girls for a while, trying to forget about her.

About two months went by before she left a letter at my door one day. In her letter, she told me that she thought I was a good man and was ready for us to be together if I was willing to let go of my drug addiction.

I didn't know how, but I was going to do it. I went looking for her that night and brought her back home with me. I took every pill and clump of marijuana I found in my apartment and flushed it down the toilet, then looked at her, petrified. Andrea grabbed me by the hand and took me to the living room where we sat down and watched the television silently—her hand never left mine. In that moment, I didn't know how, but everything was going to be alright.

Andrea and I have been together ever since. We got married a few months after that and although we've had the normal ups and downs, and I struggled with drug and alcohol withdrawal at first, we never left one another. I feel like a brand-new man and it is only because she was there to push me and support me. I know it would have never happened otherwise.

I can't lose her. If Andrea has to go back to Mexico I don't know what will happen to me. I won't even be able to stand being alone in the house without my family without the only thing that I've ever had. She is the one great thing that has ever happened to me. I don't know what to do and how to keep it together. I feel like I'm circling the drain just at the thought of her going away. I don't have anyone in my life except for her. This new, better man that I've become only happened because of her—and I built him around her. I know that I won't make it through if she has to leave.

I won't be able to move to follow her to Mexico because I would have to stay here and work so I can continue to provide for my family. We have two children now and the youngest is only six months old. I don't know where she could work in Mexico, but even if she found a job there she wouldn't have anyone to watch our children while she is away. She only has a couple of friends left in Mexico and although she is lucky that they offered her a place to stay, she can only rely on them to have a roof over her head—nothing more.

I think I would go insane knowing that my wife and children are in Mexico and always wondering if they are in potential danger. I think I've been through some pretty rough things in my life and I could only say that this is much worse. If I had to resort to drugs and alcohol to deal with my past, what am I going to do to cope with something of infinitely more impact for me? I can't go back to being the mess of a drug-addicted man that I used to be, but then how else am I supposed to deal with all of this? If they send my family away I won't make it through. I just don't know how.

. . .

I don't think Gino's initial well-adjusted presentation was dishonest. It's just that up to this point in time he had resolved to shut down his past entirely as a way to cope with it without resorting to drugs and alcohol. In turn, he dove into his life as a husband and father and believed that he had been "cured," when in fact he had merely wrapped himself around his proverbial lifesaver to the point where he lost sight of his own demons. Although I give him credit for drastically improving his life, I am quite concerned about his pathological dependence on his wife. I agree with Gino that he is unlikely to make it without her constant presence in his life.

Gino had always been eager and "ready" to leave his family and his past behind. His case is quite peculiar in that he wasn't necessarily being held back by his attachment to his past or the trauma caused by the abuse and neglect that he suffered as a child. In Gino's mind, his situation was quite clear; he would never see those people again and he would not allow anyone to treat him in the way his family did. Gino's simple yet potentially life threatening conundrum is his lack of adequate coping skills.

Gino never learned how to deal with the events in his life. He never had a stable-minded friend or an adult to look up and speak to, therefore he never had the chance to learn how to deal with his encumbering circumstances. As the years went by and his life situation became more brutal for him, he simply had no way of bearing it any longer and resorted to drugs (and later alcohol) as a way to numb himself from his reality. Because he was successful for a time in soothing himself this way, it became his coping mechanism; the only coping mechanism that he knew. Then again, he was pushing people away with his instability and was desperately lonely. Once Gino became addicted he would always have the potential of relapse lurking in the shadows, particularly in times of high stress.

When Gino met Andrea and she provided him with the love and nurturance he never had, he instantly switched from his drug dependence to being dependent on Andrea. She became Gino's coping mechanism in the only way he knew how to cope—he became addicted once again. I have no doubt in my mind that if Andrea was removed from the equation, not only would Gino fall into a complete emotional and mental breakdown, but he would be forced to switch his dependency onto something else, as this is the only thing he knows.

Long-term sobriety from drugs and alcohol is relatively rare for an addict of his type. He will need long-term addiction psychotherapy and participation in a mutual-support group if he is to find lasting recovery. His wife would also need help and support to wean herself away from her co-dependency on Gino. Otherwise, the union will eventually fail, or worse.

It is evident to me that Gino was firmly set in his decision to not follow his wife to Mexico so that he could continue to work and support his family. Yet, he may eventually have no choice but to follow her if she were forced to remain there for an extended period of time. I cannot say that Gino would resort to alcohol and drugs as a way to cope with this devastating change in his support system; but I cannot rule it out either, which makes me quite concerned about his future.

Gino is quite simply completely and pathologically attached to his wife to the point where he would not know what to do without her. It is not too late for him to learn better through supportive counseling; but in order for that to be effective, his environment needs to remain stable and intact. If his wife were deported to Mexico and Gino were to remain alone in the United States, it is clear to me that he would quickly and undoubtedly be rendered entirely non-functional. If he were to follow his wife to Mexico he would no longer have access to professional help. In any case, he speaks no Spanish and would be far more dependent on her there than he was when she was in the United States. This factor, compounded by the crude and dangerous reality of the new environment he would find himself in there, would not bode well for Gino either.

Unfortunately, as I learned through his attorney, Andrea was not allowed to remain in the United States and was required to return to Mexico for a number of years before her residency process could be finalized and she allowed return to the United States. Gino's attorney advised him to continue to fight the case and appeal the judge's decision. I was informed that Gino agreed, yet two months later he packed his bags and moved to Mexico in order to be with his wife and children. The attorney continues to work on the family's case; although he does not know how much longer the family will be able to afford his services as Gino has yet to find work.

KARINA

Karina walked in my office accompanied by her husband Marcelo. The first thing I noticed about Karina was her severe attachment to her husband. She would not even dare let go of his hand, even for a moment. Therefore I was a bit surprised when she agreed to come into my office alone for the interview. She quickly explained that "there were things" her husband had yet to know about her. "I can't live without him," she told me, "So I'm afraid if I tell him everything, he will think I'm crazy and leave me."

I pondered the significance of that statement for a moment and then politely nodded. I felt it was too early in the session to try to get right at the thing she was alluding to. During this introduction, there was a feeling of something quite large looming in her story. I figured that when it was time, we would get to it and then it would be my turn to speak.

Karina appeared to be visibly uncomfortable without her husband next to her. She rocked back and forth in her chair, her eyes wandering around the room, intentionally avoiding meeting my own. It was as if she didn't even know how to carry a conversation without her husband at her side. She simply didn't know what to say. I tried to ascribe it to immaturity, but my gut automatically told me that this couldn't be correct. Through the years I've learned to listen to my gut—there is typically always more than meets the eye.

Karina didn't laugh, and she wasn't shy. She looked simply petrified, much like a small child left alone in a room full of adults; not knowing what to say, what to do, or how to navigate the situation. I felt sympathy for her and tried to put her at ease, not by directly confronting her about the elephant in the room, but by starting out with the easy questions.

"Let's start at the beginning," I said gently, "Tell me about the first things you remember as a child."

She broke down in a cascade of tears.

It was going to be one of those afternoons.

My name is Karina. At my 24 years of age, I feel I have been sad all of my life. I think it started when my sister died in a car accident when I was four; she and two of her friends were driving around town when they were hit by a drunk driver. Her death shocked me, but I was only a little girl and didn't really understand what had happened. It was the aftermath of my sister's death that truly affected me and everything around me.

My sister's death just about killed my mother as well. She hardly ever got out of her bed anymore and spent her time crying. She tried to keep her job and take care of us the best she could, but her grief was so deep. We had to move into a mobile home park with an uncle because my mom lost her job and we ran out of money to live. My father was nowhere to be found; I guess he took off when I was two or so—I've never met him. My sister and my mother were all that I had. I grew up a typical, white, trailer-trash kid.

Even though we were lucky that my uncle took us in to live with him, that's about all he was good for. He was quite mean to my mother and me, and he treated us as if we were a burden and an inconvenience to him. We cleaned the house from top to bottom every day and then went into the little room that we shared as soon as we heard him come back from work. We would remain the rest of the day in our room, trying to stay out of his way so that he would let us live in his house.

I guess my mom had no one to talk to. She never had any friends, and her family wasn't very supportive of her. After my sister died she didn't have an outlet for her grief other than me, so she used me as a crutch.

I wish she had used me to help herself get back on her feet and get us to a better place, but I was only a sounding board to her. She would tell me about her frustrations, her sadness and desperation, then hold me and cry disconsolately until she would fall asleep. My shirts were often wet in the back and shoulders, soaked in my mom's tears. I didn't know what to do; I didn't know what to say or how to make it better and get us out of the hole we lived in—all I could do was hug her back and allow her to unload her sorrows on me.

It never changed. At first I thought my mom would get over it and get better, but she never did. In time, as I grew up, it became too much to bear and it was me now who didn't have an outlet for everything I was holding inside. I began to cut myself when I was eight; I don't remember how I started doing it, but I remember always feeling better afterwards. That was how I unloaded my sorrows—I let them flow away in my blood. It also made me feel that there was at least one thing I could control.

I don't know if it happens with everyone that cuts, but it happened to me; the thing about cutting yourself is that it grows on you and before you know it, it wraps your brain in this dark, dense cloud. I began to think about suicide and death by the time I was in the fourth grade; I'd see other girls in my class play with their dolls and I felt galaxies away from being even remotely similar to them. All I had on my mind was blood and sadness.

As I continued to grow up I became scared of just about anything. I couldn't stop the stories from playing over and over on my mind of how one thing or another would kill me. I think some part of me was afraid and was trying to keep me from running into the shadows, looking for death.

My mom became seriously worried about me when I entered the sixth grade. She blamed it on herself, but that only sent her spiraling further down into her own depression, rather than getting her on her feet to come and save me. It was a teacher who pressured my mother until she finally got around to signing me up for school counseling. My life changed from there, but I don't know if it was in a good way. I began to see a number of doctors and therapists outside of school and was put on an array of different medications. Honestly, I felt like a test bunny at a lab. Nothing ever made me feel any better; I just grew numb.

I became violent by the time I got into eighth grade. I screamed and punched and kicked. I loved fighting and I looked for any chance to beat someone up, or better yet, let them beat me a little so I could feel pain. I got into trouble more times than I care to remember, but the principal was patient with me; he put me in anger management classes and counseling several times per week. It seemed like I was hardly ever in my classroom learning with the rest of the kids.

It mattered very little what the "mental health professionals" did to me—nothing really ever improved in my life. They put me on anti-depressants, anti-anxiety medication, psychotropics of all kinds… it was all the same. At best, I felt that

75

I went about life half-asleep and mostly numb, so my inclination to fight subsided. They called it a success, I simply felt drugged up. It made me even angrier.

I met Marcelo about a year before graduating high school. I was picking a fight with him and pestering him to engage. Boys generally never physically fought me, but they yelled and insulted me and I yelled right back. It was better than nothing. Marcelo refused to even do that though, and it drove me insane.

I remember that day well. I grabbed him by the back of his shirt and I pulled hard on it to get him to turn around. Marcelo turned lazily and slowly toward me; he looked me in the eye then said, "You're prettier when you're not screaming." That disarmed me on the spot.

I blushed and I walked away in anger. I left him alone for a long time after that and then slowly, he began to look for me. Other kids in school treated me like a pariah, so I didn't know how to react when Marcelo just wanted to talk and get to know me. In fact, I pushed him away and insulted him on countless occasions, but he kept coming back. Eventually, I began to let him in.

At first, Marcelo and I were friends. I had never had a friend before and it took me a while to get used to it even when I yearned to have a friend so badly. Once I opened up and decided to trust

Marcelo, I couldn't stop talking. I wanted to tell him everything about my life, everything I thought and feared and lived. He'd tell me about his life and his family too; everyone moved here from Mexico when he was ten years old and had been here ever since. His parents worked at a meat-packing plant and he was in charge of looking after his brothers and sisters while his parents were away. It sounded like a simple, mostly peaceful life, but Marcelo hated it. His father was an alcoholic and would hit him and his mother whenever he returned home drunk. His dad also wasted most of the family's money at the bars, so they were barely surviving. His life was a similar hell to mine.

Marcelo and I eventually became romantically involved, and by the time we graduated from high school, we found jobs and moved into a place of our own. We planned to go to college somehow and make things work for ourselves and our families.

Life was hard. Even though I had become a happier and more peaceful person with Marcelo, I still didn't know how to deal with life and I often exploded, yelled, and even hit him. He never hit me back. All he ever did was protect himself or restrain me so I would calm down and stop hurting both of us. For having had a life about as screwed up as mine, Marcelo had turned out so differently than me.

Over time I've become pathologically dependent on Marcelo. I don't know what I would do without

Marcelo. I don't even know what would've happened to me if he hadn't shown up in my life at the time that he did. I always push out everyone from my life—it's almost like I want to alienate others. I don't care what I have to do; Marcelo is like my sun and my world revolves around him—I don't think I can make it without him. I didn't even learn to drive until he came around. He is the only one I trust to the point where I can't even make decisions on my own. Sometimes I even ask him what I should choose to eat.

Ever since they told me Marcelo might have to go back to Mexico things have gotten back to being really bad for me. I feel myself slipping into dark thoughts and I've begun to cut myself again. I can't deal with the thought of not having Marcelo around. I'm also afraid I'm turning into how my mother used to be after my sister died; I rarely leave my house anymore, I spend my days crying, desperate, thinking about killing myself. This time though, I don't have Marcelo to share it with because I can't tell him that he is the problem; him and his damn immigration problem. That, and the fact that he might have to leave and I don't know how to live without him. I can't tell him.

I don't know that I have what it takes to survive in Mexico, but I don't see myself surviving here in the United States without him either. I don't know where we would find counseling and a doctor and medications for me—I don't even speak Spanish.

But I figure that if I'm going to die, it may as well be by his side.

· · ·

From the very beginning, Karina's life was molded by her mother's clinical depression. She was too young and had very little recollection of what her mother used to be like before the death of her sister, so she lacked any clues that could point at a healthier way of being for her. It was, one could say, inevitable.

Karina is an extremely unbalanced woman who continues to suffer from an array of serious mental health complications. She has little faith in psychotherapy and medical treatments, and is quick to proclaim her conclusion that these methods have helped very little, if at all. Thankfully, it was mandatory for her to attend counseling sessions throughout her school career. Once she graduated from high school, Marcelo took the responsibility of making sure Karina continued with her treatment. Even though she didn't really let the counselor in, I believe it is only due to medical treatment and psychotherapy that Karina has been able to keep from committing suicide. And it is only because of Marcelo that she has had any semblance of normalcy in her life at all in the past seven years.

If Marcelo were removed from Karina's life, I have no doubt she would go into such a great shock she would be unable to handle managing even their basic living arrangements, like keeping a roof over her head. On the other hand, the stress of a life in Mexico and its environment, along with the lack of treatment and psychotherapy, would undoubtedly send Karina into a rapid decompensation from which I doubt she would be able to return.

In the end, things worked out for Karina, at least momentarily. Marcelo's attorney advised me that Marcelo was allowed to remain in the United States and become a legal resident. I can only imagine the joy and relief Karina must feel knowing the cornerstone of her life won't be uprooted to another country and she along with it. She is one of the lucky ones with the resources, both internal and financial that allowed her to battle on. Most families in her situation are not so lucky.

Yet as it is the case with many of my patients, this is nothing but a small victory for them, and I hope that they see it as such. Karina is in dire need of continued psychotherapy and likely an updated medication evaluation to assess her current mental state and needs. I know that Karina will not follow up with this on her own; she has never believed in the efficacy of treatment and has only cooperated with it because it was expected of her by others. As arduous and perhaps unfair a task as it may be, I can only hope that Marcelo continues to oversee Karina's mental health treatment. It is the only way she will ever retain any threshold of functionality.

LOURDES

Lourdes is a typical 17-year-old American girl—cell phone in hand, fashion conscious, seemingly in control of her world. She is also quite the atypical 17-year-old American girl—mother to a nine-month-old baby, caretaker to a disabled and severely mentally ill half-sister, struggling student, fast food restaurant worker and the only American citizen in her family. She presented as strong beyond her years, yet much like when one crams in more groceries than a bag can hold, Lourdes was visibly ripping apart.

Lourdes' desperation and determination to find help was remarkable. As soon as she walked in the office, she sat in the chair directly in front of me and without a blink she said, "What do you need from me?" A bit surprised at her readiness to start with a process that most people don't typically ever look forward to, I simply replied, "All I need is the truth. The truth is usually nightmarish enough."

That's all it took. Lourdes leaned back on her chair as her cheeks became soaked with a steady stream of tears. "You've got to help us. They can't send my mom and Carla to Mexico. We can't go to Mexico, we'll all die," she told me. "No Lourdes," I said, "You've got to help me."

81

I saw the look of understanding in her face. Flashes of shame, resignation and then desperation darted past her expressions as she sat in the chair across from me, attempting to tame her tears. And so this is how the story of Lourdes, the typical/atypical American girl, began to unravel in front of me.

My name is Lourdes. I'm 17 and I'm the only one in my family to have been born in the United States. My mom is from Mexico and she had my sister Carla while she lived there many years ago. Even though my mom and sister shared their culture with me and tried to keep it alive in our home, I grew up an American. English is my first language even though I can understand Spanish; I like different music and I prefer different foods. I love my mom and sister, but we are just different

My mom brought Carla to the United States in the early 90s—they fled Mexico. My mom was married to a guy that beat her and Carla. She said he used to be a "normal man," and that everything started very innocently with him simply trying to network with people, but he fell in with the wrong crowd. My mom said that her husband became very powerful around town because he became close to the gangsters. With that came a lot of drinks and drugs and this guy (who suddenly had become a very irritable man), let out all of his anger on my mom and sister. My mom told me that he would take my sister away for days and tell my mom that he would kill Carla if she didn't obey him. She said that eventually her fear of him hurting Carla took over, and she grabbed my sister one day and ran away—all the way to here.

I was born a few years after my mom arrived in the United States. She had to work two jobs in order to provide for me and Carla and we didn't get to see her very much—we spent a lot of time with my grandmother. I didn't resent my mom for being gone so much, even though I was little; I knew life was tough for us. Carla has been sick with rheumatoid arthritis since she was a kid and has never been able to have a normal life. For as long as I remember, she couldn't use her legs as she is still so tiny. So she spent her time between a wheelchair and her bed. She was also on multiple medications, and the hospital was like her second home—we were there all the time.

I've cared for Carla for as long as I can remember. Even though she is much older than I, I was her company day in and day out. We had the same friends and we always went places together. Carla has always been my responsibility and surprisingly it never bothered me even as a kid—I love my sister. I was even willing to fight other kids if they made fun of her or made her cry. Sad thing is, I often did have to fight because so many kids didn't understand us.

Carla and I hated staying with my grandmother. She may have been trying to protect us, but she would never let us do anything—she even kept us locked in the house. She was very careful with Carla, but she was very controlling with me; my mom agreed with me and hated the way my grandmother treated me, but we had no choice because she was the only one we had while my mom was at work. I know she was trying to help raise me and keep me safe, but it made me feel even more alienated and lonely than I already was. I felt smothered and angry and I would often sneak out the windows and run away from my grandma's house for the day.

School was my only escape from my grandmother and I actually had really good grades until the fifth grade. I don't remember exactly what happened, but I began to lose interest in learning. I do remember that I was really into sports, but they wouldn't let me play because my grades weren't so good any more. Instead of this motivating me to be better, it disappointed me. I felt controlled, just like my grandma tried to control me by not letting me go outside to play. I had no outlet, no way to clear my head, so I lost my motivation to do well in anything.

I grew bored with school and began to skip classes in the sixth grade. I would pretend to go to school, but I would go to my friend's house instead. Some other friends would meet us there and we would go walk around the city. I remember feeling free and able to breathe. I liked it and I looked forward every day to ditching school, and my grandma, and being away from rules. The days I did go to school I would get in trouble for fighting other kids—I don't know why I was so irritable. I was even put in anger management classes in the seventh grade and I continued to take those classes for the next four years.

My friends were troublemakers and I sometimes joined in the fun. They liked to pull pranks on people and even though I thought it was funny, in the end I would be the one in trouble for it. It happened so often that eventually the principal at school began to give me suspensions. I don't think my grandma or my mom knew what to do about me anymore. As much as they talked, yelled, grounded me and kept me locked up, I still wouldn't listen. I've always loved my mom and sister very much, but I just needed to get out and away from everything. It felt like a breath of fresh air.

One time my friends and I decided to skip school and go "somewhere far." My friend's boyfriend dropped us off at an outlet mall on the outskirts of the city and we walked around and played until our feet hurt. Then we realized we had no way of getting back, so we had no better idea than to break into a car and drive back. That was the first time I stole a car—and we got away with it.

I thought the world was out there for me to grab. I felt in command of things, powerful, smart. I began to feel that maybe I didn't have to live inside the box my grandma and school had custom-made for me, that maybe I could do something bigger—something that *I* wanted to do. I grew to really look forward to all the things that got us excited; I quickly grew addicted to bad things.

I got away with things for a long time before I got into any trouble. Each time I got away with something, I pushed a little closer to the edge, until I began to get in trouble with the police. The last time I stole a car I was caught and charged. My mom was so disappointed in me—I could see the shame in her eyes. For the first time I felt like a filthy thug, embarrassed in seeing that I was a failure in my family's eyes.

I tried to do better and began going to school frequently again and doing homework. I gave it my best shot until the tenth grade when I dropped out and enrolled in a GED program. I didn't see my friends as much, but I was still social—I wouldn't hang out with them during the day, but we would still go to parties together. It was at one of these parties that I met Martin; we liked each other right away and dated for some time. I got pregnant six months later and I have a nine month old daughter now. I see Martin from time to time, but he is not really involved in raising my daughter.

I'm lucky that my mom didn't turn her back on me after all I've done. I depend on her to help me raise Ana, because I really have no idea what I'm doing. I don't know what I'd do if they send my mom and sister back to Mexico; I guess that I would have to go with them.

I've never been to Mexico, but I know all about that place. I know people who go back are targeted by gangs because they're thought to have money, and I know they're brutal in their ways of coercing people to do as they want. I know people who return to Mexico aren't really seen as Mexicans anymore and they're not welcomed back into the community. My mom says that if people don't accept us, they won't care about us—and we'll be in even more danger. If we had to go back to Mexico it would be just us, all alone, without anyone to rely on. One of my grandfathers lives in Cuernavaca, but he's remarried and has a different family now. He would maybe give us a place to stay for a few days, but we wouldn't be welcome to live there for long or to rely on their support.

I still help care for Carla plus taking care of my daughter. If I barely know what I'm doing here, I'm really going to be lost in Mexico. Besides, Cuernavaca scares me to death. That's where everyone who gets kidnapped in Mexico is found. They find them dead. Cuernavaca is the only place my mom knows and the one place where we could maybe find work and a way to survive, but it's also where drug lords and gangs hang out the most. It's in the news every day; people get killed, people go missing, or people that went missing for a long time turn up in pieces or without their heads. A kid I knew from school moved back there and it wasn't long before people found out he had moved back from the United States, and shortly after that he was kidnapped. I was friends with his sister and kept in touch after they moved away. She told me that they received calls for a few weeks demanding $10,000 from them, and even though they didn't have it, they were scrambling to get the money together. They must have taken too long though, because they found her brother beheaded in a park. They didn't even shoot him, and he didn't die quickly. I don't want to go live there. One of my mom's uncles and other people she knew has also been murdered in Cuernavaca. Even worse, Carla's dad still lives there and he's sworn to hurt them if he ever sees them again. I'm terrified for what can happen to Carla and my mom. I'm terrified for what can happen to all of us there.

How could Carla, my daughter and I live there by ourselves? If we barely see my mom now because of work, we're not going to see her there at all—she'll be working every chance she gets so we can survive. There isn't anyone that would care for us for a long time. Carla is disabled and my daughter isn't even a toddler yet; I would be in charge of both of them. I wouldn't even be able to work and help my mom because I couldn't leave Carla or my baby alone. It would also be my job to hide us, to make sure no one knows we come from the United States—to keep us safe. I don't even know how to keep myself safe here. Lately, all I can think of doing is closing my eyes tight and praying for a miracle.

I'm very protective of my daughter, but the one that worries me the most is Carla because she is

100% dependent on us. She needs someone there for anything she could possibly need to do, from eating, to bathing, to even moving around in her bed. I love her, but taking care of her is not easy. It's also not cheap to take care of Carla; she needs medicines for her rheumatoid arthritis and cerebral palsy. She also needs pills for the very severe depression she has; otherwise she pretty much goes down the drain. On top of her physical pain, Carla is really hurt by not being able to have a normal life. When she's medicated, things are a little easier, her body doesn't hurt so much and it's easier to cheer her up –but it's not like this all the time. Over time, Carla has grown a very dark side; she tried to kill herself once and she talks about it when she feels depressed.

I don't know how Carla would be provided for in Mexico, but I know we can barely afford her medicines here. If she were to get off her pills I just don't know what she would turn into… I wouldn't know how to take care of her—to save her. I don't know how I could stop her from trying to kill herself again. Last time we lucked out—we caught her getting ready to drink a handful of pills. I was able to talk her out of trying to kill herself again. But that was then. Who knows what could happen now? I don't know how I would deal with it if she tried to do that again—I may as well kill myself alongside her. She's seeing a counselor and is becoming a little bit more stable. That's another thing we couldn't be able to give her in Mexico. That's another reason why we can't take her away

89

from here. If mom gets deported, I don't know what would happen to any of us.

I'd like to say that I'm as tough as I've always pretended to be, but I'm not. I'm falling apart and I don't know how to start putting my pieces back together. I don't even know how to stop myself from continuing to fall apart. Every day feels as if I'm only half awake—my mind half somewhere else, a black hole sucking the energy and the life out of me. I don't know how to fight it. I keep bearing the weight and thinking that it will get better, but it's not getting better and I'm cracking under the pressure. We have to stay; there is no other way for us to survive. We have to stay.

. . .

I witnessed how Lourdes' story ended. It's one of those things that stay with you for the rest of your life. The family's attorney called me to go into court and testify on her case as an expert witness. We spent hours in court that day; the family holding onto one another for dear life—their future basically hanging from a thread above their heads, ready to fall on them, whatever it may be.

Lourde's mother was not allowed to remain in the United States. In fact, she was given 90 days to return to Mexico. I know I was there an as expert witness and needed to remain impartial, but I am also a human being and I was shocked at the decision to deport Lourde's mom. There were so many lives on the line on this case, so many. Their attorney advised them to file an appeal and they followed his advice in a heartbeat. I think I would have done the same.

Their case was eventually re-opened and as far as I know they're still fighting it 14 months after that one "final" hearing. I've seen Lourdes a handful of times since that day in court. I was requested to offer counseling while their case progresses. The family can't afford it, but she won't get by without it so I offered my services at a reduced, rather symbolic rate.

Lourdes is still hanging on somehow. I had fully expected her to fall into a million pieces by now, but to my relief, she turned out to be infinitely stronger than I initially thought. She is only hanging on by a thread, though, of that I'm certain and it worries me. She looks exhausted and I wonder if every time I say goodbye to her after our sessions it may and although she's still hanging on, I can tell that it's merely by a thread. Every time we conclude a session I wonder if I will see her again. It's a terrible feeling to worry about your patient's life, about the outcome of their plights and its rippling effect in their lives. I can't imagine what it feels like to be the protagonist of a nightmare like that one.

MARIA

Maria was tired. She was so tired she could have just handed her two children over to me and simply walked away, perhaps indefinitely. I studied her quickly as she sat in front of me; her back hunched forward, her elbows resting on her lap, her downward gaze ... this was someone who appeared ready to give up but was not yet prepared to admit it.

As soon as I asked her how she was doing, Maria began to cry. She told me of how she and her children live in a basement room where the wall plaster is falling apart. She said she worked in her son's school cafeteria, but she only earned enough to pay for their small room and her son's medical treatment. Her look turned bitter when she told me that although she had family here in town, "They had never been able to protect me."

Maria was ready to tell me her story and an eerie feeling came over me as I noticed that right then and there, Maria had already made up her mind about something. Try as I might, I couldn't yet see exactly what it was, and I grew concerned that perhaps she would not tell me. I noticed deep scars around her wrists as she fidgeted with her hands on her seat, and suddenly I understood.

I looked over at Maria's children and then pretended to look down, but I had actually closed my eyes for a second hoping that we would not be among the last see Maria again. I resolved to help her and to do anything in my power to show her a different perspective on her life. I'd stick my hand in the mud, and if she took it, I'd help her pull her out of the hole that was about to extinguish her life.

"You have beautiful children. I can see they're very attached to you, too," I told her.

"They need to learn to look out for one another," she told me.

An icy cold chill ran down my spine.

My name is Maria and I'm 30 years old. I was born in Cortez, Colorado, where my parents owned a small paint and hardware store. I'm the middle of three children and even though we all get along today, I remember lots of fighting and angry words around the house while I was growing up. I grew to accept it as the norm in our home, but the anger in my family members' voices as they yelled at one another always made me scared.

Until I was about nine years old I sleep-walked and I had night terrors every other night. I'd scream and cry in my sleep and I would scratch my legs until they were bloody. During the day I'd have stomach aches and felt jumpy. I wasn't a normal kid—I was always afraid. It wasn't really the tangible things that scared me, but rather everything I couldn't see. I was terrified of anger outbursts, for example. Uncertainty about my safety made me feel sick and I was haunted by a feeling that something was about to harm me. My parents took me to different doctors, but none could tell them what was wrong with me.

My dad wasn't a good man and my mom put up with it. He was quite the character all right, but not one bit in a good way. When I was a kid I remember thinking he had scary, mean-looking friends, and as I grew up I realized they were all drug dealers, thieves, or scammers of some sort. Everyone knew—even I knew—so I know that Mom was well aware of it. I don't know why she put up with any of it; he was such a violent man and he turned her into the ridicule of the town. No one had any respect for her, and as the years went by, I too began to see how pathetic she was.

I wish my mom would've been less passive; my dad beat the hell out of all of us. His disciplinary method of choice was spanking and he made sure he would punish us severely for every little transgression. It didn't matter if we broke a plate on each other's heads or if we walked up the stairs a little too loud—he'd come and beat us with his belt. I remember how once, just to tease him I put the remote control in his boot; I had black and blue legs for a week.

I never did well in school; when you become afraid of your dad hitting you every day, other things don't seem as important. I didn't care very much about my low grades, but I also had a hard time grasping all that information. They put me in special education by the time I was in fifth grade because they said I had a learning disorder. I didn't care about learning, not even then—I was disillusioned with school. I thought it would become a safe place for me, like a second, better home where I would make friends and feel protected. It was none of that. I didn't fit in with any of them. Kids told stories of family outings and playing games and all I had to show for myself were bruises—and I couldn't even show anyone. I gave up and kept to myself. Other kids made fun of me for dressing the way I did to cover up all of the marks on my body.

My dad died when I was 13 and I didn't know what to feel. All my life I was terrified by him. But he was the only dad I ever knew—the only one I had. I was left with a very palpable hole in my life and I didn't know how where or how to begin patching up my dad's absence in my life—or the nightmarish years in his presence.

I snapped. I got into fights in school and started drinking. The rolling snowball that was my life became an avalanche. I could never drink enough to fully numb myself from all that I carried inside of me, but I kept trying. I was sad and angry at the same time, and I felt that everyone gave me a reason to lash out and try to beat them at their own games.

It wasn't enough. Nothing ever took away all the garbage from inside me, or let me forget about it for a moment. Eventually, I started to cut myself, and the physical pain became a release to my inner mess. It became my way to soothe myself and the ache I felt, and I did that for five years. Nothing was right about me during that time. But it never really made me any better—it was just a temporary fix. My mind grew darker and darker as the months went by and I began having fantasies about cutting my wrists and just ending it all. I hated everything and everyone, including myself.

I kept drinking, and I began using marijuana. I made sure I spent as much of the day as numb as I could get myself to be and I became really good at it. I felt lost in a landslide. One thing led to another and I became sexually active by the time I was 15 years old. I was promiscuous, yes. People called me a "ho," but I didn't care; I was too angry. "If they want a 'ho,' I'll show them a 'ho'"—that was my motto.

My mom had a boyfriend living in the house by then, and I didn't get along with him. I had to lock my bedroom door and push the dresser in front of it because he would usually come home late and drunk, with an excuse to argue with me and beat me. He punched me so often I finally had enough and moved to a friend's home. My mom was passive as she had always been and never even tried to defend me.

By the time I turned 18 my drinking was way out of control. I felt really guilty for leaving my brother and my mom alone with that guy, but I couldn't go back there. I couldn't make it better for them either, so I drank in order to stop thinking. I can't say that my life was very eventful around that time because I don't remember much of it. Truth is, it probably was; I did drugs regularly and partied and slept around. Maybe it's a good thing I don't remember much of it.

Eventually I met a decent enough guy and we had a son a year after moving in together. I had a healthy baby boy, but he was born with a cleft palate. I thought it was a minor surgical matter, but boy was I wrong—I was not prepared for the medical care involved with someone so young. My son was clearly in pain and uncomfortable and I couldn't understand him or how to help him.

The decent guy I thought I found turned out to be nothing more than the spitting image of my dad. He lived at the bars, and when he was home, he beat me and insulted me. He didn't offer any help in the baby's care. I was in hell all over again, only this time I was the mom in the story. I had stopped drinking for my baby's sake. But as it was, it took all I had to deal with life without running for a bottle of vodka. I had even begun to think about suicide again.

One day, this boyfriend of mine decided to go on a trip with his friends and never came back. I couldn't believe it. My hopes about our relationship had already come crashing down, but I guess I didn't expect him to do something like that. By this time my son had gone through four major surgeries to correct his cleft palate and he was still waiting for a bone graft. Life was suddenly unbearable for me, and I didn't know how much longer I would last.

My drinking got out of control. My friend George and I would get together and drink almost every night, and we did just that for about a year before we decided to get together as a couple. At first I wondered if I was repeating a pattern, but then I saw my son and George bond as if they had always belonged together. I knew that at last I had finally done something right. My son has never liked to be around people, much less let them be close to him.

My son trusted George and I saw this as a true blessing. Eventually, both my son and I completely fell in love with him. The minute we moved in together, George treated my son as his own—they even dressed identically. My own son has never liked me nearly as much as he did George. It was unbelievable how bright and happy he looked when he was around him. It made me wonder if I looked the same way to him.

I wish that had been the start of "happily ever after." George and I continued to party pretty heavily for another year, but we began to slow down after our relationship progressed. I stopped drinking altogether when I got pregnant with our first (my second) child, and I gave birth to a healthy baby girl in 2008. George and I settled down; we stopped going out and would only drink on big holidays, like New Year's Eve or the Fourth of July. We even decided to get married. I didn't think something so wonderful could happen to someone like me.

After I requested that he be allowed to stay here legally, George was required to return to Belize. It's been two years since he left. He lives with his family and helps them run their little restaurant. One of his brothers is a pastor and George helps out at his church too—he's in charge of the repairs and maintenance of both places.

The kids and I followed George when he first went back to Belize. We lived with his family for 18 months and my son even went to school there for a while. Life wasn't easy, but we were all together––maybe we could've even stayed there.

We had to come back to the United States because my son still needs medical care for his cleft palate. We specifically returned so that he could have another surgery. We tried to go back to Belize to live after that, but we couldn't afford to fly my son to the United States for every step of his treatment—so we had to stay here in Colorado.

We don't have anyone here; we only had George. My mom isn't any help at all and my son is terrified of her current boyfriend anyway—a man who is a lot like my dad used to be. My siblings aren't reliable either, and my son's dad... well, I never saw him after he went on his trip.

I'd run away to Belize if it weren't for my child's need for medical treatment. I don't care if we won't have as many opportunities or money because I just want us to be with George. We all need him. I try to visit him every six months, but I can't always take the children with me. If my grandma agrees to watch them, then I can go see George. But it's also heartbreaking to leave the kids and my home in the United States as well.

The kids and I lived in a shelter for a while after George left; we couldn't afford a place to live. My grandma let us stay with her for a few weeks, but we weren't welcome to stay there indefinitely. I found work in a school cafeteria and the kids and I were able to rent a room in the basement of one of the kitchen ladies' homes.

Being without George is unbearable. I don't know how to handle it all; I don't know how I've made it this far. He was the one to coordinate all of my son's treatments, visits, and surgeries, because I'm just not as good at making sense of it all. George still tried to take care of it over the phone from Belize, but he can only do so much. What's left for me to do by myself really overwhelms me. I don't have the tools most people have to deal with life—I don't know what happened to mine. I can't understand things or make decisions alone and a lot of information really beats me down, especially if it's something as important as my son's health. I'm frozen in panic, afraid to make the wrong decisions.

I've started to consider suicide again. I know I'd leave my children alone, but I don't know that I'm much good to them here with things as they are. George was the strong one, the role model, and our guiding light. I'm just a rehabbing alcoholic trying to keep it together, playing house. I love my children, don't get me wrong, but life for me is very simple—I'm nothing without George.

I cut the side of my wrist a few nights ago and it felt relieving. I'm about to go down the drain again. I keep wanting to stop at the liquor store and just forget about everything. But I know that will just end everything, for all of us. George was the only good thing I had in my life and I'm hanging on with the last bit of me I have left, and it's only because I hope that we can all be reunited again soon. If that is taken away from me… it would be the end of this story.

...

Maria's legal case took an interesting turn. Shortly after the judge denied the petition to allow George to return to the United States before the requisite ten year period, Maria grabbed the children, packed her bags and moved to Belize permanently.

I think this was her last attempt to save her own life, and I admire the fight she had left in her. Maria could not have lasted alone in the United States another month. She admitted this herself when she told me she had cut her wrists not that long ago, and that it had felt good. Had she remained in the United States alone, Maria would have eventually relapsed into her drug and alcohol abuse, as well as her self-mutilating behaviors. She had never availed herself to therapy or mutual support groups. She had no reliable social supports. Maria's depression and post-traumatic stress was unchecked and untreated. She placed all of her hopes and dreams with George and had become dependent on him in an unhealthy way.

People don't often understand how some adults simply cannot deal with "life." In Maria's case, childhood was a rather brutal experience and life had become unbearable. She did not have any reserves of self-esteem and didn't feel capable doing anything on her own. Her whole existence was shot through with feelings of failure, and she never learned any healthy coping mechanisms. Maria never knew how to deal with daily life struggles and the complexity of raising kids in addition to caring for herself as well. So she taught herself how to become numb to the pain of her life that she had for so long carried like a ball and chain. In doing so, it only helped her demons grow to the point where she was nearly haunted right out of her own life.

Maria considers George to be the one positive thing that has ever happened to her, and as such, she only trusts and relies on him. As a scientist/practitioner, I'm rather surprised she was able to live apart from him for two years. As a human being, I'm rather saddened by it—the separation set her back and caused a great deal of damage. I don't know if she will be able to fully heal the extent of the harm inflicted on her throughout her lifetime, but I do know she will have a more stable and peaceful life with George in Belize. Hopefully it will ripple onto her children's lives and affect them positively, as there is still time for them to be spared a significant amount of scarring.

I agreed with Maria in that life would be much more difficult for her in Belize; her children would have a more simple education and the opportunities for their future will be considerably limited. She said one thing, however, that I will always remember; "Better a simple, happy life around people that love you, than a million opportunities in hell."

Good luck, Maria.

REFUGIO

Refugio came into my office with his entire family. He was clearly the patriarch of the family unit, but I found very interesting that it was actually his oldest son Lazaro who handled all the arrangements, forms, and questions. When my assistant took some paperwork over to Refugio to fill out, he smiled sheepishly, pointed at Lazaro and told her "Give it to him, I don't understand these things." When she explained to him that the forms were in Spanish, he smiled again as he shook his head and said, "I don't understand, let Lazaro do it."

Refugio's wife and children remained in the waiting room as I beckoned him into my office. He took a few steps before he turned around to look for Lazaro. When I explained to him that I needed to interview him in private, Refugio looked at me with dismay, as if I was missing a big, obvious point. "Lazaro needs to come in," he simply stated.

Lazaro hardly spoke for the entirety of the interview, in that I hardly asked him any questions. It was Refugio who I needed to get to know, and the first and most important thing I learned about was his pathological dependence in his son. Refugio had gone from relying on Lazaro to fill out forms and handle the family arrangements to absolutely requiring his presence in order to feel safe and whole.

Refugio sat immobile in his chair with a lost and forlorn look in his face. As he told me his story about his life in Guatemala, I noticed he wasn't looking at me, but rather past me—Refugio was reliving each moment in his mind as he told me about his life. His body began to tense as his hands clutched the arms of the chair. Refugio was no longer in the room; as he spoke of his life, he was transported back to his past, and was clearly experiencing every bit of his gruesome story again.

"Save me," he suddenly said. But rather than looking at me, he had turned to look at Lazaro. I reached over to my right and grabbed a back-up notepad. It was going to be a long afternoon.

My name is Refugio. I'm an old man. I was born and raised in a village by the foot of the mountains in Guatemala. Like most families, my dad worked in the fields and my mom took care of the home. We are Mayans, and grew up surrounded by our culture and speaking our native tongue, Quiche.

My brothers and I were able to attend school, but we didn't go past the fifth grade. Our family was poor and couldn't afford to keep sending us to school. They also needed us working in the fields to help support everyone. We worked long hours every day only to be cheated out of our pay. We planted,

106

tended, and harvested crops but we rarely got money for it—we mostly got paid in sugar and coffee. I was always grateful that we never lacked food to eat, but we were seldom able to afford anything else. We couldn't even pay for electricity; we had to cook by firelight.

I was 16 when the war began. I remember many things, but my fear of the military is what I remember the most. They were brutal, vicious men, and like all the Spanish speakers, they had little regard for us natives. They always suspected us of aiding and collaborating with the guerrillas; they weren't wrong, but it wasn't out of choice. Guerrilleros were savages and came down to our village at night, demanding to be fed. It wasn't anything complicated; if we didn't help them, they would kill us. We had no choice, and as we helped the guerrilleros in order to save our lives, we prayed no militia man would ever find out—they would kill us too.

I saw the war—all of it. The fight between the guerrillas and the military was savage, as was the way both sides treated us. The military hunted for the guerrilleros in the mountains, but anyone they saw on the way was fair game to them—and they were known for their torture in order to get information. Guerrillas hunted for the military in the village and in the areas nearby. They would blow up bridges and burn buildings, aiming to kill the military, and while they did so, they also killed many of us and left the rest without a single way out

107

of there. The anticipation, knowing something could happen at any moment that could hurt us, even kill us, was unbearable. I don't know how we survived.

Every time the military came into the village, they would go from door to door questioning people, trying to find out who was helping out the guerrillas or forcing people into joining their ranks. I can't remember how many times I ran away and hid in the mountains for days, waiting for them to leave. The memories of every trip back down to the village are seared into my brain. As I walked down there I would find dead bodies scattered across the foothill—the people the military had tortured or simply killed and then discarded like trash. My fellow Mayans desecrated. It made me ill.

One of my close friends was killed by those animals. He was suspected of cooperating with the guerrillas and beaten to death with clubs. When I heard that he had disappeared, it wasn't desperation but terror that washed over me. I knew he hadn't disappeared. I knew where I would find him—and I knew I'd find him dead.

My friends and I went to the mountain to look for his body and we gave him a proper burial, even though we had to do it in secret. My heart was broken to bits; my friend hadn't cooperated with the guerrillas any more than we were all forced to do. I was afraid to lose anyone else I knew, or be next myself. I was so frightened by the military that on my way home I began to shake and I felt as though I couldn't breathe. I had run as fast as my legs would allow me so I could hide from them. I don't know if they were looking for me, but in my mind I was already a dead man; I only needed to fall into their hands.

My life went on in that same manner for years and years. The daily fear, the tension, the panic—it was our way of life. Eventually I married and had children. We got by with barely enough to eat and no time to properly care for our children. Life was difficult—too difficult.

Just like my father and his father, I worked in the fields to make a living and my wife took care of the house and the children. My wife was also a Mayan and we raised our children as such. This is our culture, this is who we are.

My son Lazaro is the oldest of the five kids we had. Poor kid, he bore the brunt of our way of life for all his siblings. Even though our kids' first language was Quiche, we sent them to school so they could learn Spanish and receive an education. Many of the students were also Mayan, but the teachers were of the white ruling class and treated them quite badly. Lazaro was always getting in trouble for defending his siblings or the other Mayan kids from the Spanish speakers.

Sending five kids to school wasn't easy on us or them. The teachers never used corporal punishment with the children, but they always put them down for being Mayans. Lazaro told me that the teachers often call them "stupid Indians," and had little patience with any of the Mayan children. My own kids often came home crying, feeling less than the rest simply for who they were, just like it happened to me when I was young. They all stopped going to school in the fourth grade. We could no longer afford to send them, and they could no longer bear the treatment.

Lazaro and the kids rarely left the house. The Spanish-speaking children were cruel to them and would hector and bully them. I remember one time Lazaro came home crying after we had sent him to the store; some kids had been taunting him—not to take his money, but simply for sport. I understood his pain and I myself wanted to go find those children and put an end to this abuse, but I knew it was a losing battle, even among children.

I travelled to the United States when Lazaro was about 12 years old. It broke my heart to leave them, but I had to find a way to support them and give them a better life. Between the military persecuting us, the racial abuse, and the gangs, we lived in more poverty and more fear than ever. I couldn't let my children grow up the same way I did.

I left the family with my father and I prayed that they would survive until I could bring them to me. Lazaro and the children worked in the fields with my dad, but they got paid in tortillas and sugar— they depended on me to survive.

Although the war between guerrillas and military had diminished in its intensity, life was still dangerous and traumatic in our village. Gangs infested the area and the military still visited homes forcing young men to join their ranks. Lazaro told me our home was visited by the military when he was 14 years old. He said he ran to his grandfather's house and he took Lazaro to the mountains to hide. The military had been recruiting children. Upon his return to the village, Lazaro found out that several of his friends had been taken by force.

The military weren't the only ones harassing people. Gangs pressured the youth to join them. They were ruthless parasites; you'd often see them terrorizing the locals in one way or another. They beat, robbed, and raped people like it was a game. It broke my heart whenever I heard Lazaro cry on the phone, telling me he was afraid to go anywhere. I knew exactly how he felt.

Finally, Lazaro told me one day he would be travelling to the United States to meet me and he would not take no for an answer. He could no longer handle life in Guatemala, living in terror and poverty. I understood perfectly, but I wanted him to wait so that there would be a man in the house. I had been planning to go back to Guatemala so I could bring the family with me, but I didn't have enough money yet.

It turned out that Lazaro wasn't asking me for my permission or any help—he left our home and began his journey to the United States. He didn't care about travelling alone or not having money; he had reached his breaking point... I knew.

Once he began his journey he was impossible to locate. I nearly died from the tension of not knowing where my son was or if he was even alive anymore. There was no stopping him; I couldn't even make him wait for me. The worry about the well-being of my children was suddenly taken over by the worry for the life of my first-born son. There he was, 15 years old, and traveling all alone. Not a word of his whereabouts did I hear.

Thank God Lazaro made it. He called me from Arizona to let me know he would be making his way to Colorado to meet me. The very next day he appeared at my doorstep. How? I don't know. He never wanted to speak of his journey.

As soon as Lazaro arrived he signed up for ESL classes and began to work alongside me in construction, doing whatever work was available to him, when there was work available. I was granted asylum a few months after his arrival and was able to submit the paperwork for him to be in the United States legally. He was granted a temporary working permit, but it will soon expire. There are complications with his case and we don't know if he will be allowed to stay any longer.

Lazaro's arrival was the best thing that could have happened for me. Together we were able to bring the entire family here. I've never been able to come back from everything that happened to me in Guatemala. I'm an old man now and I still relive those memories as if they were happening right now. Life is too hard; if it wasn't for my family, I don't know how I would make it through another day.

Lazaro is only 18 years old. He is barely an adult, but he has been an integral part of our survival here. He adapted so well, so much better than I did, that we have all become dependent on him. He is the only one that has learned English well enough, so he handles all of our living arrangements. We were able to put all of the rest of his siblings into school, and Lazaro takes care of all of that as well. My wife continues to care for the home and our family, so Lazaro and I are the main providers. I couldn't do it without him. He even switched jobs and began doing cleaning at night so that he can help his mother during the day. She doesn't drive or speak English, so Lazaro has become her only assistance in handling our life here.

I'm sick. I know something is wrong with me. Even though I'm far away from Guatemala, I still live with the same fears—I relive those memories every day. I go to work and I spend time with my family, but I do little else; I just can't. I don't have the mental capacity or the interest to handle people, crowds, activities. Maybe I've been too scarred by the war. It's like it's still happening, every day, in my head. I need Lazaro here; he is my rock.

I know we're lucky to be alive, and it wouldn't have happened without Lazaro. His decision set everything in motion and in one way or another saved us all. I can't let my son go back to Guatemala. I can't leave him at the mercy of the gangs and the government corruption; he will die. We have all been so close to death at one point or another. I can't let him go back there.

I don't know what would become of me if I have to let my son go back there to that awful place. The anguish and fear of it all would eat me up alive. The worry of losing him barely allows me to think of anything at all. I still manage to go to work, but my mind is always somewhere else. We can only afford to live here because Lazaro is here with us and he always finds a way to make everything work. Without him, we may as well be sent to our deaths as well.

...

Obviously, Refugio is a severely traumatized man. Even though he has not lived in Guatemala for many years, the horrific events of his past are being replayed over and over in his mind as if they were happening right now. I agree with Refugio in that his family has been the one element that has allowed him to "keep it together" through the years; in particular, his son Lazaro.

114

Refugio is extremely dependent on his eldest son. Try as he might, Refugio simply does not have the mental and emotional capacity to fully immerse himself in the culture and community. This is often the case with older immigrants to this country. As Lazaro so readily adjusted to their new environment, Refugio came to rely on him for any and all of their dealings to the point where the family does not know how to operate without his guidance.

At his age, I would not expect Refugio to be able to fully heal from the extremely traumatic and severely scarring events of his past. While psychotherapy can provide him with some degree of peace as he works through some of his traumas, I believe the stability of his environment is what will truly provide Refugio with quality of life in his remaining years. If he were to lose his son Lazaro, I would expect Refugio's mental health to decompensate to such a degree that he would become nearly non-functional. Additionally, in my long experience, Latino immigrants virtually never avail themselves to psychotherapy.

Lazaro's legal case was postponed for six months and then later for an entire year. He has been allowed to remain in the United States while he awaits the decision on his legal case. While the prolonged tension and uncertainty are severely damaging to Refugio and the rest of the family, at least they are able to maintain some semblance of normalcy with Lazaro still in the United States.

Refugio's story is a complicated one. He is 56 years old and thinks himself too old for the struggle of sorting through and healing the experiences from his past. Although I attempted to reason with him, he appears resigned to the fact that he "will never forget," as he puts it, and will carry these memories and the damage inflicted on him for the rest of his life. "I just want to live the rest of my years with my family, safe," is all he kept repeating—and I understand. I also believe that when he spoke of keeping his family safe he was speaking specifically of Lazaro. For the sake of this emotionally crippled refugee, I hope that Lazaro can stay.

SARA

I vividly remember my encounter with Sara because of the gaggle of people that surrounded her when she first came into my office. Aunts and uncle had arrived with this little girl and her parents in order to offer support. Seeing Sara's comfort in approaching and hugging her relatives and the warmth and care with which they responded to her, I understood that I was in the presence of something quite rare and extraordinary—this entire family operated as a unit and cared fiercely for one another.

The calm little girl I saw standing outside my office door shifted into a quiet, suspicious creature as she took a seat. She began fidgeting with her hands as she desperately looked at all her family members walking out of the room in a single file. It took a full tank of charm to put Sara at ease and convince her that it was okay to talk to me and that maybe I'd even possibly understand what she was going through.

This fifth grader had been living with the anxiety and worry of an adult. She cried profusely while admitting that she had been secretly researching "everything" she overheard her parents talking about, though she didn't understand what any of it meant. Little Sara had bravely gone out into the world looking for answers and now sat in my office

wringing her hands and looking at me imploringly
for help, as she simply did not know what to do with
the bucket-load of information she carried.

My name is Sara, and I'm 11 years old. My parents are from South Korea, but my brother and I were born here in the United States. My parents moved here a few years before we were born; my dad told me that his brother had invited them here because he saw my parents struggle a lot in South Korea. It's true, my mom explained to me once that life in South Korea is tough, and even though both of them had gone to school they weren't earning enough to survive.

My mom works at a nail shop; it's not like her assistant job in South Korea, but she told me that she likes talking to all the ladies that go in the shop. My dad worked as an architect for as long as I remember until he got sick. He has Cirrhosis and Hepatitis B. At first it wasn't noticeable, but he has gotten so sick in the past two years that he had to quit his job. My mom tried to support the house with her nail shop money, but since she had to cut back her hours to take care of my dad, now she only makes enough to pay for rent. We depend on my aunts and uncles to eat and pay the rest of the bills.

Everyone in our family is really close and we all get along well. It's like one really big family full of older brothers and sisters—I wish we could all live in one big house. My aunts and uncles even help take care of my dad when they're not at work since my brother and I are in school all day. I've noticed that it embarrasses my mom to ask them for help; I think she feels like she's bothering them, but we don't have a choice. Besides, they're our family—they're not going to let us live in the streets.

My family would say that I've always been a little shy, but they were never concerned about it until recently—I've changed a lot. Our family is in trouble because my dad, sick as he is, might get sent back to Korea. I've never been there, but I know I don't want to go. My dad will die if we have to take him there.

I guess I don't feel like talking anymore. My family says that whenever I do speak it's barely a mumble and I'm usually staring at the floor. I don't do it on purpose, but it's true. I just don't feel like seeing anyone. I don't laugh very much anymore either. According to my parents I used to be "bright and outgoing," and maybe they're right, but I feel miles away from that girl now. I've seen my dad get sicker by the day for the past two years, coming back from the doctor with a little less hope every time. Of course I'm sad—my dad is dying. And now I'm angry that they want to take him away from his doctor and our family and send us to Korea. For what? So that we can all die together?

I used to love school. I loved being around kids my age and I loved the smell of notebooks. I loved my classroom so much I thought I'd become a teacher someday, but I don't really care anymore. My grades are really bad now and my parents are angry with me, but I don't know what to do about it. I just don't care. I don't care about books or drawings or school papers—I just want to know how to get my dad to stay.

I don't know what to do about it, so I cry. I have nightmares all the time about us going to Korea and living in the alleys. I've had nightmares about my mom not being able to pay for the hospital there and my dad dying. I don't want to go to sleep anymore. I lay in my bed and my head goes racing on its own trying to figure out how to get a new liver for my dad and how to get us to stay here in the United States. I stayed up one night and I wrote a letter to the president, but I haven't heard back.

I know I'm Korean, but I don't feel Korean. If my dad got deported we would have to go back with him and I'm scared of that. They'll treat me like an outsider for being an American and thinking like an American; only my looks are Korean—I can't even speak the language that well. I don't know how I would go to school or do the homework there, but I do know that kids would pick on me for being different. That's their country and their culture; I'm just a foreigner.

I've seen it once the internet, how kids abuse other kids in Korea. There are a lot of bullies over there and they don't punish them like they do here––I'm scared that something will happen to me. I feel alone in the world with my problems; I don't think people understand what I'm going through and what can happen to me if I go to Korea. My parents have enough problems on their own, so I choose to keep things to myself and turn them around in my mind over and over—but I can't find a solution.

If we move to Korea my dad will die. It's true, I've heard my parents talk and I've looked online. I don't know where my mom would work, but she wouldn't be able to earn enough to support us and to pay for my dad's treatment. It's not like she's been able to do that here either, but at least here in the United States we have the rest of our family to rely on, and they come through for us. In Korea we'd have no one, and no one would care because we wouldn't even be considered Koreans.

My dad is waiting for a liver transplant here in the United States; if he gets it, he could live. I've looked and I know they can do the same thing in South Korea, but I heard my mom talk about how they expect you to pay up front for everything there; at least here in the U.S., you can make payments. I know we don't have the money, you see? So we couldn't pay up front, which means my dad would die. If we stayed in the US my dad could live because they would let us make payments on his liver and the surgery.

If I went to school in Korea I'd have to be set back a few years because I hardly speak the language. I would be the only 11-year-old second grader in the school and the bullies would notice me. I talked online with some Korean-American kids that have lived in South Korea and they say that teachers still punish you physically there. I read that online too. I also saw that it's common for kids to be violent with each other. I don't want them to beat me up. Kids in schools there try to fit in at all costs to avoid getting picked on, so no one would help me if I became a target. I don't even know if anyone would even want to be friends with "the foreign girl;" as far as I know, I'd be alone.

I don't know how to deal with this anymore. I don't want to put any more burdens on my parents, but I can't handle this on my own. I rarely ever laugh anymore, I don't smile and I can't sleep. I mostly cry—I'm scared. All I want is to stay here in my home, go to school in the language I know, and be with my dad and family.

We went to court last week. The judge didn't tell us whether we could stay or go, but rather, he put off my dad's case for another six months. I don't know if that's good or bad, but I'm glad we don't have to go South Korea right now. I feel lucky; maybe the hospital will call and tell my dad they found a liver for him.

...

Sara's level of anxiety and depression is beyond what most any typical 11-year-old child endures.

She had been crippled by worry and fear on so many levels that I expected her to spiral down into a full blown depression within weeks of having seen her. Although the family seemed to care about my advice to start taking Sara to counseling, they admitted that they were running out of financial resources and the manpower to accomplish their various responsibilities.

I was relieved when I later learned that Sara had begun to see the school counselor and was also referred to a mental health clinic in her area that offered discounted services. Although she was greatly affected by her family's situation, Sara was still at a point where she could be saved from degenerating into the destructive behaviors many troubled adolescents resort to as deviant coping mechanisms.

I never saw Sara again, but I often remember her and hope that this little, shy, inquisitive Sara got her wishes granted and her family was allowed to remain in the United States, and that hopefully "the hospital called dad to tell him they found him a liver."

American Citizen Cruelty Toward Immigrants

A'MER

A'mer was remarkably calm, well-spoken, and self-reflective—which was somewhat surprising for a person in his situation. It appeared as though he had spent a good deal of time contemplating his circumstances, and although it became apparent that he was resigned to his current life situation, I didn't get the feeling that he quite understood it.

I was also surprised that unlike many men I have met from his Arabic culture, A'mer did not exhibit an overly traditional masculine persona. I asked him about the dynamics of his family life, and he indicated that his father was clearly the head of the household and decision-maker. He also told me that his father treated his wife with affection and was respectful with her, and that she was his partner in all respects.

"So did you spend more time with your mother or your father?" I asked him.

"My mom," he responded. "My dad usually worked until late."

A'mer went on to describe his mother as a calm and quiet woman who was affectionate with the children and devoted to her husband. He even smiled while he recounted several small events in his childhood. It all sounded almost picture-perfect, and I began to wonder just what had been the series of events in his life that led up to his present circumstances.

A'mer appeared to be at ease while he related his childhood and adolescent history. As likeable as he appeared to be, I couldn't find anything noteworthy in his history that helped me to make sense of his present situation. As is normally the case in such matters, I only had to wait just a little longer.

"Everything changed when the Iraqi soldiers invaded Kuwait," he said. It was at this point in his story that A'mer began to pick at his cuticles, even though he appeared consciously unaware of doing it. He shifted his position in his seat and sunk down ever so slightly in the chair, as if looking for cover.

A'mer then began to report his memories of the Iraqi invasion of Kuwait in a matter-of-fact kind of way. His countenance was stoic as he told me everything that happened in his life during that year. His eyes betrayed him, however, and I knew that this had been the event which had instilled in A'mer an abiding sense of fear. His wartime experiences steeled him, and may have provided the conditioning for him to withstand the events that occurred many years later in his life.

When I asked if his wife was with him, A'mer turned quickly, to look at the door. It was as if he expected to see her to come through the entrance of *my office at any moment. He was quite tense and with eyes wide, he said, "Why do you ask?"*

A brief moment went by before he began to calm down a bit. It seemed as if he realized that his wife would not be coming into the building. He slowly relaxed back into his seat. His hands loosened their grip on the arms of his chair.

"She's not the same girl I met at the diner. She hasn't been for a long time," he told me, his eyes moist behind a watery curtain. His sudden change in demeanor caught me off guard, and I felt a sudden surge of compassion for him. I wondered to myself, "Just what has this man gone through?"

My name is A'mer and I'm 45 years old. I was born in Syria, but my family moved to Kuwait when I was merely a baby, and this is where I was raised. My father worked in the kitchen of a hospital and my mother stayed home and took care of my six siblings and me.

Life growing up was rather unremarkable for me. I grew up in a traditional Muslim home, so I don't have any stories of alcohol or drug abuse in my family. My mother always seemed to hold a lower status than my father. She couldn't work outside the home or do much for herself—her duty was to the family. Nonetheless, they respected and loved one another; I rarely saw them fight or treat one another with anything but kindness.

I was a normal child with average grades. I had friends in school, but I rarely saw them outside of class. It was just the way things were. Besides, my mom had her hands full with my six siblings, and I never had any shortage of playmates. I think I was a happy child. I don't have any particularly sour memories from that time. I know we didn't have money to splurge on toys or newer clothes, but we never lacked for food, a roof over our heads, or clean clothes to wear.

After I graduated from high school, I enrolled in the University of Kuwait and I eventually graduated with a degree in accounting. I found work at one of the many corporations in Kuwait and I stayed there for nearly ten years. My siblings and I went our different ways in making something of ourselves, but we all continued to live with our parents. We just liked being together. We contributed to the house's expenses and went on independently about our days, but we always gathered in the evenings and spent a lot of time together. I never felt overly attached to my family; we simply got along and supported one another. No one was in a hurry to leave.

I remember when the Iraqis invaded Kuwait; I was there. I remember driving to work one day when I ran into a roadblock set up by Iraqi soldiers. They were stopping and searching everyone, then turning them back home. I remember being utterly confused about what was happening, but I didn't fear for my life or well-being. That would come later.

I returned home that day to find that my siblings had also been turned back from different roads. My dad was the only one who wasn't stopped on his way to work that day, but only because the hospital was about one kilometer away from where we lived. I'd be hard-pressed to forget a day like that. We huddled together watching the news, afraid of what we might find out. Our encounters with the Iraqi soldiers had not been hostile, but we didn't know how long that would last and we began to wonder what would happen to us.

It was a like full-on war, the invasion. The power and water systems were shut down the day after the Iraqi soldiers blocked the roads. We lived in darkness for the first week and heard little else outside other than the sound of bombings and fighter jets. Tanks and soldiers lined the streets and highways. People were being searched and questioned. No one wanted to leave their homes, and that's exactly what happened. Many people stopped working, including us. The streets weren't safe any longer.

The Iraqis occupied the streets with their tanks and checkpoints for seven months. Countless fights broke out between the soldiers and the Kuwaiti resistance and many citizens died in the process. It wasn't difficult to find oneself in the wrong place at the wrong time, and many people were victims of friendly fire, angry mobs, or bombings. Two of my brothers were injured during that time. They were in a market when a bomb exploded nearby. The blast destroyed everything nearby and my brothers were buried under the collapsed eaves of a supply store for about two hours before other survivors helped them out of the rubble. One brother broke two ribs, the other one his left arm.

We panicked—I panicked. We stopped going out unless we absolutely required to do so and my mother convinced my father to stop going to the hospital for his work shifts. Even one kilometer was just too dangerous a distance to endure in the streets. We survived by carefully scheduling trips out to markets and buying supplies, and even then, it was my other siblings who normally went scavenging. I was too terrified and therefore a liability. Since nobody wanted to leave their homes, we survived by selling whatever goods we were able to find to the families in our neighborhood at a higher price. It didn't make us rich, but it gave us enough to get by and feed everyone.

Our scavenging trips to the markets were like stepping out into a post-apocalyptic nightmare. My city was no longer the peaceful place where I grew up. Some areas had been obliterated in bombings, and some still remained, but in ruins. The façade of buildings and houses were covered in black ash and some even bore the scorching black marks of fire. We often saw citizens and soldiers, shot dead, and lying in the streets. There were burned-out tanks on the sides of the roads and fires still burning somewhere in the distance.

Every day I feared for my life and that of my siblings. I found myself constantly trying to will myself into waking, as if this was some horrid, outrageous nightmare rather than our everyday reality. Although we made some money from the supplies we collected on our scavenging trips, before everything turned chaotic we had to pull out what little money we had from our bank accounts. After a few months, however, we ran into the same problem as most everyone else: we were slowly running out of funds. We worked hard to find and sell the supplies we had gathered, but it wasn't enough. Slowly we began to run errands for a price. We would go to the markets for our neighbors so they could remain safe in their homes.

We didn't want to do it and we feared every step of the way, but we had no choice. Sometimes I would smile at the irony of our situation—being forced to go outside where danger and death lurked in order to make a little money, to keep a roof over our heads, so we could be safe. It seemed like we got the short end of the deal—no work, no money, sometimes not even electricity or water. We were living like rats.

I often thought of escaping, but couldn't. I beat myself up over it many times. I wanted to flee. I wanted a better life, a normal life, but I couldn't abandon my family. I knew we would all be killed if we tried to flee together. Hell, I probably would have been killed had I tried to flee on my own, anyway. It was an impossible dream and no matter how hard I tried, I couldn't figure out a way to save myself and my family.

Then one day the Americans joined the Kuwaitis in the fight to liberate the country. I felt a hope I hadn't known in a long time, but life was still very much the same nightmare I had come to know in the prior months. I was stopped at a checkpoint once, and to my horror, I was blindfolded and taken to an interrogation site. They questioned me regarding my associations, beliefs, and whereabouts for the past few months. Luckily, I had nothing that they were interested in and they let me go. I'm sure many of the men who were in the same room as me did not have the same fate.

I lived in Kuwait for six or seven more years after the war ended. The place was a disaster and it took forever for everything to get cleaned up. I settled into a comfortable little existence as an engineer, but I never did end up feeling normal or secure. I always had an unsettled feeling that something bad was just about to happen. Eventually, I decided to explore my options outside of my country in order to provide a better life for myself and my parents. They were never the same after the war, and became more fragile and dependent on us as the years went by.

After college, a few of my friends had moved to the United States and I kept in touch with them. After the war and the many hardships they knew my family had been through, these friends worked hard to convince me to travel to the United States and try my luck. Eventually they succeeded. I moved to Texas and lived with them for some time while I got used to my new life and the environment there. I worked as a cook in a small diner, and although I felt cheated out of a good career in my field of study, I kept telling myself that my situation was only temporary and tried to focus on the peace of mind that I got from being able to provide for my parents and help my siblings.

I met Sara while working at the diner. She was a waitress there. She was always in an upbeat mood and treated people kindly. We became friends quickly, and about a month into our friendship, we began to date.

Sara was very direct and intense in her approach, which was new to me. The women in my culture are impossibly submissive and acquiescent. She told me she was in love and wanted us to start making a life together. I was surprised by how quickly things evolved, but I truly liked her and her honesty and thought we would be good for one another. I agreed to take the next step in our relationship and let her take charge. She had lived all her life in the United States and knew, much better than I, about how things worked here. She picked out an apartment that was a little too pricey for us, but I thought I could find a second job and make things work. I wanted to be good to her.

Things moved along real quickly, but they were good. So good, in fact, that Sara and I got married a few months after we moved in together.

I took on a second job and Sara quit working at the restaurant and found a higher paying job at a warehouse. This is when things took a turn for the worse. She used to be a good girl; she was sweet and caring, and even though she was intense in her feelings, she showed nothing but love for me. Once she found work at the warehouse she began to spend time with her coworkers and I saw her change just as quickly as she had fallen in love with me.

Sara began to come home late at night smelling of marijuana. Even though I was her husband, she would not be questioned about her whereabouts, and if I ever made so much as a comment about her not being home, she would explode in a fit of rage and begin screaming at me. I feared those fits of rage. Her eyes looked wild and angry and she turned into someone truly unpredictable. I tried to keep quiet and keep things peaceful between us, but there was no telling what would make her angry, and once she became angry, there was no telling what she would do. Oftentimes she threw things at me while she chased me out of the apartment, yelling.

She then began to bring her coworkers home to party and turned me into their waiter. She wouldn't let me join them or get to know her friends very much, but she expected me to go buy more liquor and things for them to eat. She treated me like her servant, and if I ever refused, she would humiliate me by yelling and throwing food at me in front of her friends.

In observing and listening to her friends, I realized that they were dangerous people who frequented dangerous circles. They spoke of selling drugs, stealing, the many times they had been in jail, drinking and partying. I didn't know who to fear the most, Sara or her friends.

One time I came home from work and I found Sara home with two of her friends. When she saw me come in she got up from her chair and approached me decidedly, handing me a piece of paper that said I was to pay her $10,000 upon receipt of my Green Card. She wanted me to sign it. I looked at her astounded, humiliated and deeply wounded. I had married her for love and I thought she loved me as well. When I told her this she began yelling and told me she would report me to Immigration if I didn't agree with her, then she completely lost it, grabbed a knife and chased me out of the apartment.

Sara had become someone I no longer recognized and I was afraid she would follow through with her threats. I didn't sign the paper, but

I became even more submissive to her demands. She began to call me at work demanding that I bring her money. Otherwise, she wouldn't let me back in our apartment. I was already giving her most of my money and she blew it on alcohol and marijuana. I had nothing else to give her except the money I had to help my parents and siblings. She knew it and she didn't care—she wanted "her money," and she expected to have it or else.

I don't know how she spent her salary, because she left all the bills and costs of our living arrangements to me. If I ever couldn't buy the food she liked or give her money to go out, she would become enraged and react. How she reacted was always a horrible surprise.

She kicked me out of the house many times, but kept all of my clothes and money. She left me out on the street with nothing but the clothes on my back. I had nowhere to go except for my friend's home, but they didn't know how to help me. They feared she would follow through on her threats as well. All they could do is give me a place to sleep for the night and try to give hope that my situation would improve.

Ironically it only became worse. Sara's friends were always around and they egged her on to pressure me for money and run their errands. Sometimes they even wanted me to go pick up marijuana or pills for them. I would refuse and lock myself in the bedroom, but they would come shouting insults, banging on the door.

I began to develop a tick. I was terrified. She and her friends terrified me. I became jumpy at the sound of her voice and began to blink almost uncontrollably throughout the day, especially when she was angry and yelling. I couldn't handle it anymore. When my residency paperwork came back for us to sign, she demanded that I give her $1500 or else she wouldn't sign it. When I told her that she was my wife and in any case I didn't have that kind of money she threw a glass at me, then walked to the kitchen and lit the paperwork on fire.

I knew at that moment that she did not care about me or my well-being and that my life would be in great danger if I stayed around her any longer. I waited for her to leave the apartment with her friends, then grabbed my clothes and a few of my things, and left to my friend's house.

I haven't seen her since, but she will call from time to time demanding I give her money. She keeps telling me she will tell Immigration about me and make sure they send me home. My friends have never gone through anything like this, so they don't know what to make of it. They don't even know if she can do something like that, but we're all afraid. She will call just for fun and threaten to have one of her friends find us and beat us at any time, in any place.

I can't walk down the street without looking behind my shoulder to see if anyone is following me. Any car that drives by, any strangers that approach my direction petrify me. I would stand there frozen in a panic every time, my legs wanting to run for my life as fast as they will take me, yet unable to move an inch in any direction. I can't live in peace at home and constantly look out the windows, scanning the streets for any suspicious cars or people. Even tiny noises in the middle of the night wake me because I can't control the fear that someone is trying to break in and is coming for me.

...

Fear can be a moving and empowering emotion, if channeled properly. In A'mer's case it taught him a passive way to self-preservation. The imminent dangers from the war around him during his youth were too much of a risk. In accepting his circumstances and choosing to "hide out" in the hopes that things would improve, A'mer bowed down to his circumstances and relinquished his power to change them. Likewise, when his wife humiliated, mistreated, and threatened him, the lessons from his previous experiences kicked in and he simply endured her treatment, as he feared the repercussions of confronting his situation.

Although A'mer suffered from a great deal of trauma during the Kuwait occupation, it appears that his relationship with Sara was the trigger and multiplier of A'mer's rather severe post-traumatic stress disorder symptoms. It is quite different to live in a city under attack and to have someone explicitly running at you with a knife, chasing you out of your own home.

Unfortunately, A'mer's symptoms of post-traumatic stress disorder are exponentially greater than his understanding of them. He explained to me every single one of them, from his inability to sleep to freezing into a panic attack while out among a crowd of people. He failed to understand that his symptoms dated from his life back in Kuwait and that his relationship with Sara, although damaging, simply "set on fire" the symptoms already hiding within him. I recommended that he seek out counseling, and to my surprise he told me that he had been considering it, but was so afraid of leaving his home that he couldn't find a way to make it happen. As an exception due to his situation, I offered treatment services to him over the phone. He accepted in a heartbeat.

After a grueling battle in court, in which his short marriage to Sara was used over and over as an excuse to try and nullify the impact of her mistreatment of him, A'mer was allowed to remain in the country and become a legal resident of the United States. The resolution of his legal case noticeably lifted a load of weight off his shoulders, yet some time later and to his surprise, he continued to feel many of his post-traumatic stress disorder symptoms.

A'mer continued his weekly sessions with me for a few more months, then dropped them to twice per month and then once per month to ensure he "is still making progress."

He is.

ANGELA

Angela couldn't have been more wound up if she tried. She oozed tension as she walked into my office, and although she tried to be polite, her impatience, pressured speech, and the multitude of questions she spewed were beyond her control. She repeatedly questioned me about the evaluation procedure and frowned as she listened to my response, seemingly waiting for a "catch"—for me to try to take advantage of her in some way.

To her visible surprise, I didn't try to manipulate her and gave her the straight talk she seemed to need. I explained that we would need to dig into her past to find out what is driving her. She opened her eyes wide and said "okay," as she picked a chair in which to sit. I wasn't sure where to begin. I had the feeling this interview could go one of two very different ways; it could either be like pulling teeth for a few hours, or she could come unraveled and unload her entire story this very afternoon. For both our sakes, I hoped for the latter.

Angela turned out to be quite a pleasant woman. She told me about her "unremarkable, yet peaceful past," as she called it, and as the clock ticked I had the feeling I was in the presence of a truly good-hearted woman. I knew she had gone to jail for a time, however. Her attorney had informed me as much. I silently wondered what could have happened in her life to take such a wild, life-changing turn.

As if she knew what I was thinking, she gave me an awkward half-smile and said, "Not your garden variety jailbird, huh?" I shook my head and frowned. What was going on?

"Look," she said, "My family is falling apart. My husband is gone, my daughters are two steps away from God-knows-what, and I don't know how to keep it together. We've been going at this legal case for a long time and I don't know what else to do to help it along. I don't even know if it can be helped."

Tears began to stream down Angela's face. She wiped them off nonchalantly, but they kept coming down and soon it all became more than she could keep up with. She steadied herself and looked away as her leg shook violently.

"Listen," I told her, "Perhaps you don't need to know what all else to do. Perhaps you don't need to do anything else right now at all. Let me do my job and see if I can help. When was the last time someone offered to help you?"

Angela began to weep inconsolably. I knew no matter how many people offered to assist her, the weight of the burden was hers alone to carry. And it was about to crush her.

Angela is my name and I'm from Mexico. Like most small town families, my father worked in the fields and my mother took care of the house. My sisters and I went to school until the sixth grade and after that we worked in the fields with our dad and cleaning houses with our mom. We were raised to work hard and earn a living. No handouts for us— ever.

All in all it was a great childhood. Life wasn't easy, but my parents gave us everything they could, even the freedom to be children despite the need for us to work. There isn't much to tell about my life while I lived in Mexico. It was quiet, and although we often lacked resources, it was rather peaceful.

I married young, but he is a great man. I met Arnaldo when I was 15 and we were together for three years before we got married. We didn't have money to live in a place of our own, so we lived with my parents until my first daughter was born when I was 21 years old.

We were happy. We were so happy! But as the years went by, we became more and more aware that we could not provide any better for our children than we had while growing up. Our lives were good, but we needed to give our children better opportunities if they were ever to have a nicer life than us. So we took my two-year-old daughter and a handful of clothes and resolved to leave everything and everyone we ever loved and look for a better life in the United States.

Arnaldo wanted to come by himself first and establish himself a little before sending for our daughter and me, but I refused. If we were going to make a new life, we were going to forge it together, like the family we were. We had left everything behind. All we had to rely on was each other.

So the three of us came together to see what this new world had in store for us. We were lucky that Arnaldo found work right away through a friend of his. He offered work for me, too. I had no one to leave our daughter with, so I had to stay home for some time. She was still a baby, anyway.

Many years went by, and Arnaldo was the main breadwinner. Our daughter grew up healthy and happy, and as the years passed, we gave her a brother and two sisters. Our children are quite the handful, so it's always been my main responsibility to care for them. As they grew old enough to go to school, however, I began to take little odd jobs here and there when I had the opportunity, to help us save more money. I dreamed of watching my kids graduate from high school and then go on to college—maybe after that, get good jobs in places like the offices I used to clean from time to time. Yes. That was why we moved here and why Arnaldo broke his back working every day. So they could have better and be better than us.

Our life has been quiet all these years. We aren't big drinkers or partiers like so many others. We were lucky to be able to make some friends, though, and after a few years, two of my siblings and my father moved here. I guess when life is peaceful, one doesn't think much of it and it is not until we are engulfed in chaos and turmoil that we truly come to cherish our previous, quieter circumstances. I thought I had been grateful all these years, but I truly never knew what I had until I recently lost it all.

A neighbor friend of mine told me her boss was looking to hire another cleaning lady and asked me if I would be interested. I was scared at first, because I never had a permanent job before, but my friend told me it was only part time and likely wouldn't be more than 15 hours per week. I thought that still gave me plenty of time to take care of my family and help our funds grow, so I decided to meet with her boss. Within 45 minutes I was the new part-time cleaning lady. Best of all, they happened to be swamped with work that week and needed my help. I was so excited.

Her boss fired me after a week though. I don't know what I did wrong. She told me that she had simply realized she did not have enough work for me and could not keep me on the payroll. I thanked her and I went on my way; I was thankful for the week's worth of work anyway, and she told me she would pay me that Friday.

Friday came and I never received my check. When I called her, she told me she would be sending my check with my friend, but that didn't happen either. I asked my neighbor often if she had received my paycheck, but nothing. I was disappointed and I felt cheated out of hard work, but there was nothing I could do about it. After a few weeks of chasing down the pay I'd earned, I had to let it go.

Three months later, I got a call from the boss lady. She told me I could come by her office that afternoon to pick up my long-overdue paycheck. It was the perfect time. My son had just been diagnosed with severe asthma and we needed to buy a nebulizer and medicine for him. We had been worried about how to make all of that happen. I thought things were looking up.

Arnaldo, my daughters, and I drove over to this woman's office to pick up my check. To my horror, she had the police waiting for us and they arrested my husband and me for working undocumented. They put me in jail for four months and locked up Arnaldo for six months before they deported him back to Mexico.

I don't know where to begin the horror story. My children were left alone and Social Services was called. I don't know how my brothers managed, but they picked up my children and watched over them throughout the whole time. Unfortunately, they couldn't get my son's medical treatment started because they didn't have a power of attorney. My baby got very sick in those four months.

We lost everything. We obviously lost our apartment and my brothers weren't able to store all of our things, so they grabbed what they could. Each of my kids had a bag full of clothes and a handful of toys and pictures. We regressed to the time when we first arrived and had just a little more than the clothes on our backs. It broke my heart, but I kept trying to remember that, at least my children weren't alone.

The time I spent in jail was, without a doubt, the worst time in my entire life. I had never had problems with the law before and I had only seen these things on movies. It exceeded anything I ever imagined that reality to be.

My cellmates were unstable, scary women. They would get up in the middle of the night, shaking, walking about the cell, looking to see if I was awake. I was always awake. I was afraid to sleep. I was afraid they would hurt me. I became jumpy and hyper-vigilant. I expected danger to come at me any minute, from any direction. I could feel the tension breaking down my body, tensing up my muscles every second of the day until it felt that they would snap. I was exhausted from lack of sleep, yet terrified to even blink and be caught off guard. I don't know how I made it through that time. Actually, I think part of me didn't.

I begged the guards to put me with other Hispanic women, but they didn't come around that particular jail too often. Every once in a while I would see a Hispanic girl brought in and they were nice enough to put her with me if they could. But just as quickly as they arrived, they would be gone. They wouldn't even be there half a week.

To their misfortune and to my luck, two Hispanic women arrived and were told they would stay there until they were told otherwise. It was one drop of relief in the ocean of desperation. I tried to savor it, terrified as I was.

I was so relieved to be able to speak to someone and even though in the outside world we may have had nothing in common, in there we were the only three Hispanic women and we stuck together like our lives depended on it. I have no doubt that it truly did.

None of us slept at night. We were too afraid. We took turns sleeping during the day so that there would always be someone watching out for us. We spent our nights sometimes talking, sometimes staring silently into space, praying. We never left our cell unless we had no choice, and when that happened, we squirreled around and through the hallways as fast as we could. We wanted no one to notice us, not even speak to us.

I was astounded by how horrible this place was. Women got into brutal fights with one another all the time, for no good reason. All it took was someone to look at someone else wrong, then the insults began... then, even chairs flew about. I've never been through anything like that, ever. I had never been afraid for my life before. I was always on edge and was sure my turn was coming.

It seemed like the women weren't sorted according to their offense. For a time I had to share a cell with a girl who told me she had killed her boyfriend, and another who told me she had killed her baby. So there I was, in jail because I was trying to work to put my kids through college one day.

I was warned to never tell anyone about anything I saw happening around me. Otherwise, I'd be considered a snitch and the other women would make me pay. Daily you'd see girls fighting and about to kill one another, or someone get beaten bloody for no good reason, but you couldn't do anything about it. It didn't matter if they deserved it or if you feared for their lives. If you said anything, you'd be next.

I don't know how I made it through, I just don't. I thought about death every day and even though I feared the other women, towards the end, I thought about getting into a fight and letting them beat me— —just to get it all over with. I've never known myself as being in a darker or more desperate place than during that time. I know it was only four months, but every day felt like weeks to me.

We lived like farm animals. I didn't know why we weren't allowed to wash our clothes or that we didn't get to keep them. We gave them away to one another every so many days, and got a set of "used but clean" clothes in return. I know they washed them, but they smelled dirty and even the underwear was sometimes stained. I remember freaking out the first time I got my "fresh" clothes; I thought I'd undoubtedly catch an infection of some sort if I wore that underwear. I couldn't deal with it. I sank into my bed and covered my face so my cellmates wouldn't see that I was crying. Of course they noticed and they laughed among themselves about it. Clearly they had all been in this situation before.

I always felt so hungry. We were only given so much and it wasn't good. The beans had rocks in them, the lettuce had dirt and if you were lucky, and didn't find either of those on your plate, the food itself tasted rotten. Even when I felt starved and I forced myself to eat, it later made me ill. I would try to buy food for myself sometimes and keep it in my cell, but either my cellmates would eat it or it would get taken from me by the bigger women as soon as I was done buying it.

I resigned myself to swallowing the food and "being fine" so that I wouldn't become sick and vomit moments later. I found a worm in my stew once and slugs on my lettuce twice. I was lucky to catch them before I ate any of it.

Meal times weren't only bad because of the food. They were truly so dangerous. The women had sections separated for their groups where you couldn't sit or even walk by. Fights often happened in the eating hall and things would get nasty really quick. The other Hispanic women and I would run back to our cells without finishing our food just so we could get out of the way and not get hit.

Some of the longest and most horrible months of my life went by and I was finally released from that hell. It felt as though someone had been holding me under water until I was about to die, yet at the very last moment I was released to fill my lungs with air once again. I felt alive once more, though in the back of my mind I knew that even when I was free from that place, it still had its claws buried deep in my mind.

My brothers picked me up and took me to see my children in our new home—their basement. It didn't matter to me at that point that we had lost nearly everything we had worked so hard for. I just wanted to see my children. I felt such a surge of hope when I was finally able to put my arms around them. Not only had I not felt something like that in months, but it was rather as if someone had erased it from my memory completely. I felt almost as if I had been born again, only I had been born out of a nightmare. I knew I wasn't my old self anymore, and what would I turn out to be? I was yet to find out.

Even though I was no longer in jail, the memories wouldn't leave me, and they maneuvered me around my daily life like a finger puppet. I couldn't sleep. Whenever I finally become exhausted I would close my eyes, but was awakened quickly and in a startle by dreams; of being back in jail, of women fighting and screaming, of my cell mates lurking around me, waiting to hurt me. I'd break into a cold sweat every night, and many of those were accompanied by my own screams as I awoke from those dreams.

Life wasn't much easier during the day. Somehow I didn't know how life worked anymore. My mind was gone, my attention and focus completely checked out. I found my mind trailing back to those months in jail; wondering about what happened to many of those women, wondering what would have happened to me had I stayed any longer, wondering what had I become.

I worried to death about my husband. I knew that if women's jail was a horrific nightmare, a men's jail was guaranteed to be much worse. I worried about his well-being and I caught myself wondering, through the day, if he was still alive. So many violent things happened in there so quickly.

When he was finally released, they informed me that they were going to transfer him to the Federal Detention Facility, as he was now in deportation proceedings. They held him there for a month and then they sent him back to Mexico. He's been gone for over a year.

My brothers hired an attorney for me to see if he could help me avoid deportation. I've been to court many times in this past year and there is yet to be a resolution. Not only do I feel uncertain about my future and that of my children, but desperate in that we basically continue to dangle from a string, our fates in someone else's hands, unable to leave, unable to decide. Waiting for someone to tell me what will happen to me and my children. I'm ready to give up.

Things have gone from bad to worse and I'm no longer able to think straight. Arnaldo hasn't been able to find work in Mexico, and I am not allowed to work at all. I clean a friend's house twice a week and that gives me a little money to help in the house, but my kids and I are completely dependent on my brothers. I can't even afford to get them backpacks for school or give them lunch money. I've failed as a parent, and it rips me apart.

I can tell my two oldest daughters aren't coping with any of this well. None of us are, really. But now they've begun to cut themselves. They're not little scrapes either—they're big, thick cuts. They were never like that. They were there when the police arrested us and I think everything went to hell for them after that. I fear for them. I'm terrified they'll decide to slit their wrists one of these days. They don't seem to be too far from that. I follow them around when they're in the house, but it's impossible to control them all the time. Sometimes they'll lock themselves in the bathroom for a half an hour and I know that's not normal. I know what they're doing and I can't get them out. What's going to happen to them next? Drinking? Hanging out with boys so they can escape from something they should have never gone through in the first place? How do I save them?

I can't handle this any longer. Arnaldo is far away. My children are hurting themselves. And all of us are living hand to mouth, at the mercy of my brothers. We aren't bad people. We've never had problems with the law, but we also didn't come here to live like this. I don't care anymore. Send me back. Send us all back. I'd rather my children have the same humble life I did than keep them here sick and unstable. I wanted us to have a good life and a future, but this is none of those things anymore.

It's been two weeks since my last and supposedly final court hearing. The judge decided to deny my request to stay and said I have to go back to Mexico. In the meantime, I can stay while my attorney files an appeal. I agreed to stay and fight for the sake of my children because all of them (except for my oldest daughter) were born here.

I don't know what to do. I don't know how much longer I can live like this, waiting for the axe to fall and either chop off my shackles or my head. I want to leave and go be with Arnaldo and start all over again, but I don't know if that's best for my children's future. I want to keep fighting for them, but at what cost? I'm barely there for them now and they themselves are falling apart, too. Is the "better life" here worth any of this? What kind of a life can it be? Right now, I really don't know.

...

Life did to Angela in three months what I've seen take much longer for many wartime survivors. Worst of it all is that she has very little hope left for any of her life circumstances changing, ever. The Angela I met was seriously in the process of accepting that there was no going back to the way their lives used to be, and there was very little chance of it becoming any different than the nightmare it had become.

I still have hope for Angela, but I know that she does not stand a chance on her own. Her circumstances are difficult in that she does not have the funds to seek out a medication evaluation and counseling. I pointed her in the direction of some organizations that may be able to help her get the medicine and therapy that she needs. It is in her hands now, but that is what concerns me the most, since she appears to be virtually ready to give up.

In speaking to her attorney some time later, I learned that while Angela had yet to seek out counseling, she had agreed to pursue her legal case further. Apparently her siblings had done their best to convince her to do it. Honestly, I don't know how long that will last without her receiving competent professional support. My guess is not very long. It saddens me that such a strong, resilient, and resourceful soul could have been reduced to little more than utter hopelessness in such a short time. The four months that Angela was imprisoned was the originator of an almost insurmountable trauma for her, as well as the cause of her severe symptoms of post-traumatic stress disorder. These factors, compounded by the reality that she encountered upon her release, only damaged her further and caused her symptoms to quickly degenerate into various other, more severe mental health problems, including major depression and generalized anxiety disorder.

Although the idea of continuing to pursue her legal case would seem like the correct thing to do for her family, without professional support, Angela is very much like a ticking time bomb. Not only is there a risk for her to throw in the towel, pack her bags and take her children to Mexico despite her family's effort to keep her here, but once in Mexico, I simply don't know what would become of her with her current mental condition. All I can say is that Angela is here for now, and just like her brothers convinced her to continue the fight for her future, I hope they can also convince her to engage in the long struggle ahead to stabilize her mental and emotional health.

DELIA

Delia came into the office accompanied by her two sons. "Twins!" I exclaimed enthusiastically as I welcomed everyone into my office. The boys took a seat next to each other, then one of them stood up, and seeing his brother's anxiety, quickly allowed his mother to take the middle seat.

Although Roberto and Ernesto were identical twins, they were far from being alike. Ernesto and his mother answered my questions candidly while Roberto stared at the floor, his hands tucked tight between his thighs. I followed Delia and Ernesto's conversation, but I stayed focused on Roberto—as casually as I could, of course.

Delia was speaking about her relationship with her husband Julian (at least the parts she had told her kids, I suspected) when suddenly Roberto's gaze followed an invisible trail on the floor leading to the main window. I watched as his body tensed up and he unconsciously gripped his mother's jacket. Delia paused to look at her son, while Roberto's eyes grew wider, wilder, and terrified.

Suddenly he let out a scream of sheer terror and hooked his arm to his mother's while he attempted to hide the rest of his body behind hers. He gripped the back of her jacket with both hands while he pressed his forehead against her back and muttered

159

to himself. I was incredulous and had no idea what was going on.

As if they had done this a thousand times, Delia turned around and cradled her son in her arms. She held him tight and stroked him soothingly. At the same time Ernesto shot up from his seat towards the window. He gave me a tentative look, and I nodded back in approval. He closed the blinds, and then went to kneel next to his brother. He spoke to Roberto, soothing him, promising he would protect him. It all happened too quickly for me to even begin to react.

I had no place in that interaction. I sat back quietly, observing, ready to intervene if I was needed. To my surprise, Roberto soon relaxed and returned to his initial composed demeanor. This time, Ernesto took the seat next to him and hooked his arm under his brother's arm. The three of them looked at me apprehensively, as if expecting me to pass judgment on what I had just witnessed.

I asked Roberto if he liked movies, and then asked Ernesto if he could go with his brother to the next room and watch a videotape with him for a while. The twins got up obediently and quietly made their way down the hall. I chanced a peek out of my door—Ernesto had his arm around his brother.

Delia picked at her fingers while a tear rolled down her cheek. "You know, their father couldn't care any less about supporting them in any way.

They're lucky if they get one phone call a week from Julian." She began to weep, sadness saturating every one of her tears. *"How could I leave them here?" she said. "They've got no one to take them in. They're just kids."*

"So where did this Julian come from?" I asked her.

My name is Delia and I'm 35 years old. I was born and raised in the little town of Francisco I Madero in Zacatecas, Mexico. My father worked in agriculture and my mother was in charge of taking care of the family and our house. I have two older brothers, and we went to school until the sixth grade. After that we helped my father work in the fields.

I married Julian when I was 19 years old. He, too, is from Zacatecas, but he had become a United States citizen several years before I met him. We were married for eight years and had twins together. Julian had built a house for us in Mexico and the children and I lived there while he worked in Montana part of the year.

Julian came to visit us two or three times a year. He would always tell me that he wanted to take me and the boys to Montana to live with him, but he never did anything about it. I think it was after our third year of marriage that he asked me to move to my parent's house. The plan was for him to sell the house he built and come get us, but he never did.

Instead, he sent me a letter saying he didn't want to be with me anymore.

Julian didn't care about his children. The twins and I lived with my parents, but they didn't have any money to support us, and Julian rarely sent anything to help support our kids. My mother helped me out by watching them during the day, so I could go work as a maid. I struggled, but I fed and clothed my children the best I could.

Julian never returned to visit his children. One of the rare times he called, he said that he would be visiting to see the twins on a certain date. The boys were so excited. They got ready and made presents for their dad, but he never showed up to get them. They were crushed. They asked to call him on the phone and Julian told them I had lied to them and that he had never said such a thing. My boys resented me for that for a long time, until they were old enough to figure out for themselves that their father was a liar.

I waited for Julian to come back to me. I hoped he would change, even though he showed no interest in me or his children. Years went by and life didn't get any easier. I continued to struggle to provide for my children and deal with the heartache, but I could barely hang on. My parents kept reminding me of our family in Denver, but I couldn't bear the thought of separating from my children, and I couldn't rely on my family in

Denver to care for them while I worked. They had jobs and families of their own.

I hung in there for as long as I could, but eventually I had to leave my children and move to Denver so I could provide them and my parents with a better life. My parents took care of the twins and I worked long hours to provide for everyone and put my kids through school. I lived with my heart broken, spending every day far away from my children. I couldn't bring them with me. The journey would have been too dangerous for them to come on their own and there was no one I could trust to bring them across. Besides, I wanted my children to have better opportunities than I had, and I could put them through school and perhaps even college if they lived in Mexico. I resigned myself to living separate from them. I tried to focus on the positive things, but as time went by the sadness began to gain ground, and like a weed, little by little, it began to kill everything good inside my heart.

When the twins were 14 years old, Julian went to Mexico to get them. He called and told them that he wanted them to become American residents and have the opportunity to make a good life for themselves. He told them they could go to high school there and he would give them work at the restaurant. My kids called me to tell me about it; I remember very clearly how they tried to not be excited about it, as it could've simply been another empty promise. My own heart brightened at the possibility of being reunited with my children and I, too, began to fantasize about the possibility of getting back together with Julian and becoming a family. I also tried not to get excited about it, and instead told the kids that it was something that would take time to plan and discuss.

Or so I thought. Julian went to Mexico and picked up the twins without my permission. My parents couldn't stop him. In fact, I don't quite know how he did it, but he sweet-talked them into believing some lie that he had my permission and that everything was fine. When my parents told me, I freaked out. Julian hadn't told me any of this. I didn't know where my children were, if they had made it to Montana, or if they even wanted to go with Julian. I never felt more terrified in my life.

My kids called me about a week later. They had no idea I had nothing to do with any of it. They were intimidated by being in a completely foreign place, but they seemed excited to finally get to spend some time with their father and do all the things that he had promised them. I couldn't take that away from my children—not after they pleaded with me to allow them to stay and be with their father. It felt a little bit like a slap in the face, but I tried to understand that they had never before had Julian to themselves. I didn't say yes to their request at the time, but I didn't say no either.

My kids soon came to understand that the life their father had promised them was far from the reality that he lived. He didn't allow them to go to school. He told them they didn't need any more education and instead gave them full-time jobs at the restaurant. They worked long days and many times only had a day off to rest. Julian didn't make himself available to care for the twins or build a relationship with them. Instead, cousins and uncles took care of my kids. According to what my children have said, Julian seemed plainly uncomfortable around them. It disturbed my kids big-time. They never said their father was abusive and mean to them, but they didn't know how to handle their father not wanting to be around them.

Julian was mean to me though. I think he liked to torment me. He would call to tell me about how he got to see the twins every day, and found ways to tell me I was a lousy mother for not going back to Mexico to see them or bringing them to the States. "Have you ever seen him ride his bike? He shoots down the street like a rocket. His cousins have to chase after him! Oh yeah, I guess you haven't been back to Mexico to see them. Who taught them to ride bikes then? That's a parent's job." Every one of his words burned in my mind, and they still do to this day.

Roberto, one of the twins, didn't adjust very well to his new life. Julian even mentioned several times that Roberto often seemed disoriented. Many times on the phone Roberto told me that he wanted to come to Denver to live with me, but his father wouldn't allow him to do so. I tried calling my sons more regularly after that conversation, but Julian began to refuse to allow me speak to them. I became quite worried for the twins. I told Julian that I wanted to go up there to Montana to visit them, but he would not have it. He told me that he would call Immigration on me if I ever showed up at his house. "It shouldn't make much difference to you, it's not like you've done anything to see them lately," he would tell me. He knew exactly what to say to crush my spirit. He knew I was powerless before him, as I had always been.

Three months went by and then one day I got a call from one of Julian's cousins. Roberto had experienced some sort of nervous breakdown and was in the psychiatric ward at the hospital. He said the twins had been working about 12 hours daily at the restaurant, when one day Roberto just lost it. He was held in the psychiatric ward for a month. Ernesto called me one day while his father was out and told me that their uncles regularly ridiculed them and were always quite harsh with both of them. Ernesto told me that Roberto had enough of it one day, grabbed his bicycle and left, telling them that he was going back to Mexico. Roberto was then befriended by a man in a small town who drove Roberto back to Montana. Ernesto said that the man drove for well over two hours to get him home.

I didn't care if Julian called Immigration on me. I was going to go to Montana to see my children. I managed to get Roberto transferred to a hospital in Denver and I brought Ernesto back home with me as well. Roberto stayed in the hospital for another month. The doctors there prescribed him with a variety of things, but they did him little good. He was released to go home with a medical regimen to follow, but it didn't help much. Roberto's nervous breakdown crisis had been dealt with, but he was far from being back to normal. He'd walk around the house absent-mindedly with a glassy look in his eyes, as if lost inside of himself. He was always anxious, fearful, and impossibly jumpy, which put us all on edge.

Ernesto told me that Roberto had never been this way prior to them going to live with their father. I wanted to kill that man. I feared Roberto would never go back to being himself again, and as time went by, my fears only grew. As the first of many symptoms, Roberto developed an insatiable appetite. He stopped talking altogether and dedicated himself to eating. He ate day and night, sometimes without stopping to warm up his food or cook it. I caught him eating frozen peas once. The microwave was right next to him.

Roberto became anxious and shaky and didn't want to be inside the house. I would let him go for walks at first, but he would wander off for hours and Ernesto and I would frantically rush off looking for him. We began to take walks with Roberto as a family, but we could hardly spend all of our time outdoors, and he would grow restless once we tired. He began to throw himself against the walls and eat feces out of the toilet.

It wasn't long before Roberto began to hallucinate. He constantly saw women disguised as men who would rush towards him and try to eat him. He would be walking down the hallway when out of nowhere he would scream and come running, looking for me or his brother. One time I found him in his room, looking like a crazed person, drawing skulls and scribbling on the walls. He wouldn't stop muttering to himself, and when I finally got his attention, he pulled me over to the wall and gave me a pencil. He said he was drawing a protection so the women wouldn't come eat him. It destroyed me to see my son so tormented. I didn't know how to continue to be strong for him. I kept taking him to see his doctor and he continued to prescribe him different things, but nothing cured him. When we were lucky it merely calmed him down a bit.

We are slowly coming to terms with the reality that Roberto isn't going to be himself, ever again. We've come to measure good days in our ability to keep Roberto calm, and when times get rough, the family and I try our best to navigate through it and take care of him. I feel blessed that I don't have to go through this alone. I couldn't do it without my son and my family here in Denver.

Roberto is no longer the happy, social boy I knew. Actually, he spends most of his time alone in his room. The doctor told me that we should never leave Roberto alone, so Ernesto and I take turns watching him. My family also helps whenever they can. Even though Roberto clings to Ernesto and me, he feels safe enough with our relatives to spend time with them without much problem. They've learned how to assuage Roberto and help him feel calm.

Julian never really cared about his children. Just like when we lived in Mexico, he won't help me support them and will have no part in Roberto's treatment. Nonetheless, he continues to try and control us. He will call the children from time to time only to try and convince them to return to Montana. Whenever Ernesto refuses, he becomes angry and begins to insult my son. I don't know exactly what he tells him—Ernesto won't say—but it always leaves him with a crushed spirit for days afterwards.

Sometimes Julian will call me and demand to know, "What are the doctors doing to Roberto?" He then becomes angry and tells me that I'm letting them take advantage of me, and that I don't know what I'm doing. He'll bark orders about what I need to tell the doctors and how I need to handle Roberto's condition. Then he'll threaten me to call Immigration on me, and says he'll come take Roberto away if I don't do as he says. He tells me that he has friends in Colorado that are keeping an eye on me, and that he'd know if I disobeyed him.

I don't know what to do. I believe Julian. He already took my sons away from me once. Worst of all, just look how things have fared for my children—not well. I've ignored Julian's demands and have continued to follow the doctor's advice, yet I'm afraid that Julian will find out somehow. I don't know what will happen to Roberto if he takes them away. I don't think he will make it through this time. Roberto already lives a nightmare inside his head. Ernesto, my family, and I are the only people he has to make him feel halfway okay. I'm terrified to think of what Roberto will do to himself if his father takes him away. Julian didn't care for him while he was healthy and living with him. He wasn't even aware that Roberto had taken his bicycle and ran away that day. If Julian takes him away, I don't think I'd ever see my son again.

I can't take my sons back with me to Mexico. Ernesto is starting to make a life of his own and Roberto wouldn't survive there. I don't even know how I would be able to provide for his medical care and medicines. What would happen to Roberto then? How could I keep my son safe in a remote little town with nothing but gangsters and criminals all around?

My children are legal residents through Julian, and they deserve to be here. Roberto needs to be here. His life depends on it, and on me. If I knew there was a way he could be safe here without me and I could still provide for him, I'd resign myself to going back to Mexico, even though being away from my children would crush my heart. But no one will watch and care for Roberto as if he were their own son. Our family helps us, but taking care of

Roberto is so intense and involved that none of them are willing to take on such a huge responsibility. I can't say that I blame them. Roberto is *my* son, after all. He can't go through this alone. I can't let that happen.

...

The twins refused to say much about life with their father, but it was evident that they had both been severely damaged by the months they spent in his home. The pressure, frustration, and helplessness Roberto experienced in Montana was clearly overwhelming for him. As for Ernesto, although he managed to avoid a breakdown, he still bore deep wounds from that period of time. Rather than starting his own healing process, however, Ernesto's wounds only became deeper as a result of having to deal with the aftermath of his life in Montana along with helping to care for his severely mentally ill brother.

Everyone in the family had been quite scarred, actually. Delia had endured constant emotional abuse and neglect from Julian for many years. Once her children moved to the United States, she suffered ongoing, severe psychological and emotional battery from her husband to the point where she plunged into a severe depression, the effects of which are still visible.

The problem in a situation like this is that Delia and Ernesto are called on to be the strong members of the family, and in their fight to save Roberto, they completely neglect their own trauma. This in turn causes them to deny themselves the possibility of any healing and further wears down whatever ability they have left to "keep it together."

It isn't often that I see how one person can so thoroughly damage this many people at once. All Delia, Roberto, and Ernesto have left are one another, and I believe there is no way for them to survive unless they remain together and continue to support one another.

Delia is right in that Roberto's schizophrenia can best (and perhaps only) be kept under control here in the United States, where he is afforded proper medical services as an American resident. Ernesto's case is similar in that he, too, is in need of psychological treatment in order to treat his trauma history, yet these services would be unavailable for him in Mexico. Both of these teenagers need their mother, particularly Roberto. The stability of his environment is of utmost importance considering his exceptionally fragile mental condition.

It was heartwarming to learn that Delia was allowed to remain in the United States and become a legal resident. She and her children can now begin a life removed from Julian's shadow and threats. She can continue to care for Roberto, and to provide adequate medical care for him. Delia can now focus her energies in providing her son and herself the opportunity to begin their own healing journeys. Most importantly it seems that, once and for all, they will be able to finally cut all ties with Julian who, to this point, had continued to be a destructive presence in their lives. Prior to the judge's decision, he forced them to maintain contact with him under threats of Delia's deportation or removing the twins from her care.

Delia's legal residency is not a magical cure for the family's somber plight, but it is a start. The road ahead is still quite long and tenuous, but perhaps with the degree of peace and safety they will now be able to feel, they can look forward with renewed hope.

FERNANDO

*Fernando is a young, kind, and amicable man.
You would expect him to have many friends and
social activities that take up his time, but Fernando
spends almost the entirety of his days working. He
lives with his long-time friend Juan in a small
apartment in the west part of town. Fernando told
me that he worked in construction during the day
and delivered pizzas at night. When I asked him for
the reason why he felt he needed to work 15 hours a
day, Fernando's affect became somber and
nostalgic. He simply told me, "my daughters."*

*Fernando's demeanor automatically changed as
a very dark cloud seemed to roll over him. He
switched his gaze to the floor and slowly shuffled
his feet while telling me his story. I quickly
understood that Fernando had felt significantly
alone and isolated throughout his life, brought on
by inconceivably brutal events suffered in
childhood. It was also quite apparent that his
marriage to his wife Sonia had served to diminish
his already low self-worth and rekindle his
childhood trauma issues.*

*I could see the light in his eyes flicker as I
informed Fernando that in order to help him, I
needed to know everything about him. He continued
to stare at the floor while he half-smiled and said,*

"There's nothing good to tell, doctor." He closed his eyes for a moment, leaned forward, and covered his face with his hands as he let out a big sigh. He looked at me imploringly, almost begging me to stop before we even began, but then resignedly said, "Okay doctor, what do you want to know?"

My name is Fernando, and I'm in my mid-30s. I grew up in a small pueblo in northern Mexico where my dad owned a store. My mom and I helped run the store and also take care of the farm animals and the house. It was a big load for a little kid. I even had to watch over my younger siblings, who were a handful.

Unlike most people from small pueblos in Mexico, I was able to finish high school and went to college for one year. My dad wanted us to do well in school so we could receive scholarships to go to college. He meant well in thinking about our future, but he put a lot of pressure on us to do well and study hard. This always made me feel uncomfortable at home, even though I did put a lot of effort into school and I enjoyed it. In the end I was the only one in my family to finish high school and go to college. I knew learning wasn't the favorite thing to do for many of my siblings, but I always wondered why they weren't driven by fear like I was. As for myself, I couldn't even think of letting my dad down, so I studied a lot.

My dad worked hard and pushed the whole family to work hard. He was very strict and rigid. Whenever my dad told me to do something, I didn't even think twice about it. I was passive and submissive as a kid, yes. I was very obedient and I preferred to not stand out. I just didn't want any trouble, and I didn't know how to deal with praise. I'd go into hiding if someone gave me too much attention.

My dad rarely punished us with any kind of beating or anything, but he didn't give us a lot of affection, either. He always seemed so cold and distant regardless of his good intentions. I never spoke to him about anything that was happening to me. I never felt comfortable talking to him.

My mom was affectionate with us, but she was also the one in charge of discipline. My mom was tough. She would snap and hit us if we ever did something she didn't like. She always looked overwhelmed with the stress of caring for so many children and running a family that large. I think she figured that hitting us was the quickest and most effective way to correct us. My mom wasn't a woman that would stop to consider things for very long—she didn't have the time. Sometimes I laugh about it now, but back then she seemed deadly to me. I remember that if there was ever an issue and she didn't know whose fault it was, she would hit everyone around. I was always afraid I'd get hit just for being in the wrong place at the wrong time. She had a strong hand.

I remember one particular time like it was yesterday. I was six years old and I had fallen off a tree I was playing on. The ground was rocky and uneven and I fractured my skull and had to go to the hospital for stitches on my arm and cheek. My mom was livid. She was so angry that she hit me for hurting myself. My dad could not believe her reaction and beat her for beating me. It turned into a circus—a terrifying, nightmarish circus. Between the blood gushing out different parts of my body, the pain, and my parents beating one another, I was convinced the doctor would have to amputate my arm and my parents were going to abandon me for being bad. I was six; these things get burned in your mind.

I liked spending as much time as possible away from my parents, so I got involved in a church group when I was 13 years old. I liked being around other kids, and it wasn't as boring as it sounds. The priest, Father Diego, would invite us over for Bible study and we would barbeque and watch videos or movies about religion for young people. I really liked it over there, and I made several friends. It felt good to feel like I belonged somewhere and that people were glad I was there.

Father Diego was young and from time to time would have alcohol and mixed drinks at his reunions. The older kids would stay later and get drunk, and at the end of the night, the priest would ask one of us to spend the night there with the excuse that he didn't want to feel lonely. First timers felt lucky to be picked to stay–special. Sometimes he would even have one of us over for dinner.

It's kind of addicting, isn't it? Feeling special like that? Father Diego always seemed just a little weird to me and I was never comfortable around him. There was always a voice in the back of my head pointing out that his Bible study gatherings seemed more like undercover parties. I continued to go because I liked to spend time with other kids and I liked to be away from home, but I never felt comfortable around that priest.

Then he began to come around my house and would ask my parents' permission for me to spend the evening at his house. I thought it was weird and I never wanted to go by myself, but my parents insisted. They liked me hanging out with a priest and being involved in church. I guess they figured it was the safest place for me to be—little did they know.

Once at his house Father Diego gave me rum and brandy to drink. I got so drunk that I got sick and vomited and he kept pushing drinks on me with the excuse that it would make me feel better. I was drunk to the point of incoherence and he took my clothes off, against my will. I only remember some things about that night. He touched and molested me and sucked on my member before making me perform oral sex on him.

I just wish that it had been a one-time nightmare, but it happened four times that year. I couldn't tell my parents because I was too embarrassed and afraid of my dad, and I could only avoid so many of Father Diego's requests before my parents would make me go to his house.

I grew to hate it—all of it. The church group was supposed to be my fun, good choice to hang out with kids instead of drinking and partying on the street. Instead it had turned into a secret terror with no way out.

My mom wouldn't stop insisting that I frequent Father Diego, so I quit the church group altogether. It was the only way to rid myself of that sick situation. Some of the kids approached me when they found out and very coyly asked if I had been molested. I denied it, of course. Now I look back and I bet we were all molested—at least most of us. But just like me, no one would speak about it.

I was finally free of Father Diego, but the damage was already done. Even though I know it isn't right, to this day I feel a deep hatred for homosexual men and women. Religious people disgust me as well–hypocrites! I still read the Bible searching for truth, but I haven't been to any church since I was 15.

That last year in church group made me feel filthy. After I quit going to their meetings, I began to hurt myself as punishment for what had happened to me. It felt good somehow when I would burn my arm with a cigarette. I felt extremely guilty and ashamed about the abuse until eight years ago. To be honest, I still struggle with my memories. I never spoke to anyone about this until two years ago when I couldn't take it anymore. All this time and I've never been able to forget about it, to get over it. All these years with those memories eating away at me. It's amazing the power we have to destroy one another so easily.

Of all people, I told my mom. Normally I would go to my brother to talk about most things, but I didn't think he would understand. I couldn't tell my dad. I just didn't dare. My mom was all I had. Part of me felt weak for not "manning up" and getting over it. It was the past after all. The majority of me, however, needed desperately to be freed from those memories, and even though I didn't know how, I thought telling someone was a start.

I don't know what I was expecting from my mom, but whatever it was, I should've known better. I didn't find the understanding and comfort I had hoped for, but rather a long introspective silence followed by an exasperated call to simply forget it ever happened as it could not be fixed. Sometimes I wonder if she feels partially guilty about it. After all, she was the one that insisted on me going to that pedophile priest, even after I would refuse to go.

I was 19 when I moved to the United States with my sister and her husband, and I couldn't have been more glad to leave home. I wanted to put all the miles I could between me and that town. We stayed in San Francisco for a while with an uncle. He gave us work cleaning offices with him. We were only welcomed in my uncle's home temporarily, however. We were expected to get on our feet and move on as soon as we could.

I met my friend, Juan, while cleaning offices with my uncle. He worked at one of the small offices doing maintenance. He told me once that he had friends in Denver who often told him that there was plenty of work there and life was cheaper than in San Francisco. We talked about the idea of moving and "making millions" every time we saw each other. Eventually our dreams got the best of us and we decided to take a chance and moved to Denver, Colorado.

I met my wife, Sonia, not long after I moved to Denver. We dated for a while, but things moved quickly and we got married in less than six months of being together. Life with her was good in the beginning, except that she was insufferably jealous. I spent most of the day out working, but she didn't care. She paged me over and over to try and keep track of me, and if I didn't answer her calls, or call her back right away, she would get really, really angry.

Sonia didn't drive, so I took her anywhere she needed to go. She expected me to do so. I lived on-call for her day and night. It didn't matter that I worked two jobs. I had to take her to work and pick her up even if I was really tired, otherwise she would get angry with me. I cared about her, but I felt that she was only out for herself, and worst of all, would become unhinged if I didn't comply with her wishes. It became a burden to tend to her every need just to avoid her wrath.

Oddly, I felt lucky to have someone in my life to care for me and love me, even if she was mean and controlling sometimes. I tried to understand her and did whatever I could to make her happy, because I wanted things to work and have someone with me. Sadly, things only got worse. Sonia became progressively more controlling and even ordered me to stop delivering pizza so I wouldn't have the chance to see other women. I took a job painting houses to make her happy, but then I wasn't earning enough to cover all of our costs and yet make sure that Sonia was contented, so I had to go back to pizza delivery. She hated it.

Sonia transformed into someone I didn't know. She began to insult me all the time and for no reason. Whenever she wasn't happy with me she would call me a "wetback" and tell me that I had no right to be in the United States. She put me down for not speaking English well, for doing labor work, for not knowing how to do my taxes. She put me down any chance she got. We had children together by this time, and she took advantage of that, too. She would threaten me and tell me that she was going to have me deported and she would never let me see my daughter again. I don't know what I did to her for things to turn out like this, but I believed her. I feared her, so I did whatever she asked of me.

I begged her to allow my parents to come visit us after our first daughter was born. My dad was terminally ill and wanted to come meet her and say good-bye. Although she eventually accepted, Sonia never welcomed my parents or even tried to make them feel comfortable. She was rigid in this idea that they would sleep in the living room while we continued to sleep in our bedroom. I was humiliated that I had to let my parents be treated this way, but I felt powerless to make it right. My dad died six months later and Sonia simply informed me that I was not going to attend the funeral. I remember that day. She was irritated because I kept trying to make her understand. She yelled at me in frustration and told me we didn't have money… then she left to go shopping.

Sonia was the law in our house. As soon as I came home from work, I had to hand over all the tips I made and on paydays I had to give her my checks. She made it so I always had to ask her for money to buy anything for myself, and when I did, she would always get angry. She would then grab my daughters and go stay at her parents' house for a few days, sometimes a few weeks. She still demanded all the money I earned during that time, and threatened to have me deported if I refused.

Sonia liked to control me and the children and was very cruel and critical of me, but she never bothered to care for herself. She wouldn't shower, she put on a lot of weight, and even though she stopped smoking marijuana, she began to chain smoke cigarettes. If we ever had sex it was only because she wanted to and it was a rare occurrence. The times when we actually did she would laugh at me and call me useless because I didn't have a lot of experience.

You would hope she was at least at good mother, but no. She didn't care about our daughters too much. I did most of the cleaning, feeding, and bathing of my kids. My daughters would even come tell me that "mommy cannot cook" and ask me to please make them something to eat. I have no idea why I stayed with her as long as I did. I was afraid of what she would do in retaliation if I left. I didn't have the courage to get up and leave.

Finally we discovered that I couldn't stay with her anymore. I just couldn't take it. Eventually we divorced, but even after this, she continued to look for ways to have fights and belittle me. She continued to demand money and threatened to stop letting me see my daughters if I didn't give her whatever I earned. I had to beg her to let me have time with my daughters and she would sometimes agree to meet me at a park so that I could see them, but only if I brought her money. I remember being in between jobs one time and didn't have money to give her that day at the park, and she wouldn't let me get close to my two daughters. I had to sit and watch them play from the other side of the park.

Even though I stayed with Sonia a lot longer than I should have, I left her before my U.S. residency was finalized, and because of this, I might get sent back home. To be honest, the one good thing about being sent back to Mexico would be being free of Sonia, but I wouldn't see my daughters again and I wouldn't be able to support them. I could always live with one of my siblings, but after being out of Mexico for so long I don't know if I'd even be able to find a job. I'd become a burden for my family, on top of it all.

My three daughters rely on me. I give Sonia money every month and I even pay half of her rent. I'm the one that got her the apartment where she lives because my boss helped me; they wouldn't give her one on her own. I don't feel bad saying that I really don't care about her anymore, but she has my children and I worry about them a lot. I'm always afraid of her doing something to them or flat-out neglecting their needs, but I'm here. If anything ever happened, at least I'm here and I could save them. If I had to move to Mexico I may as well sign away their lives to her.

...

186

At no point in the evaluation did Fernando want to go into detail as to what he would do if he had to return to Mexico. I believe he simply could not bear the idea of losing this battle. Fernando wasn't a fighter by any conventional standards. Rather, his persistence stemmed from concern and love for his daughters.

As difficult it was to hear Fernando's story of abuse at the hands of his ex-wife, I cannot say that I am surprised about the dynamics of their relationship. Fernando suffers from various mental health disorders stemming from early childhood and the interactions with his parents. Fernando learned to become passive and acquiescent early on in life in order to avoid the mental and physical punishment he otherwise suffered at the hands of his demanding and volatile parents. It is my opinion that this conditioning, along with some innate character traits set Fernando up to be an abuse victim. Additionally, the sexual abuse perpetrated numerous times on him by a priest only served to make Fernando believe himself powerless at the hands of any aggressors.

Fernando grew up to think of himself as meek and worthless, and developed the notion that he was not fit to navigate life through his own devices. This brought about his defining mental health disorder: dependent personality disorder. I believe this to be the initial reason why he attached himself to his ex-wife Sonia and remained with her for so long despite the fact that he was quite done with her cruelty and abuse.

Sonia's strong and controlling personality resembled that of Fernando's mother and was familiar to him. Fernando wasn't strong enough to feel that he could stand up for himself and manage life on his own, yet he felt comfortable in this relational pattern despite the abuse. He knew what to expect and how to behave in order to keep himself safe because he had been doing it for years, in his family of origin.

To Sonia, who met the profile of a spousal-abuse perpetrator with her controlling nature and isolation of Fernando, this was the equivalent of getting a fully trained puppy and only served to give her free reign in the relationship to do as she pleased. From the moment he bowed his head and allowed her to fully control him, he sent the message that he would go along with anything asked of him in order to avoid anything that smacked of confrontation—and Sonia received the message loud and clear.

I have a lot of respect for Fernando in that he eventually found it in himself to separate from and then finally divorce Sonia. It takes a great deal of courage to take a stand against an oppressor, despite the fact that she still has not let him see his kids and that he continues to pay her the blackmail she demands. But the divorce signifies a huge step nonetheless for this spousal abuse victim, and the fact that Fernando did so despite his meek character leads me to believe that there is great hope for his recovery—provided that he is willing to open up and seek out professional help.

JAVIER

My first impression of Javier as he walked in my office was... nothing. He was the most unremarkable man I had ever seen. Nothing in Javier was outside the norm. From the way he walked and dressed, to his pedestrian manner and the way he spoke, nothing about him had even a trace of a distinctive personality. He was a tiny drop of water lost in a vast ocean, and for some reason I got the feeling that that was exactly what he wanted.

Indeed, upon chatting with Javier for a while, I came to the conclusion that this was not a man who wanted to stand out in any way. Although cooperative and exceedingly honest, Javier was unbearably meek and passive. Once past the initial introductions, Javier's voice began to quaver while he spoke, particularly when being asked about his opinion on any given matter. It wasn't that Javier came off as unintelligent. Even that was average in him. He simply wanted to hide. I wondered whether this was a "built-in" part of his character, or if a particular life event triggered this affect in him. Soon I would find out.

Javier began telling me his story, his eyes darting wildly to the sides of the room, as he related events from his childhood. He remained quite rigid from when he arrived up to the point in his story where he met his wife, whereupon he immediately switched his gaze to the floor. Tears began to roll down his cheeks. "My friends say she's not a good woman and I know it. I don't know why I still want to be with her," he told me.

My name is Javier, and I'm 30 years old. I was born in Mexico, in a small city by the name of San Fernando. My father worked as a migrant field worker and did odd jobs for a nearby butcher shop whenever he was in town. My mother took care of our home and of us. I'm the third of five kids. My oldest sister's job was to help care for the house and the rest us. I was responsible for looking out for my two youngest siblings.

Our parents made sure we went to school every day. I don't think they valued education all that much, but I know my mom wanted us away from the house for part of the day so that she could take care of her multitude of chores. I think I did okay in school, regardless. Even though my parents didn't push us to be good students, I received average grades and never really got into trouble. Some of my brothers and sisters weren't interested in school and repeated some grades before they dropped out altogether. I was the only one who attended school until the ninth grade. That's all that was available to us at that time.

My dad wasn't home very much while I was a kid, and he would never tell us what his life was like while he was away working. All I remember is what life was like when he was home from travelling, and it wasn't good. My father drank a lot and used to beat all of us pretty regularly, especially my mom. For, as often as he was far away, my father was a very possessive man. He didn't like any of us, especially my mom, to talk to other people. He would burst out in fits of anger whenever he drank, and he'd make up stories of how my mother was probably cheating on him. And then he would beat her for it. None of it was true. My mom was too afraid of him and too passive to do anything like that, but it didn't matter. She couldn't even be happy or laugh when my father was around, because he automatically suspected her of having been with another man, and he'd beat her. "Why else are you in such a good mood, then?!" he would yell at her each time he slapped her—and he'd do it even in front of us kids.

So Mom could never feel happy around my father, and with time, any feelings of joy or happiness disappeared from her altogether. She became a sour, humorless woman and she began to hit us too. With one of my dad's belts, nonetheless. While she did not drink, she had turned into her own version of my dad, and she could be quite brutal.

I was terrified of her. I stopped speaking or making any noise altogether so that I could avoid getting in trouble with her. In my mind, my mother was like a volcano—always fuming, hostile, and ready to explode and destroy anything within her reach. I felt a deep fear every day, all day long; a true and abiding fear of my mother and her reactions. It was like living in a pressure cooker. I tried my best to handle it, but the only way I found any safety as a kid was to back away from everyone and keep to myself in the corner of my room. I had one blue toy car and it kept me company all day long. I used to imagine that I was the tiny driver and that I was driving away to a happier, better place where people smiled, and where no one yelled.

If I hadn't had any siblings, I probably would've been spared many beatings. My brothers turned out to be just as angry as my mom and dad and would constantly bicker and hit one another. My mother had zero tolerance for any of that, and she made sure we knew about it. She would come into the room and beat everyone that was in it, whether they had something to do with the problem or not. She got out her own anger and frustrations that way. I would have bruises for days for no good reason other than being in the same room with my siblings. The only way to stay safe was to go hide in a corner on my own. It was ever so lonely.

Kids at school weren't nice to me either. I didn't speak much to anybody and I think they found me weird for being so quiet. They picked on me relentlessly while at school and then would follow me home to pick a fight with me. Since I wouldn't fight back to avoid getting in trouble, they got away with beating me. Every time I would return home with a bloody nose, I would try to explain it to my mother, but she would beat me for getting into trouble and damaging my clothes.

As a kid, I didn't feel that I amounted to very much. Everything and everyone that crossed my path had a way of reminding me of that. Kids beat me, my mom beat me, and my teachers made fun of me in front of everyone for making mistakes. It was difficult not to think of myself as anything more than pond scum—an unwanted waste of space. Like a cloud rolling over, I too became quite grim, like my mom, like my siblings. And to my surprise, I quickly began to forget what it was like to feel happy and loved.

As I became older, the persecution from the boys in my neighborhood got worse than my mother's worst beatings. I don't know why they had it in for me, especially since some of them were friends with my brothers, but they just wouldn't leave me in peace. I avoided going outside my house, at all costs. All it took was for one of them to see me for the persecution to begin.

This abuse lasted for years. It started when I was about six or seven and it became regular and more brutal as I grew up. Their games began to change though, when I was about ten years old. It was like they no longer wanted to take out their anger on me, they simply wanted to have a laugh at my expense, to humiliate me and make me cry.

It was always the same three or four kids. They would chase me into the alleys and then they'd make me pull down my pants. After that, they would spit on me and on my private parts. I wish it had only happened once, but it was a constant feature of my daily life.

I don't know how I'm even able to talk about it. The memory of it brings back those feelings as if it was happening to me now. I felt so ashamed, reduced to nothing. I felt hated, helpless, and alone. I tried to tell my father about it a few times, but he showed little pity for me. In fact, he simply told me to "fight back," and to not let any of those boys beat me. Right.

Life felt like a constant threat and I lived in a continual state of fear. There wasn't a single good thing about my life during those years. I resented my mother and father for not protecting me. To make matters worse, did they really have to beat me for not fighting back whenever I came home bloody? I had no one to care for me and no one I could trust.

After I finished the ninth grade, I began to work in the agricultural fields full-time in order to avoid my mother. I stayed away late into the evening and I worked like an animal for little pay, but I wasn't allowed to keep it. I was expected to turn it in to my parents so I could help support the family. Every once in a while they would let me keep a bit for myself, but it was just so I could buy shoes, food, or clothes that I wouldn't have otherwise. Life was a chore. There was no joy in it for me.

By the time I was 15 years old, I had had enough. I couldn't live another day in this manner. I migrated to the United States on my own "in order to follow my dad's footsteps," and become a field-worker like him. I told my parents I wanted to better help support the family, and while that was true, I really just wanted to get away.

I arrived in Colorado and lived with various relatives for different periods of time. Life wasn't easy, but it was much better than the life I had left behind in Mexico. I even found a job at a bakery instead of the agricultural fields and worked hard to keep it for the next five years.

I even began to date a woman from work when I was 17 years old. She was six years older than me and had two kids, but I didn't care. I had no previous experience to compare this relationship with, so I just went along with it and let her "drive." She would have me come over to her house after work and we would spend the evening together, though she would never let me stay and spend the night. I learned a few months later that she had a husband who worked the night shift at a gas station. I was disgusted with her and myself for being so stupid.

And yet, I guess I just didn't really care much, because I continued to see this woman. Two months later I moved into an apartment with her and her kids. We lived together for some time and although she relied heavily on me to support her and her children, life was all right and I didn't complain. She was only separated from her husband and not actually divorced yet, but she kept promising me over and over that she soon would be completely done with him.

One day she went to visit her parents in Mexico with the excuse that they had not seen her children in a few years. I paid for her trip and I supported her and her children for the entire month that they stayed there. I later learned that she had returned to Colorado without me knowing about it in order to finalize her divorce. She waited for that, and then called me from Mexico to let me know we were through and she was not coming back. I felt stupid before, but now I knew that I was.

I met Monica a few years after that. For a while I reverted to working all the time and spending my free time alone at home. I didn't want to involve myself with anyone. My family was worried about me though, and would often drag me to outings and other events. It was on one of these occasions, at a party actually, that I met Monica.

I remember very clearly not wanting to go, but I had little choice. My family had resolved to "fix me up," and they were going to drag me out no matter what I had to say about it.

One of my cousins introduced me to Monica. She was a pretty girl and seemed nice. I was actually a little surprised that she wanted to talk to me at all. My cousin left me alone with her and I wasn't sure of what to do. I spoke to her for a while and then tried to return to my family, but they would eventually redirect me back to Monica. At one point they even left the party altogether so that I would be alone with her.

I didn't know what to do. I didn't know anyone at this party except for Monica and I had no way of getting back home. We spent the next couple of hours together and I began to feel at ease with her. At the end of the night she drove me home and we exchanged phone numbers. We even made plans to have lunch the next day at a Chinese restaurant that she wanted to show me.

Things progressed quickly. I walked out of our lunch at the Chinese restaurant glad to have a friend. But Monica wanted more, and I learned that quickly when she leaned over to kiss me in the car. I wasn't sure how I felt about any of that, but she very decidedly took charge and I automatically gave in, as is my nature I guess.

Monica and I spent every free minute of our time together. Within a week she told me she loved me and within two months we were getting married. She was a nice girl and she truly seemed honest in her feelings for me, so it was easy to get swept away—no one had ever really showed me this kind of love or interest before.

I became excited about our relationship. I even got a second job so we could afford a nicer place and I could better provide for us. Suddenly everything looked so promising. I was going to have a nice life, a family of my own and a wife that adored me. But I was wrong. Not long after we got married, Monica started coming home late and drunk on a regular basis. She would tell me that she worked late and then went out for a drink with her friends, but I was hurt and jealous nonetheless. Something didn't ring true in what she said.

It never stopped. She continued to call several days a week to tell me that she was working late at her boss' office and I would just tell her "okay," even though I knew something wasn't right. Then it got worse. She became mean and began to go away for entire weekends at a time and would tell me that it was because she didn't like being in the same place as me. She stopped telling me that she loved me or showing me any affection whatsoever. Suddenly she couldn't tolerate my very breath. I was heartbroken.

I tried to win her back and would invite her out on dates to fancy places, but she refused me every time. She didn't even want to be intimate with me anymore. One time she even told me that I sucked in bed. Whatever little self-esteem I had initially gained by being with her all came crashing down around me. I knew she was with other men every time she went out.

It wasn't long before she became violent. First, she would just explode, yell and insult me, but it quickly escalated and became much worse. She began to push me and hit me on the chest with her fists whenever she became angry with me. Then she started slapping me across the head and the face. She even kicked me once. It's never been in my nature to defend myself, so I just took it. I was also afraid of what else she would do if I didn't let her have her way, because she often threatened to call the police and have me deported.

All in all I still felt love for her. I didn't want her to leave me. I tried to make her happy, but my very presence exasperated her. I bought her flowers and wrote her letters, but she ignored them. One night I was telling her that I loved her as I begged her not to leave me, and she pushed me away from her and told me, "Well, I don't love you." Then she pulled a knife and warned me to get out of the way before she killed me.

One day she agreed to stay with me if I changed my ways. She told me that she wanted to go out and have fun with her friends and didn't want me to become jealous or to question her anymore as to her whereabouts. I agreed in a heartbeat. I didn't want to lose Monica. I breathed a sigh of relief as she then smiled and gave me a hug. "Okay," she told me, then went upstairs to get ready to go out.

I dealt with it for weeks. I never asked her a question and never uttered a peep about her goings on. Things were more peaceful, but she still wanted very little to do with me. Then one night a man called while she was out and told me he was Monica's boyfriend and that I was to leave her alone. I confronted Monica about this when she came home that night, and of course she denied everything. But I knew it was true. I had always known.

She was exceptionally nice to me for the next few days, but then quickly reverted to being explosive, violent, and hurtful in her words to me. She began to yell at me again and tell me that I was worthless and nothing but a "wetback." Soon after this she finally admitted to having another man. I wanted to die.

I didn't leave her. I let her come and go as she pleased. I don't know what I was trying to hold onto to, since she clearly wanted nothing to do with me. She would only be remotely affectionate and interested in me whenever she came home drunk and nearly incoherent, and like the loser I am, I always took the scraps she gave me.

I now know that Monica stayed with me all along just for the money. She stopped working not long after we got married, yet demanded my paychecks every week to do with them as she saw fit. I allowed her to manage our finances. She was

202

smart with bills and money—but she didn't give me any. She would give me $20 for the week and keep the rest of the money to herself. She wouldn't even let me send money back home to help support my mom.

Even though we were married she always made it sound as though I owed her money and kept demanding that I find a way to bring home more money. Whenever she got mad over finances, she would tell me that I was worthless and threaten to call the police and have me sent back to Mexico. I didn't know she couldn't do that, but at the time I believed her! I felt myself physically tremble every time she threatened to send me back home. I felt powerless to do anything about my situation. She was an American citizen, and she would make sure she got her way. Of course she wasn't about to help me get my papers—that would have taken away her power.

She knew she had succeeded in terrifying me and no longer cared to hide her affairs or show me any consideration. I heard her talking to other men on the phone multiple times, laughing and speaking to them about oral sex and the things they could do together. I felt shattered. My reality took me back to the days in the alleys of Mexico, when kids spat on me and I felt hated, humiliated, and completely alone.

We were together seven months before she left me. I came home one night after work to find that she had left and taken all of our things. She didn't even bother to tell me why, even though I already knew the reason, quite well. I felt sick to my stomach and fell to my knees. I cried myself to sleep that night on the floor of the empty living room.

Two weeks went by before I heard from Monica again. She called me one day to tell me that I owed her money and demanded that I get cash ready for her to pick up at the apartment that Friday or else she would call the police on me.

I didn't owe her a thing, but I was still afraid that she would follow through with her threats, and so that Friday I got her money together and she came to pick it up. Since then she has found an excuse to demand money from me at least three or four more times. She billed me for Christmas gifts that she bought for me in the past. She billed me for gifts that I bought for my family in Mexico. She even demanded that I pay her for things that she had wanted to buy that "I never gave her," like a cell phone and myriad other things. Each time she threatened to call the police and every time I was too afraid to fight back.

I don't know how to deal with Monica's absence. I don't even know what to make of the whole relationship. I can't stop thinking about everything she told me at the beginning of our relationship. Every cruel joke, insult, and threat. That I was worthless, nothing but a wetback, a waste of space. Maybe it was stupid of me to fight until the very end to get her back, but I couldn't stop thinking about the Monica I first met—the one that was so madly in love with me—and I clung to the hope that I could bring her back. I was wrong. She never loved me. I now know that it was all a lie.

In the end, immigration problems found me anyway. Not because Monica called the police on me like she said she would, but because we didn't know I could be required to return to Mexico when she eventually filed the request for me to stay in the United States.

My chances of survival in Mexico are next to none. I have no place to go except my old hometown, and there is no work or opportunities even for the men who already live there. Even if I were lucky enough to find work, it would not be enough to support me and my mom in Mexico. I know she was a terrible mother, but she is my mother, nonetheless, and she is old and frail now. My father is dead. Her children are all that she has left. My siblings pitched in to help with daily expenses and her medical treatments, but they mostly rely on me to pay the majority of her bills. I just don't know what would happen to either of us if I had to go back.

I don't have anyone to rely on in Mexico. Although my siblings are still there, our relationships are too strained for any of them to offer me a place to live, let alone emotional support.

Sometimes I think it would've been better if I hadn't let Monica convince me to file all that residency paperwork. I would've remained an illegal resident, but at least I could continue to live here in the US and be safe. I rarely drink and I don't do drugs, and I certainly don't involve myself with criminals. Hell, I don't ever even get into anybody's way. All I've done throughout these years is work and support other people. I just want to live in peace and maybe, one day, I can finally have a place to call home.

...

Javier is a clear example of the power of our past to shape the course of our lives. From a very young age, Javier was taught that standing up for himself was unacceptable and would only be met with rigorous opposition and even cruel punishment. Additionally, he quickly learned that the people closest to him would not protect him and perhaps didn't even care for him. Javier's upbringing, extremely abusive and neglectful in nature, helped to shape him into the meek, fearful, scarred, and exceedingly dependent man that he is today.

Javier undoubtedly experienced a severe level of psychological and even physical abuse during his relationship with Monica. She forced Javier to comply with her wishes through insults, verbal attacks, and emotional manipulation, controlling him through her actions. What is worse, in Javier's mind, Monica was only confirming what he had grown to believe about himself his entire life; that he was worthless, helpless, powerless, and undeserving of love.

There are some notable similarities between Javier's disposition for abuse and the behaviors his mother modeled for him while he was still a child. Not only was Javier fully immersed into his cruel reality first-hand with his wife's brutal treatment of him, but he also observed his mother—an adult— suffer the same kind of cruel and abusive treatment at the hands of her own spouse. In order to avoid any further punishment by her husband, she modeled spousal-abuse victim behavior to Javier. She showed Javier exactly what he needed to do in order to attenuate such punishment, as he had already learned that he could not entirely avoid it.

Two things caused Javier to be singled out as a potential victim by his wife: his passive and submissive nature, along with his conditioning as a child. His wife was clearly a woman with psychological problems of her own, and evidences many traits of a person with borderline personality disorder. His dependent personality features, however, are a big factor as to why he remained with Monica for so long. She provided Javier with attention and a degree of affection that he had been deprived of his entire life. Much like a drug, once she stopped providing him with emotional nurturance, he simply became obsessed with her. His ongoing attempts to "get her back" and be once again supplied with life-sustaining love and care were notable. Again, Monica was the first person to ever show Javier this level of love and affection, and for all he knew it was not going to happen again.

As with most of my patients, Javier is in dire need of psychological assistance. I wouldn't imagine that even a good wife or girlfriend, or even a family and children, could help Javier to heal the damage from his past and basically re-program his belief system. If anything, without long-term counseling, it would make him once again pathologically dependent on them. Javier would surely feel great having a wife and children that love him, but that certainly wouldn't mean his core issues stemming from neglect and abuse would then be healed.

Unfortunately for Javier, the judge decided that he would not be allowed to remain in the United States, even though he suffered from what I determined to be severe cruelty at the hands of an American citizen. Monica had her own sworn affidavits and witnesses that testified that Javier was a heavy drinker and was abusive to her.

Of course Javier is devastated and does not want to leave. He is terrified to return to his past life in Mexico. His attorney advised him to appeal and re-open the case, and Javier obviously agreed in a heartbeat, although it is yet to be known if that means he would be eligible to remain in the United States while his case is still sorted out.

NALIN

Shy, skinny Nalin walked into my office quite hesitantly that day. I will never forget. He took the first few steps through the doorway and when he saw me, he jumped backward, much like a scared cat, apparently thinking that he had interrupted me. He then, very sheepishly, poked his head around the doorway and I couldn't help but wonder about the underlying causes of such a reticent and skittish demeanor. I reassured him that everything was fine and he was welcome to come in and take a seat.

Nalin sat down very gently and placed his hands on his lap. "You have great posture," I told him, and he half-smiled and said, "I had good teachers." I made small talk with him for a few minutes so I could observe his body language and affect. Nalin was extremely gentle, almost as if he was fearful of upsetting any small piece of the environment he had entered. I noticed that even though he had an empty chair next to him, he had chosen to place his jacket and folder on the floor. I noticed that he did not do so in order to better guard his possessions, but rather, he wanted to disturb as little space as possible with his presence.

I didn't learn much about Nalin's current life conditions because there wasn't a lot to learn. Nalin worked as a waiter and divided his time between work, the grocery store, and a small

211

apartment where he lived alone. He did not have any friends, nor did he pursue any interests or engage in any social activities. Even though he seemingly got along well with his coworkers, he never saw any of them outside of the restaurant. Gentle, shy Nalin had the most bland, boring life one could imagine.

He was telling me about his mundane existence when suddenly I blurted out, "What are you hiding from, Nalin?" He stopped halfway through his sentence to look at me—half in awe and half in horror. "They said they would kill me. I don't want to upset them. I don't want them to come looking for me," he told me.

Nalin visibly began to shake, and had it not been for the effects of his superior will and tenacious efforts at self-control, he likely would have fallen completely apart in that moment. It had been such a long time since he had anyone to talk to that he had grown accustomed to keeping his feelings to himself. Yet, as with anyone who remains that isolated for that long a time, his mind loses the ability to discern what is real and what is only imagined. Nalin had long since lost his ability to control his thoughts and emotions, and was allowing wild ideas to run amok inside his head. I could see him growing ever tenser by the minute and he even began clenching his jaws.

"Nalin, Nalin," I said, attempting to pull him out of the worried, trance-like state he seemed to have

fallen into. "*All those thoughts running through you right now ... tell me all of them.*"

And so the story of Nalin's sad and tortured life began.

My name is Nalin, and I came from Darjeeling, India. I'm 27 years old and the youngest of three children. My dad had a small tea crop and also a small spice shop at the market. My mom helped run both, but mostly she took care of us and our home.

My dad drank a lot. He was hardly ever home, so I didn't often get to see his sober side. He would come home late at night and by then he was usually already drunk. He was really abusive to everyone in the family. When he was drunk he would make up any excuse to beat us. He didn't really care where he hit us or with what object, sometimes he would even punch us in the face. We missed school many times because we had visible bruises and he didn't want other people to know what was happening at home. It always puzzled me how he would care about what other people thought of him, but he never seemed to give a second thought as to what our opinions of him might be.

My mom tried her best to protect us, but she was weak. She was just as terrified of my dad as we all were and would not stand up to him. She knew she couldn't win. She also knew that my dad would beat

213

us even for walking near him, so she tried to hide us away from him as best as she could.

I didn't understand back then that my dad was a mean drunk. I thought this was what sergeants in the military were probably like; cold, stern, strict disciplinarians. I thought dads were the head of the household (as we were told in my culture), and that all of them behaved in this way. I didn't know any better.

He scared the hell out of me. I always tried so hard to read his mind and anticipate any of his requests. I tried to stay out of his way and out of trouble, so he wouldn't hit me. I never thought of telling anyone about this, because it never even crossed my mind. I thought this was the way life was. I always felt in my heart that it wasn't right for him to beat us, especially because he looked like he enjoyed it. But I thought it was the way life was for everyone and I simply resigned myself to it.

There was something about the violence in Dad's eyes that left me very confused about the beatings he dished out, regardless of how normal I thought it was or how much I had resigned myself to it. There was no hint of love or caring in his eyes. Whenever he beat us he was completely detached. In those moments we were all strangers to him and he hated us. There was no regret or remorse in him, and never with any intention of correcting us for our own good. He wanted to hurt us. There was nothing else to it than that, and it felt like a stab in the heart.

I attended a missionary school for many years. I was so excited about starting school and the thought of being with other children all day, playing and learning had me bouncing off the walls. My excitement earned me a few extra beatings from my dad for making "too much noise," but I didn't care, because soon I would be in a happy place.

To my surprise, school was a very formal place and the teachers were unbearably strict. They didn't tolerate any misbehavior and were quick to dispense punishment if anyone gave them the smallest reason. We were hit for making mistakes, for not sitting straight, for speaking, for not speaking, for laughing, for playing with abandon, for having ugly penmanship. I began to wonder why adults were so eager to hurt children. All of the illusions I had about school quickly dissolved, as did my dreams of ever having a nicer life anywhere—they all began to crumble apart. My resolve to avoid being hit became my prime motivation to do well in school. I was unhappy, but it worked. I got good grades and sported less bruises than the rest of the kids in my class.

I eventually finished school and went off to college to study business and finance. I knew many of the students who were in the same year as me, and even though we would get together to study, I was unable to make any friends, just like back in school. It was a lonely existence, and I often pondered why it was so difficult for me to understand the dynamics of life and be able to relate to people.

I began to date girls halfway through college, but I had no idea of what I was doing. I was always so jittery around them. I wouldn't know what to say or what to do, and they were always so strong-willed. I just followed wherever they led. I think they sort of considered me their pet.

As was customary, my parents arranged a marriage for me after I graduated from college and began to work. They had struck a deal with another couple with whom they had been friends for decades. In fact, I had known Sanguita all of my life. She and her parents lived in a nearby city, and my mom and I often went to visit them. We used to play together all the time as kids, and then suddenly it stopped. I didn't think much about it and when my mom explained to me that they had moved to the United States, I put it behind me and went on about my life. I was consumed with avoiding beatings at the hands of my teachers and my dad. anyway.

After the arrangement was finalized, I travelled to the United States several times to visit Sanguita. I had not seen her since we were children. I was glad that she was not a complete stranger and, at first, I felt hopeful about the marriage. She was pretty and it seemed that she had grown up to be a good person. I imagined that she would make a good wife. I thought of countless horror stories about arranged marriages in my culture and I felt lucky to not have it nearly as bad. I continued to work for another year to save money, and when I was 25 years old, I moved to the United States. I followed through with my parent's arrangement to marry Sanguita.

The first few weeks of our marriage went impossibly well. Sanguita's parents were very nice to me. They made me feel at home, and she seemed to like me, as well. As time went by, however, they became to tighten the proverbial leash around my neck and became progressively more controlling of me. They told me what to do and when, and they really didn't like me leaving the house alone. I wanted to please Sanguita, so I went along with and did everything they asked of me, but she was picky. No matter what I did, she never fully approved of it.

Sanguita and her parents had a very well-defined idea of what they thought I should be and do and they pushed for it, relentlessly. They insisted that I get a certain job, they bought and picked my clothes for me, and told me when to eat and what. They even forbade me to go out at all at night, and if I wanted to go out during the day it could only be escorted by them. I couldn't make friends, and if I had made any friends at work, I could never bring them over.

Part of me felt it was my duty to acquiesce to Sanguita's wishes, but most of me felt there was something very wrong with this situation. I didn't see the harm in walking to the corner store, or working at the dry cleaners, or having a friend. But when it came to me wanting these things, it was simply unacceptable for them.

I often spoke to my mother and I learned that her health had declined and my father had begun to drink most of his money away with his friends from the market. I took a job at a Chinese restaurant so I could help support my mother. I spoke to Sanguita and her parents about this and they were suspiciously ready to agree with me. I should've seen it coming. Deep inside I still trusted them, because they were friends of my parents, but it turned out that I was wrong to do that.

As soon as I began to work, Sanguita's parents demanded money from me. I thought it was more than fair for me to pay my share of the expenses, but they would take my entire paycheck every week. My mom became quite ill a few months after I began to work and as astounding as it sounds, I begged Sanguita's parents to let me have some of the money from my paycheck so I could pay for my mom's medical care. They refused. They told me that my mom was old and it was time to let her die. I could not believe what I had heard. In my mind, these people in front of me began to change into what they really were—monsters. I turned to Sanguita in my horror to help intercede for my mom, but she turned around and went into her room. She either could not have cared any less, or was just as afraid of her parents as I was.

My relationship with Sanguita wasn't good after that, and her parents damaged any chance at salvaging it. They wouldn't stop telling her that I wasn't good enough and didn't make enough money for her. In fact, they often told her I probably hid money from her and Sanguita believed them. Her torment was very different than mine, but it was more than she could bear. She'd often lock herself in the room and cry for hours. Nothing I could say made her feel better and even seemed to make her angrier at me.

Sanguita's parents' demands for money escalated even though they received the entirety of my paycheck each week. It wasn't long before all of the money I made was not enough for them. I had to switch jobs and work for a different restaurant in the hopes of earning more and keeping them happy. They were the only people I knew, and I was tied to Sanguita—I didn't know what to do or where to go.

I continued to give them all of my money, but they were never satisfied. They kept asking me for more money and even went to the restaurant to ask my boss about how much money I actually made. They even had the audacity to ask how much business he had coming into the restaurant and how much money I made in tips. I was lucky that I didn't lose my job. My boss felt pity for me and crossed Sanguita's parents off as "crazy people."

There was nothing left for me to do but to try my best to please these people. Sanguita wanted nothing to do with me, and even though we slept in the same room she made me sleep on the floor. She even stopped speaking to me, and her parents treated me like I was worthless. About two weeks after their visit to talk to my boss they sat me down and very casually told me that I no longer served a purpose for them, and that they did not want me to stay any longer. They informed me I'd be going back to India, "and FYI—Sanguita won't be going with you."

Whether I liked it or not, I had made a solemn vow, and I refused to leave without Sanguita. Somewhere within me I still thought that we could salvage our marriage if only we could get away from her parents. I wanted to have a family. I wanted a home, a happy home, like I never had, where I would never hit my children, and where I could be happy. I had not picked Sanguita, but I knew the child she used to be and the woman she was now, and I knew she needed me every bit as much as I needed her. I would help her and we would both be free. I told myself I would win her back, bit by bit, over time, and then I would convince her to leave with me. We would go away and make a life where no one would hurt us anymore.

I was determined to stay entrenched in the house and I continued to go to work and hand them my paychecks every week. Then one day, Sanguita's parents took me to work, but then didn't pick me up. I was lucky that my boss allowed me to spend the next few weeks at his apartment, because Sanguita's parents never returned for me and refused to answer any of my calls.

I never stopped calling and they never picked up. One day Sanguita's parents showed up at the restaurant and her father told me that he would kill me if I didn't go back to India. He then opened his jacket and showed me a gun. My boss and two of my coworkers were watching as it happened, but they didn't seem to care. Her parents had delivered their message and they left. My boss, an old and rather frail Tibetan man, feared for his business and what could happen to him if I made a big deal out of any of this. He begged me to not report the incident to the police. My boss had been so good to me all this time that I agreed to not compromise him in any way and did not call the police.

This is how my marriage with Sanguita ended. I never spoke to her again. I tried to call a few times after that, but her father would always pick up the phone and I would hang up. I really thought I could make her happy. I thought, even though we had never actually fallen in love with each other, that we could make do with what we had and build a happy life for ourselves and that love would come to us in time. I never had the chance.

Although I haven't seen or heard from Sanguita or her parents in the last seven months, I'm afraid they will come find me and kill me. I think they know where I live.

I live in fear of making any mistakes, as then they would become alerted and come and punish me. I leave my apartment to go to work and to buy groceries. I spend the rest of my time in hiding. I'm afraid to go outside or to have friends. I am frightened that I will somehow anger Sanguita's parents, to have them spot me somewhere when I am not at work, and that they would become enraged and hurt me. I just don't know why I can't deal with it. I'm afraid of them.

I do worry about what will become of me if I keep going on like this. My mind is constantly spinning and I'm so occupied with my worries, I don't even notice that life is passing me by. It takes a lot of effort to even get up in the morning and go to work. Once I'm at work, I'm a mess. I become tense, and I'm always looking through the corners of my eyes to make sure Sanguita's parents aren't sneaking up on me. I'm jumpy and I get startled easily. I constantly drop trays of food which makes my boss very, very unhappy with me.

Sometimes I want to go back to India. I want to be with my mother, though I don't know what kind of life I could make for myself over there. I certainly don't want to end up like my father or spend my days working in a market. Then again, I haven't made a satisfying life for myself here, either… I suppose there is still hope that one day I can.

...

As the advanced, contemporary society that we assume we are here, we oftentimes seem to miss the huge cultural impact that newcomers to this country experience—the clash between those of a Third-World upbringing with that of our ultra-modern, progressive way of being here in America. After hearing Nalin's story, it wasn't difficult to spot the factors that had molded his character as he was led through the events he experienced as a child growing up in his home country.

Nalin had understood one thing at a very early age: obedience and submission to authority above all else. He lived his life scurrying around his home following orders to the letter in order to avoid a beating. He spent his time at school in very much the same fashion. His father, the feared, strict, brutally violent man he had grown to fear, respect, and obey, ingrained in him that whoever holds the power must and will be obeyed. Sanguita's parent's cruelly stepped in and filled the role of his father's voice.

Nalin's mother was gentle and weak, and was incapable of protecting her children or taking them away to safety due to her own fears and cultural conditioning. Nalin's mother had cared for her son and he spent most of his waking hours observing the modeling of her temperament and outlook on life. These would be the predominant personality traits that he would grow to absorb and emulate.

Many people living in the United States who also grow up with a similarly oppressive family dynamic would simply bail out at some point, particularly as adults who realize their options in this free society. Under such harsh conditions, most, but not all American citizens will move away, make new friends, stay in a motel, sleep in a car or at their jobs or in a shelter, but will find some way to remove themselves from such a repressive and unreasonably cruel situation. Such thoughts never even crossed Nalin's mind. In this pre-arranged marriage, Nalin felt a strong sense of duty to his wife which was imposed on him at an early age by their culture, and in any case he had grown up conditioned to fill this very role. It wasn't that there was no fight in Nalin, let alone assertiveness or determination. It was that the ever-present cultural influences in his character inhibited his embracing and inhabiting these very human traits. His mind and soul were impregnated with old-country beliefs and values that were deeply embedded from his childhood. These features, together with his naturally submissive personality, set the stage for Nalin's acceptance of his lot in life and his suffering with no conviction of finding recourse or justice.

In speaking to Nalin's attorney many months after my interview with him, I learned that Nalin had not been allowed to remain in the United

States. His Green Card had not been renewed and he was informed that he would have to return to India. I was saddened by this news, yet I was also glad for him. Nalin had no one and nothing in this country to sustain him, and his spirit was dying. Even though the possibility of creating a better future for himself in America was almost irresistible, Nalin did not have the resources, either physically or spiritually, to persevere. He did not seem to have the tools necessary to be able to truly immerse himself in the community and build a support network for himself. Had Nalin remained in the United States, surely his isolation would have only intensified and degenerated into a variety of serious mental health maladies.

Although Nalin had experienced quite a traumatic family history, in my opinion, returning to India was probably the lesser of two evils for him. The Nalin I met was in desperate need of support, and felt incapable of finding it for himself. While a return to India would put him in proximity of the hands of his brutal father, Nalin can still count on the support of his mother and brothers to help him to forge a better, healthier life for himself back home. I see this as a second chance for him—an opportunity for him to put his history to rest, cross through the fire, and start again as a different, but stronger Nalin.

RAQUEL

Raquel's attorney had already briefed me on the condition of her situation and I had prepared my office and the staff accordingly. The blinds had been closed, and my office manager had taken her post by the front window in order to watch for any cars or people that came and went. The receptionist had been warned not to disclose to anyone that Raquel was to come to our office. We were ready. Now we just needed Raquel to show up. Hopefully, she would.

Raquel came into sight on foot, leading her son by the hand through the snow. She walked hurriedly, her gaze fixed on the ground, and her young son struggling to keep up the pace. It was evident that she did not want to be exposed outside for another minute if she could at all help it.

Raquel had been advised that the front door to my office would be left unlocked for her, so that she could simply hurry in rather than ringing the doorbell and waiting outside. She sighed in relief as she closed the door behind her and picked up her son. She hugged him tight, yet ever so gently. "That was a fast walk, huh? You did a good job, thank you," she told him. The little boy hugged his mother's neck as he leaned to put his head on her shoulder. He was clearly exhausted.

227

My assistant had a way with kids and she made friends with the little boy quickly. She then took him to the testing room where she had set up toys, snacks, and a movie for him. She kept him company as she looked out the window, just as I had instructed her. We were all tense. Raquel's partner had not yet learned of her seeking legal help, but he had grown suspicious at the various "doctor's appointments" to which she had supposedly been taking their child.

Raquel sat nervously at the table in my office, her gaze helplessly gravitating towards the front door and the windows. Her left leg shook frenetically as she compulsively bit the sides of her fingernails. We didn't have much time. I cut to the chase.

"Raquel, was Glenn your first relationship?" I asked. She looked down to the floor, her lips pressed into a line. She shook her head "yes," then a tear rolled down her cheek.

A silent moment went by, and then she said, "I don't know." I looked at her quizzically. I had yet to ask her my follow-up question before she finally responded, "I don't know why I stayed with him so long, weren't you gonna ask me that next?" I could see her sadness turning into irritation, frustration, defensiveness. Raquel wasn't getting angry at me though, she was angry with herself.

"Well," I said with my signature eyebrow raise, "No. I wasn't going to ask that just yet, but it seems like you're ready to tell me about it. Can we start at the beginning?"

Raquel sighed deeply once again. She leaned forward to grab a Kleenex from the table and nodded her head "yes," as she wiped the tears from her eyes.

My name is Raquel, and I'm 24 years old. I was born in a small town near Culiacan, Mexico. My father had a small shoe repair business in the back of our house and also worked in a shop repairing agricultural equipment. I don't have a mother. She died giving birth to my younger sister (there are three of us altogether). My dad worked hard to keep food on the table and worked even harder to ensure we were "growing up right," as he liked to call it.

I lived in our little town until I finished elementary school, after which my sister and I moved to a bigger town closer to Culiacan in order to continue with school. We lived there with an aunt for a few years before my sister and I moved to Grand Junction, Colorado when I was 14 years old. My dad's idea was for us to learn English and become familiar with the way of life in the United States, hoping that one day we would forge our lives here. He always told us that he wanted a better life for his children than the one he had, and that this one opportunity for a fresh start was all that he could offer us.

We lived in Grand Junction with another aunt and her family. We enrolled in high school and attended English only classes, which made things exceptionally difficult. My dad kept pushing us, though, and we graduated high school on time. My days in high school weren't noteworthy. I was very shy and only managed to make two friends. We stuck together during school, but we never went out or did anything afterwards. While other kids gossiped about parties, their crushes, and fun activities, I had nothing to talk about. I felt completely foreign from their culture, language, and way of life, and it was difficult to even try to integrate myself anywhere.

Life at home wasn't much easier either. Simply put, my aunt and uncle were crazy. They were happy and friendly one minute, then angry, violent, and hateful the next. They were very controlling and watched my every move. You'd think I was nothing but trouble, but the truth is that I spent most of my time in my room. Even then, they constantly barged through the door as if expecting to catch me red-handed doing something bad.

My sister didn't have an easy time either. She was older than I, but also had a hard time acclimating to our new life in the United States. In fact, as soon as she finished high school, she begged my dad to let her return to Mexico, but he wouldn't have it. He tried to convince her that the only opportunity she had for a better life was in the United States, but she wanted nothing to do with it. She spent her entire time here sleeping and crying. In the end, they reached a compromise of sorts and an older cousin in Texas invited her to move in with her. The problem was that she had a large family and could only house one of us. My dad pleaded with me to understand, but I couldn't get over being left alone with the crazies. In the end, Dad promised he would try his best to find a new place for me to live, and I had to let my sister go without me. I didn't think she would've been able to handle it much longer in Colorado anyway.

After I graduated from high school, I went to live with my aunt's daughter, Cristina. I babysat her kids and I also worked at a meat-packing plant. I hated working ankle deep in cow's blood and looking at entrails every day. The smell of the place alone often made me vomit. I didn't last there very long. In fact, I actively began looking for work again after my third day at the plant. Thankfully, it was only a few weeks until I found something better and I began work cleaning a senior center part-time.

I lied my way into the senior center and told the hiring lady that all my documents had been stolen. She believed me, but gave me a couple of weeks to get duplicates and bring them to her, otherwise she couldn't let me work. Cristina told me she knew how to get fake documents and without asking me, she took my last paycheck stub to get IDs made for me. No documents ever materialized and I never saw my money again. I was angry with her for stealing from me, but I felt powerless to do anything as I lived in her house and had nowhere to go.

About two weeks later, Cristina went to New Mexico to buy false documents for her husband. When she came back, she gave me copies of one of her cousin's documents and told me her cousin was alright with me using her identity. I did—I had to. I was "Angela Cuevas" at work for the next five years.

I was almost 20 when my youngest sister came to the United States and we rented a place together. Even my older sister moved back from Texas so that we could all be together. It was so relieving to have some real family around me for a change. The little one-bedroom apartment we rented and our uncomplicated lives finally gave me hope about making things work out here in the United States. Maybe we could even bring my father to live with us some day.

I met Glenn not long after my sisters and I settled into our new place. He was an American who didn't speak Spanish, so things were a bit difficult in the beginning because I didn't get here as a little kid and my English wasn't great. He was a real nice guy, and I thought I had been lucky to find him. We dated for a little while and I got to know some of his friends and coworkers. The first thing I noticed was that they were friendly and polite to me, but each of them seemed to keep their distance from Glenn. I found it odd.

As time went by and some of his friends grew more comfortable with me, they began to comment on Glenn, and warned me to be careful. They would tell me that Glenn often lied and had a very bad, dark side, but I never noticed any of that. Glenn drank and sometimes he would drink a lot, but that was about the only thing wrong with him.

We moved in together about six weeks after we started dating. I left my sister to take over our apartment by herself, and I went to live in Glenn's house. His friends were right. As our relationship continued, he began to behave less and less like the man he initially portrayed himself to be. He began to drink every night and would get really drunk every weekend. It was as if he couldn't have fun if he didn't have a beer in his hand.

Alcohol made Glenn a different man. He became selfish, sarcastic, and caustic in the way he spoke to me. During those times the only things that mattered to him were his friends and partying, and they took priority over everything, including me. I wish the problem was only his heavy drinking, but alcohol completely changed his character. Whenever he was drinking he was angry and had a short temper. He hadn't begun yelling at me yet, but he would snap at me for any little thing and his moodiness replaced the caring, loving man that I initially met.

About seven months went by like this. I tried talking to him about the problems between us on several occasions, and at times it would work for a short period of time. But at other times Glenn would grumpily dismiss me. Yet I couldn't bring myself to leave him. I had fallen in love with him, and I thought our relationship still had hope. I tried. I tended to his every need and never complained about his drinking, but my all my efforts seemed pointless. I'd talk to my sisters from time to time about my relationship and they would remind me of the Mexican men in our town, always drinking and getting in trouble. "It's just men being men," they would say; "Find a way to make it work if you love him." I was trying.

In September of that year, Glenn invited me on a trip to Maine to visit his family. This is where I got to know the real him.

On the trip his mood would change from one moment to the next. He would smile at me and hold my hand as we drove to Maine, then get angry and stop talking to me for miles, because I changed the radio station. I thought the long road trip had made him short-tempered, but things remained the same after we arrived in Maine. He would get angry at me all the time, and although he wouldn't insult me or yell at me in front of his family, he'd make angry, hurtful, sardonic remarks. One time I asked him to let me drive his truck to the grocery store and he became outraged. He threw the keys on the floor and right in front of his family told me to pick up the keys if I wanted to take his truck.

I felt alone and humiliated in front of all these strangers and without anyone that truly cared about me. I tried to keep my composure and told him I'd go take a nap instead. I went to our room and quietly cried myself to sleep. A few hours later Glenn came to our room acting nice and loving as if nothing had happened. He began to do that a lot.

I became pregnant about a month after our trip. I don't know what I was thinking. I guess I wasn't thinking at all. I didn't have a difficult pregnancy, but it was stressful. Glenn wouldn't help me at all. Only rarely did he seem to care, and it was often short-lived.

He was obsessed with online games and spent nearly all of his free time consumed in front of the computer. He would become snappy if I interrupted him, so I tried to stay out of his way, but even then I couldn't manage to avoid his wrath. He would get so wrapped up in his games and become so upset whenever he lost that he would smash his fists on the desk, and throw things against the wall—he even broke the bathroom door once. It was scary to be nearby in the living room and hear him smash things against the wall. Sometimes I feared he would come looking for me to let out his anger.

Our relationship worsened, of course. He began to yell and insult me in anger. He wasn't holding back anymore. I'd often feel hurt and cry, but he only became meaner. He would walk up to me, put his face right up to mine and tell me I could leave if I didn't like things. That I was worthless and I would be nothing without him. I wanted to run away. I wanted to stay. I wanted to make him stop. I wanted to find a way to make things better. I felt so torn. My sister's advice never changed, not even when our own dad was never like that with us. "Men are wild—they're all going to be like that," she'd said. And it played over and over in my mind.

I was five months pregnant at the time and I couldn't handle it anymore. I needed to get out at least for a while, but I had nowhere to go. My dad had broken a leg and an arm in an accident and both of my sisters went to take care of him and his business for a few months. In my desperation, I reached out to my cousin Cristina, and she called me back a few days later and told me that all I had to do was sign some papers and I could live in this basement studio apartment for free. Glenn and I had gotten into a really bad fight the night prior and I wasn't thinking straight. I didn't even ask her what it was, I signed it and I went to live over there.

A week went by without talking to Glenn. Then he called.

He told me that he missed me and that he was sorry and wanted things to work out between us and raise our baby together. I didn't believe him at first. It sounded similar to him being nice after exploding and treating me badly. I told him I didn't know what to think. He said he would change. He didn't stop calling and checking up on me. I was not used to being alone. I thought I still loved him. Two weeks later, I agreed to move back in with him.

Glenn had promised to help one of his friends move to New Mexico and was going to be gone for the weekend, so we agreed that I would move back in when he returned to town. That Friday night the police came looking for me and took me to jail for forgery charges. Apparently I had done something very bad, something I didn't understand. I never stopped to think twice about signing those papers because they had come from my own cousin. I never thought for a moment that she would do anything to put me in danger.

I spent four months in the Homeland Security Detention Facility. Glenn was furious about it. He didn't know what I had done to get there in the first place, but mostly he was nervous that he would be implicated somehow and get into trouble. Nothing ever happened to him though. I was the one who had to be in jail with all those crazy girls yelling and fighting all the time. I feared for my life and that of my baby. I feared being in the wrong place at the wrong time and getting hurt for no good reason. It seemed like I spent my life afraid of being hurt by one person or another. I couldn't handle the fear anymore, and I was terrified of what it was doing to my baby. It was all too much. One day I finally had a nervous breakdown. I couldn't get up, I could barely speak or think straight. The guards took me to their equivalent of an ICU and I spent many hours there. The next day I went into labor—two weeks earlier than scheduled. My baby was born in jail.

Glenn came to get me once I was released from jail and we went back to living together. He was gentle and loving for a while, but it wasn't long before he went right back to being his old self. Actually, it got worse in that he began mistreating me and our son. He was never physical with the baby, but he neglected him and spoke of him as if he was an inconvenience.

Glenn was regularly disrespectful to me in public. He would make me go to his friend's parties, and if I did anything he didn't like, he'd humiliate me by calling me names, or would dare me to leave if I tried to stand up for myself. It was at one of these parties that Glenn ran into one of his ex-girlfriends and began talking to her. The next thing I knew they had disappeared together; Glenn's friends glanced over at me from time to time, pity and sympathy in their eyes.

It turned out that Glenn just left with this girl and abandoned me at the party. One of Glenn's friends offered to take me back home. Of course Glenn hadn't come back for me. He came home much later that night. He denied cheating on me with this girl, but I wouldn't have put it past him. When I confronted him about it, he became defensive and told me that I wasn't good enough for him, that the baby had made me fat, that I was stupid and boring, and that he no longer liked me. I knew he didn't love me, but he didn't have to say any of that. He ripped my heart to pieces.

I don't know why I had stayed with him for so long. I guess it was because we had a child together, and because we had been together for so long. I truly convinced myself that there was a way to make it work. Maybe it was because I refused to accept that he just did not care. I don't understand it either, but I stuck around.

Glenn took on the habit of treating me like his servant and insulting me in front of his friends. Whether I liked it or not, he would invite his friends over, and I was expected to serve them as if I were their maid. Whenever I told him I couldn't do something because I had to take care of the baby, he would get mad and yell "Go fuck yourself, then," in front of his friends. It was so very denigrating. He would make comments to his friends, referring to me as "this whore," and call me a myriad of other names. He then trampled all over me and made sure I felt as low as possible.

It's been three and a half years and I'm still with Glenn. I thought of leaving him for good about six months ago, but he threatened to call Immigration on me and then take my baby away. I know it's our child, but Glenn has never taken responsibility or interest in the baby. He hasn't even wanted to help me cover the costs of raising our child. I consulted with a community legal advisor and I was told that he would likely be able to get full custody of my son because I don't have a steady job (Glenn doesn't let me work), and because of my legal status and criminal history for that forged document.

So, even though, at first, I didn't want to leave him, now I'm trapped. Glenn has me hanging by a thread with his threats to call Immigration and take my child away. I don't know why he wants me to stick around. I'm nothing but a maid to him. He insults me and spends his time yelling at me and telling me I'm worthless. I don't know what to do. I've thought about death more often than I care to admit, but I can't leave my son alone. My sisters have been back from Mexico for some time now, but I can't flee to them because Glenn will take my son.

Even though we have been together for almost four years and we have a child, Glenn refuses to help me become a resident. He says I don't need to since I don't need to work or leave the house for anything at all. A friend of my sister's told her that perhaps an attorney could help me, but Glenn would kill me if he knew about this. I wouldn't see the light of another day.

My sister convinced me to do it, and even though I didn't have money to pay the attorney, he agreed to work on my case pro-bono. I've been meeting him secretly for over two months now. I have to tell Glenn I'm taking the baby to the doctor, then I'm panicked the whole way to my attorney's office, thinking that Glenn might be following me. I have to do this, though. This is the only way my baby and I will ever have a chance at a normal life. My son is four now, and he has grown up watching his father beat and berate his mother every day. I don't want him to grow up like this. Not having a father is better than this.

...

Fortunately, Glenn never appeared in our office that day, nor did he find out about Raquel's legal case until the very end. By that time, Raquel and her attorney had already won her legal case and she was in process of becoming a legal resident. An order of protection was filed against Glenn, and she and her child were able to move in with her oldest sister while the battle for custody began. It is my understanding that the custody fight was a much more difficult process, but in the end Raquel was able to keep her son with her full-time.

One of the things I find most surprising about Raquel's story is the feedback she received from her sisters when she spoke to them about Glenn's abuse—"It's just men being men, they're all like that." Apparently Raquel's father had been far from abusive, though somewhat neglectful. In fact, he made up for the seemingly infinite amount of time he spent away from his daughters when he worked long hours, through lavishing them with care and attention at the times when he was able to be with them. In any case, while Raquel's father appears to have been a caring and loving father to his children, he did not get to spend nearly enough time with them. By proxy, Raquel and her sisters spent much of their time with relatives and witnessed the dynamics of those more common, unhealthy relationships.

It is not difficult to see how most of her father's efforts toward being a good example to his girls were almost fully cancelled out by the examples of other family members, with whom they spent more time. As he has told them himself, perhaps the best thing Raquel's father could have done for those girls was to give them an opportunity to make a better life for themselves by sending them to the United States.

Granted, Raquel didn't have the best start on her new life by a long shot. Even now that she is no longer at Glenn's mercy, she has quite a load to untangle, and must embark on the long process of healing before she is able to start with a clean slate—without repeating any of her old, self-destructive patterns and beliefs.

Raquel long ago began to present with very clear signs of trauma reactions that have now morphed into what appears as a prominent generalized anxiety disorder. Although she has attempted to remain strong for her child, by herself she was unable to heal the effects of the mental and *emotional battery that she suffered at the hands of this man. Thankfully, she is well aware of these issues, and once she no longer feared Glenn learning of her whereabouts, she began therapy in a local clinic.*

Her sisters may consider Raquel's experiences with Glenn normal, but thankfully Raquel does not. As long as she remains psychologically aware of her inner states and continues on her path to healing, she will be able to discern healthy from unhealthy, and be able to provide herself with the chance at a new life that her father had hoped to give her.

SEO-YEON

"You can close the door behind you," I told her.

Seo-Yeon walked timidly to the table. Despite her age, there was an air of innocence about her that made her look almost completely and utterly lost. She sat with her ankles together and rested her neatly folded hands on her thighs. She gave me a tentative look and a polite half-smile, and then continued to inspect my office with only her gaze, nervousness oozing through her pores, despite her attempts to keep herself composed. I feared Seo-Yeon was perfectly comfortable not speaking, and if it were up to her, another five, 50 or 60 minutes might go by in perfect silence. Today was going to be a long day.

After a great deal of effort, Seo-Yeon warmed up and began to speak about herself. She wouldn't share anything overly personal, but I accepted her informational contributions anyway—baby steps. She told me about her love for Colorado and the mountains and how she planned to finally get into hiking. She spoke of her love of classical music and the opera and how she found it soothing. She told me her life in South Korea had been quiet and peaceful. Additionally, she enjoys simple pleasures such as walking in nature and preparing a meal.

These were all positive things, and although she smiled as she spoke of them, her face belied the front that she was trying to put on. She appeared morose and downcast throughout our conversation. It wasn't a grumpy frown, she didn't even look upset. It was more of a sad, yet confused look, and I don't think she was even aware of the expression her face conveyed. Something about her life didn't make sense to her. And she wasn't able to tell me what it was.

I allowed her the space to continue to speak about her history, and she did so in a seemingly calm manner until it she reached the point in her story where she met Patrick, her ex-husband.

At once Seo-Yeon's demeanor changed. She switched her gaze to the floor and held her hands tight against her stomach. She attempted to maintain her reserved, composed demeanor, but the mounting tension was too much to hide. She lifted her gaze and stared at me with glazed eyes for a moment, before one of her legs began to shake uncontrollably. She was allowing me to see her as she really was, and coming from this dour, enigmatic woman, this was quite a development.

My name is Seo-Yeon, and I'm 45 years old. I was born in South Korea and I have two brothers and four sisters. When I was young, my family moved to a rural area of South Korea where we farmed the land. I went to school in the village there, and after I completed my education, I stayed home for some time to help the family. I liked walking through the fields, perusing the food and wares in the market, and preparing our food. It was a peaceful life.

I worked as a clerk in the office of a tailor for two years, and after that I worked in the PX store at an American military base. I spent most of my free time with family or friends. I liked to go hiking in the mountains with them. It truly was a quiet, peaceful life, and I expected to remain with my family and live the rest of my life in this manner. It wasn't exciting or glamorous, but it was serene, and in serenity I found happiness.

Never in a thousand years did I expect to move to the United States.

I travelled to the U.S. for a visit in March of 2000. I wanted to start the new millennium doing something adventurous. I travelled through Colorado and California and I fell in love with the mountains and the forests. I began to daydream about a life in the United States, and though I knew there was no way for me to stay in the country, I secretly hoped that I could.

I returned home after a few months and all I could think of was travelling and seeing more of the United States. I worked hard and I was able to return and visit a few more times. My girlfriend, Ji-Min, a childhood friend, had long lived in Colorado, so I always had a place to stay when I was here. Eventually, I fell in love with the mountains in Colorado and decided that I wanted to live here. To me it was such a magical, beautiful place. It took some planning, but I was able to move in with Ji-Min in 2003.

Ji-Min introduced me to many of her friends, and one of them had been Patrick. They had known one another for several years. Patrick was 72 years old at the time, but Ji-Min thought we had much in common and would get along famously. She set up a blind date for us and we met at a restaurant. Ji-Min came with me the first few times to help me communicate and to make me feel comfortable, but later I learned to manage on my own.

I knew some English from working at the military base and from listening to tapes. When my English got better, Patrick and I started to meet alone. We talked very slowly and we often had to repeat a few times what we said. Patrick was hard of hearing and I was very self-conscious of my English. It was uncomfortable for me to talk loudly so that he could hear me, but I tried it anyway.

We dated for a month before Patrick asked me to move in with him. I accepted. He told me he loved me and said he wanted to marry me. It was beyond a dream. He gave me a ring and we were married by a judge at the end of 2003. Although I had met many of Ji-Min's friends by then, she continued to be my only true friend and the only one who attended the wedding.

I didn't make many friends during the time I was married, but I tried to keep in contact with the few friends I had. Life wasn't exactly like I thought it would be. I didn't go mountain climbing like I had dreamt of—the winter in Colorado was too cold for that.

Our life together was simple. We cleaned the house together, we cooked separate meals but we ate together, we went shopping or to a restaurant... simple things. I didn't work, but I had money that I had brought with me from South Korea, and we kept separate accounts. We also kept separate rooms. We would have sex in his room, but he wouldn't let me stay. He would ask me to go back to my room afterwards in order to sleep.

At first I liked having sex with Patrick, but things changed quickly around springtime. He began to take Viagra once or twice a week so he could have sex. He couldn't have an erection otherwise. Intercourse was no longer pleasurable for me. He was very rough and would hurt me. He would chew on my nipples and bite my thighs and vagina to the point where I would bleed. I'd tell him "no" as loud as I could to make sure he would hear me, but he wouldn't stop. I'd try to push him away, but he held onto me so tight that I couldn't make him stop.

Sex would go on for several hours and afterwards I couldn't wear any underwear; even showering was very painful, my whole body hurt. Every time he wanted to have sex it was the same thing, and I'd grow so tense from the pain that I had headaches afterwards.

I tried talking to him. I told him that I hurt and that it felt like he was raping me, but he didn't care. Sometimes, he lay on the edge of the bed and spread my legs to where I thought he was going to rip them apart. He would then ask me to masturbate in front of him and I would say no, but he wouldn't stop pressuring me until I did his bidding. Viagra gave him erection for at least two hours, and he never wanted to stop. He said that because he was so old and I was so young, he wanted to keep going until the drug wore off.

I would try to stop him, throw pillows at him, but he was an animal during those times and not a person at all. I didn't know this wasn't normal in a marriage because I had never been married before. My parents never spoke about such things, or anyone else. I felt inside that it was wrong what Patrick was doing to me, but couldn't be sure. I only learned that the feelings were correct after I finally gathered the courage to talk to someone about it. I did this one day after Patrick admitted that he knew he was hurting me, but he liked the sex so much that he couldn't stop himself.

Patrick overdosed on Viagra one time and we had to take him to the hospital because he feared a heart attack. The doctor agreed and told him that he could potentially die if he didn't stop taking so much of the medicine so regularly. It was as if a dark cloud had rolled over Patrick that day and never left. I was the same to him as always, but after that day he began to treat me differently. He acted as if I was the one to blame for his predicament and became quite cold and distant with me. He'd even say he didn't need me anymore. It really upset me. It made me feel that he only wanted me around for sex, and not for the companionship a marriage also entails. He even told me to go meet someone else. I couldn't believe it. I felt insulted and worthless.

I moved out a week after Patrick came home from the hospital. I only took the clothes that I was wearing and a small bag with my underwear. I thought we just needed time away from each other, so I stayed with Ji-Min for a little while. I called him every day to check up on him and I even began to hint and ask when he could start taking Viagra again. I had made a commitment to him and I thought I had to stay married to him and make things work somehow.

I felt I had a duty with him as his wife and I worried about him, so I went back to see him, despite how he had treated me. He was indifferent to me. He wondered why I had come back. He told me that I didn't need to worry about him, and to go my way. I couldn't believe it. He was supposed to be my husband and we were supposed to be together. I tried to work things out and decided to stay with him, but he really didn't seem to care at all that I was there. I went back to Ji-Min's house after just two days, again, without taking anything with me.

A week or so later Patrick told me in a phone conversation that the doctor had finally cleared him to start taking Viagra again, but that he didn't want me back in any case. In fact, he said he had found another woman! I felt as if I had been stabbed in the heart. I went to his house and confronted him about it and he said that he was sorry, but that the woman had moved in with him already. Offended and humiliated, I asked for my things, but he said he had thrown them away. He divorced me not long after.

I've been receiving letters from the government ever since the divorce became final. I'm afraid the police are watching me and I have become so fearful that I get tension headaches that put me in bed for days. I'm a mess, I've lost my appetite, I'm terrified of noises. I think it's the police coming to take me away. My heart is heavy and life feels rough. I think I need to show evidence of the way Patrick treated me because no one believes me, but I never told anyone except for my one friend. My culture raises people to be private and discreet. We don't talk about husband issues—not even to a doctor. I know now that if this ever happened to me again, I would tell someone and find a way to keep myself safe, but I didn't know then. I thought it was a normal marriage and I had a duty to him.

I have no family here, which means I don't have anyone's support to help solve any of my problems, and I just have to figure things out on my own. I think I'm going crazy. I don't even feel like myself anymore. I feel as if I've become a different person, a stranger even to me.

I lost all desire to be around people after the divorce. I've been staying home all day listening to music and watching television, trying to soothe myself. After I moved out on my own I never heard from Ji-Min again, which makes me angry because I thought she was my close friend who would always be there for me. I don't know how to deal with what I've been through. I'm even afraid of having sex with other men. I fear they will treat me the way Patrick did.

Life without Patrick is better in some ways. I started working for a dry-cleaning business and I was able to rent my own apartment and make my life more stable. I feel pity on myself sometimes, but I shudder when I think of what my life would be like if I were still with Patrick. I guess it's better this way, even if I'm alone. My parents are ashamed of me though. I'm not welcome back to stay with them since I dishonored them and married Patrick against their wishes, never mind my divorce. I don't know if I would be more miserable alone here in the

U.S., or back in South Korea where I would be close to my family, yet rebuked by them. I couldn't bear to see my parents reject me or treat me like a stranger. I just can't see them if they'll treat me like that. It would just destroy me.

I still think that Colorado is a beautiful place and I believe staying here is my one shot at making a decent life for myself. I know I'm getting old, but I think I can start over one last time. All the bridges behind me have been burned; my family, my marriage, my one friend... I have nothing left, but maybe I don't have to give up yet. Maybe I can still hope for a good life.

Although Seo-Yeon's life while growing up was rather quiet and peaceful, and she speaks of this in a very positive manner, it would appear that her uneventful, isolated upbringing prevented her from acquiring the life experience necessary to recognize her husband for what he truly is: a predatory abuser. To this day, Seo-Yeon exudes naïveté and without a doubt, it is this very characteristic what made Patrick gravitate towards her. His violent sexual behavior was a window into his character and soul. I believe he knew from the very beginning he could dominate Seo-Yeon—and he did.

Although her marriage lasted less than a year, it had been Seo-Yeon's first serious relationship, and this caused a great deal of damage to her. To begin with, Seo-Yeon had no point of reference against which to compare her relationship with Patrick. She was completely inexperienced and naïve in her sexual development. Due to her upbringing, she could have tolerated his other "traditional," but equally abusive and neglectful ways of being with her, but his violent sexual nature went beyond the pale and forced her to take action.

Her distorted perceptions about the proper role of each partner in a marriage led her to endure a great deal of emotional as well as sexual abuse, thinking that this must simply be the way couples normally relate to one another in private. Secondly, and perhaps more concerning, Seo-Yeon now had a point of reference for all future relationships—and the bar was set as low as it could go. As I have seen in the past, people tend to follow patterns. While Seo-Yeon may not tolerate again the kind of abuse she suffered at the hands of Patrick, in her eyes, anything that would be only somewhat improved might seem significantly better. Even when, in fact, it may be just as neglectful and abusive in other ways.

Seo-Yeon evidenced most symptoms of clinical depression and the isolation in which she lived only served to exacerbate her condition. I tried to talk to her about it, but this is where the cultural gap wedged itself in. Seo-Yeon listened to my observations and advice attentively, and then with one polite nod she dismissed it all. She may have confided her very personal story to me, but she would not be making herself any more vulnerable by admitting to her weaknesses and vulnerabilities, or admitting that she needed help. Seo-Yeon's reserved and exceedingly private nature, in a large part inculcated in her by the cultural influences of her upbringing, had taught her to keep problems behind closed doors—to never speak to others of any shortcomings, personal issues, or other potentially "dishonorable" matters.

As it is the case for the majority of cruelty cases, Seo-Yeon was permitted to remain in the United States and become a legal resident. Although, I do believe that life would have been exponentially more difficult for her back in South Korea due to the conflict with her family, I have to say that I continue to worry about her and her reticence to seek out professional help. Seo-Yeon believes she can get over her past simply by putting time between her and "it." Yet sadly, the only thing this stubborn mindset has delivered to her so far is severe isolation and a worsening of her depression, yet she fails to understand this.

Seo-Yeon dreams of starting her life over "one last time," and I believe that having received legal residency represents the chance that she was hoping for. In turn, at the very least, I truly hope that at some point she can begin to reach out and associate with people. And perhaps, in time, she can come to understand the critical importance of availing herself to the support of counseling. Without a doubt, I feel that these are the keys for

Seo-Yeon to truly have a chance at starting a new life.

Mail Order Brides

DINA

Dina was a sight to behold, in an awkwardly charming way. She was not an unattractive woman, and was tall and lean. She had light blonde hair cascading down to her elbows, tied in a neat ponytail. She was also dressed in dirty, tattered clothes. Dina carried herself with dignity—the remnants of an identity as a worldly, educated person. Yet as if looking through a very dirty window, these attributes were made almost invisible by her prominent anxiety, fearful presentation, and her overall doleful demeanor.

Dina didn't say much. Actually, she hardly spoke at all of her own initiative. She sat quietly on her chair, nervously looking around the office through the corner of her eye. It took more work than I initially expected to get her to warm up enough to begin sharing her thoughts.

"I know I'm supposed to tell you all about my life, but I can't. It's just hard for me to trust people anymore," she told me. I noticed she leaned forward and visibly tensed herself while she told me this, almost as if putting herself into a fetal position. Something had made her quite apprehensive at the idea of sharing her inner world with others—I needed to find out what that was.

"It's not like we have to jump straight to the rough parts," I told her, "You look like a sharp woman. Do you enjoy reading?"

She nodded her head "Yes."

"Well, can we do this as if we're reading a book? Let's start at the beginning. Tell me the good things you remember about life when you were a little girl. Where are you from?"

Dina looked away for a moment and began to cry. She wrapped her arms around her legs and cradled herself. She cradled herself throughout the entire interview.

My name is Dina and I'm 27 years old. I was born and raised in Minsk, Belarus. My father worked as a civil engineer and my mother was a music teacher. My family was far from conventional, and my brothers and I were lucky in that regard. Rather than following the conservative and strict family dynamics of our culture, my parents were always quite warm, encouraging, and open with us.

I have little to report about my years growing up. I did well in school, had friends, and played sports. My parents were good to one another, and even though I'd see them argue from time to time, it was never anything that scared me. After school I continued on to college and I graduated with a business degree. Life was good, but it felt incomplete. I had friends, I went to parties and outings with friends, and I had a good relationship with my parents and brothers—yet I felt lonely.

I realized I craved companionship. I needed the love and attention only someone else could provide for me, and I craved to lavish someone with the same. I began to wonder if there was something wrong with me; I mean, why hadn't I met someone special? I was old enough. For a while I sat there examining every bit of myself, looking for the missing piece, the broken piece; I looked at my friends and then back at myself, trying to figure out what made me so different—but in a bad way.

And then I realized what I was. I didn't think like them. I was missing the conservative, conforming, stern chip in my brain they all seemed to have. I was relieved and suddenly miserable at the same time. I didn't mind not being like them, but I realized it meant I probably wouldn't find someone with whom I could share my life. I began to feel even lonelier all of the sudden.

I had been playing with the idea of signing up with a marriage agency for a while. I daydreamed of how I would meet a charming, smart guy who would sweep me off my feet and go discover the world with me. It made me smile to think of it, but I chalked it up to fantasy. It took me six months before I convinced myself to give it a go; the more I tried to meet a suitable man in my own culture, the more I realized that such a man did not exist.

I became a member of this marriage agency for two years before anything happened. I met plenty of men online, particularly from America, but I didn't feel any of them cared about me as a person and I was in no hurry to attach myself to anyone unless he was a good man. After all, I had a decent job and I was starting a small business of my own. I made enough money to take care of myself and my parents. I wasn't looking for a way out; I was looking for a good partner.

Eventually, I met Mark. We emailed back and forth for a while, along with the rest of the other men that I met on their website. Mark was different, though—I felt a connection with him. He cared to get to know me, to hear what I thought about things. We both had a lot in common; we liked music, we wanted to travel to the same places, we had a thirst for adventure... I began to get excited whenever he called or emailed me. I began to have hope that the man of my dreams existed after all.

After a few months getting to know one another, Mark came to visit me in Minsk. He stayed for about six weeks—the most magical six weeks of my life. We spent every day together and went to museums, art shows, movies, dinners... even the circus! I loved every second of those six weeks. Mark did too; I could see we were falling in love with one another. He began to tell me about the kind of life we could have together in the United States and all the adventures we could go on. I loved it; it was exactly what I wanted—someone to go on this huge adventure of life.

Mark and I remained in constant communication after he returned to the United States. We emailed, used video chat, and spoke on the phone every minute we had a chance. It felt so real. I began to worry about my feelings for Mark; I didn't want them to grow any more if we were going to remain apart like this. As if on cue, Mark invited me to come live in the United States with him. He promised me heaven and earth if I accepted to be his wife. We talked about children and opening a bakery—it was like a fairytale, only I felt I could trust him. It felt real. I said yes.

As soon as I arrived to his house in Boulder, Colorado, I noticed things were very different. He was very different. He hadn't seen me in five months, yet he seemed to care very little about welcoming me into his home, or trying to make me feel comfortable. It was supposed to be my home too, but I couldn't take out a glass or a plate without him looking as if I was intruding in his life. And I felt as exactly like that; an intruder.

Mark's house was full of posters of naked women and Star Wars action figures. It was also very dirty. I didn't know what to do; it made me uncomfortable to see naked women everywhere and I even asked him if he could take them down since I was here with him now, but he paid little regard to that. I tried to clean the house to at least make myself comfortable that way, but he would stop me within minutes, telling me that everything was fine as it was. It wasn't fine. Nothing was even close to being okay.

Three or four days after my arrival, Mark gave me a bunch of written instructions on how the house was to be cleaned and the laundry done. He also wrote down the foods he liked to eat and the time he normally had dinner. I had become his maid. I felt he had made me come all this way just to be his maid. I grabbed his stack of papers and asked him if he planned on helping me with the household chores. I told him that the situation made me feel like I was nothing more than a servant. He told me that he worked hard at his job and simply couldn't help me; that it was my job.

Mark cared very little to make sure I was okay. One time I asked him for winter shoes as mine had been ruined by the snow, and he told he would have to think about it. Two days later he came to tell me that his mother would take me to find some shoes, but she just dropped me off at the mall and left me by myself. She said she had no time to help me. I didn't know what to do; I barely spoke any English and didn't even have money to try and find my way around the mall. Mark's mother never came back either. I had to call Mark over and over until he picked up his phone, and then I had to wait for him to get off work.

Things only got worse between us and by this time we were already married. He began to yell and insult me, calling me names I didn't even understand at the time. Whenever I couldn't get my point across he'd call me a stupid Russian woman and continue to yell. I'm not even from Russia.

Mark had a tendency to control me every way he could. When he finally agreed to give me a bank card he intentionally kept the balance near zero so I couldn't buy anything without asking him to transfer money. He would then go inspect the things I wanted to buy and tell me that I spent too much money on myself and I that couldn't buy new things. I only wanted to buy socks, underwear, or clothes to wear. He only allowed me to shop at the used clothing store, and then only rarely. Even then, he would only give me $10 or $20 to buy whatever I needed.

I also found hidden cameras in the house and when I confronted Mark about it he would get angry and tell me that it was for our protection in case someone broke in the house, and that I could leave if I didn't like it. He was lying. The cameras were only in the living room, where he confined me and made me sleep whenever he was mad at me.

He forbade that I used the internet, even to email my family. After a while, he finally agreed to let me to get online, but under his supervision. He would literally sit by me while I used the computer. While

I wrote, he examined my purse and questioned me about any notes or business cards—anything he could find that gave him a reason to suspect me of wrongdoing. I felt as if I was in jail. I could never do anything I wanted, and I was always suspected of doing something bad. It crushed my spirit.

Mark kept me locked in the house during the day while I was studying English. He forbade me to go anywhere and told me that he would know if I lied to him. I sat home like a prisoner, reading, cleaning and cooking for him. Whenever he would come home from work though, he would become angry with the way I had done things at home and accuse me of "just sitting there being lazy," and eating his food. I was terribly lonely before, but at least I wasn't isolated like this.

Whenever he was angry he would throw things around the house, which made me very nervous. He began to tell me that I should go back to Belarus, and many times told me to get out of his house. It felt so unfair, as it was supposed to be our house together. He began to grab me by the arms and shake me whenever he was angry, and one time he threw me against the kitchen pantry. I must have looked quite scared, because he warned me not to call the police, or else he would have to call the INS and have me sent away. Whenever he would say such things it would scare me to death.

One time Mark got angry at me because I wanted to talk to him about our problems. I just wanted to try to understand him better so he wouldn't get mad at me all the time, but he didn't even want to talk about it. He began to yell and pushed me backwards; my ankle rolled sideways and I fell down the stairs. I reached out for anything that would help me stop the fall and brought down a bunch of picture frames with me. All the glass shattered over me and cut me everywhere. Mark began to clean up without saying a word, without asking me if I was okay. He then calmed down and asked me not to call the police and told me that it would be very expensive if I did. I hadn't even thought of calling the police; we don't do that in my country. He seemed really worried that I would however, or that I would tell someone and then they would call the police. He demanded that I not tell anyone about the incident and labeled it an accident. He then threatened to call INS again if I didn't do as I was told.

Life was not what I expected it would be, to say the least. I felt myself getting more and more depressed and I felt powerless about my situation. The only saving grace was in finding a job at a nearby grocery store. It wasn't the "career" kind of job I had done back home, but it was better than nothing, and it gave me a way to provide things for myself that I needed. It felt like a little ray of sunshine.

Mark and I were on our way out one day when I asked him if we could stop by the bank so I could open a bank account with my paycheck. He was livid. He grabbed my hand and twisted my arm yelling at me, questioning why I wanted my own account separate from his. He was too strong. I screamed in pain as my knees buckled. He let go and looked at me worried—then ran to the phone. "You won't be the one to call the cops," is what I heard him say as he rushed to the kitchen. He called the police himself, and when they came they asked Mark to leave the house for the night.

I was scared. I didn't know what was going on or why he had to leave. I hadn't asked for him to leave. Mark took off and took all my documents with him. Two days later I got a letter from him saying he had withdrawn my visa petition and was filing for divorce, without my permission. He also said that he would only give me my documents back if I agreed to leave the country, and if so, that I should sign his letter and leave it in the mailbox. He said he would buy the plane ticket and make arrangements for someone other than him to take me to the airport. Clearly he didn't want to see me again.

Then one day soon after, Mark's attorney came and asked me to leave the house in exchange for getting my documents back. The police had already told me to not stay in the house; they said it wasn't safe for me to live there anymore, but I didn't believe them. I didn't know what was happening, or why any of this was happening. Mark came back the next evening and told me to leave his house. I didn't know where to go. I stayed with friends for a couple of nights and then at a hotel before I ended up at a battered women's shelter. Mark cancelled the credit cards and had my phone turned off.

During that entire time I tried not to think about it; I thought I had to try harder and just learn to adjust to life here. Only now after speaking to the women in the shelter do I realize I had suffered terrible abuse. I'm going to need lots of time to recover after all of this to be the person I used to be. I used to feel strong and capable, and now I feel like I'm nobody. I don't know what is happening to me. This time I don't even know how my life is going to turn out or if I can ever trust anyone again. I can't deal with this; I can't even speak of it. Most of the time I pretend like it never happened—like it was a bad dream that I've now shaken off. Only it wasn't a dream and I haven't been able to shake it off.

. . .

Dina's story is an example of the twisted dynamics inherent in these abusive relationships that I've become accustomed to seeing. Honestly, it baffles me how everything degenerated so quickly for her after her arrival. Dina is an educated woman who had a good job and even a business of her own back in Belarus. She was in no hurry to flee her circumstances—she was simply lonely.

This is exactly what Mark saw in her. I don't think he is a psychopath or a predator, but certainly meets the profile of a spousal abuse perpetrator. He has deep insecurities and strong tendencies toward power and control. An abuser can only abuse if his victim is vulnerable and open to receiving such treatment. And this appeared to be the case with Dina. She is not a weak woman, but she had fallen in love for the first time in her life, and abusers like Mark are adept at putting their best foot forward. She had no previous relationships with which to compare Mark, no particular standard to go by. In fact, the only example she had known of what a healthy relationship looked like was her parent's relationship. She never saw them argue or learned from them how to handle situations like the one she found herself in. She simply saw how her parents loved and cared for one another, and while that is a wonderful thing to witness, her education was... incomplete.

I believe that getting Dina outside of her comfort zone was a key element for the events that followed. Had this relationship occurred in Minsk where Dina had the support of her family and her own financial independence, not to mention her intact notion of self-worth, things might have been different. It would have been unlikely that the relationship continued past Mark's initial mistreatment of her and his attempts to control her. Yet, her personality structure was such that if certain factors were in place, she was vulnerable to tolerating the cruel and abusive treatment that she endured with Mark.

While Dina later made some friends in the United States, she didn't share with them the truth of what was going on and was virtually alone and unprotected. Not only that, but she was emotionally and financially dependent on her abuser. She was so shell-shocked that she didn't consider going home to her family; plus, that would have been humiliating for her. She had nowhere to turn to because Mark was supposed to be the one she could rely on. Instead, he turned out to be a source of deep trauma for Dina.

Dina was still in such shock about what this relationship turned out to be that she simply couldn't wrap her brain around it. I could see that on some level she knew she needed to reach out for help beyond the group therapy available at the battered women's shelter, but she was simply not ready for it. That worried me. I don't know if one is ever ready to explore the dark parts of our lives; perhaps one can only be willing to do such work at certain points in their lives. I knew Dina would never get through her ordeal unless she was willing to deal with these critical issues. The intensity of the horrors of her life with Mark might subside with time, but she would have difficulty with normal relationships in the future because of the natural resistance in trusting others... and she would always wonder why, unaware of the proverbial monster hiding under her bed.

Dina was allowed to remain in the country and become a legal resident of the United States. I don't know if she will choose to stay here though. She told me her belief that she doesn't feel she fits in either in Belarus or in the US. "Back home I have family and friends, but there's really no place there where my thoughts and beliefs fit in. Here in the States I'm allowed to be myself, but I don't really have anyone or anything other than bad memories."

I tried to explain to Dina that a bad start didn't mean things would always be negative for her here. I tried to impress upon her the importance of seeking out the help of a therapist so that she could begin to truly heal and continue her journey, wherever she might choose to do so, and to head in a more positive direction.

ILIE

Ilie walked into my office visibly unsure of what to expect. She meekly looked about and I noticed how she fearfully took a seat, careful not to disturb anything around her. Her thin frame was covered in a sweater and a light jacket—not nearly enough layers for this frigid day in the middle of January.

I smiled at her, "Aren't you cold?" I asked.

Ilie gave me a shy half-smile, and went onto tell me that those were the warmest clothes she had. "We left in a hurry," she said. "We didn't have any money and in the months my daughter and I lived with my husband I didn't want to ask him to take us shopping." I looked at my notepad for a moment. I knew where this was heading.

"Why didn't you want to ask your husband?" I asked.

Ilie's eyes suddenly became glazed, covered by a sheet of tears about to fall and roll down her cheeks. Her lips began to tremble as she looked away and unsuccessfully attempted to contain herself. Her legs began to shift ever so slowly, as if they were bearing a great burden.

"He wouldn't have liked it and I tried to keep Anastasia and me from bothering him. He... he gets angry quickly," she said.

"You fear him," I said, to which she began to cry.

"Do you have reason to fear him?" I prodded. This was going to be one of those days that made me wish I had become a boxer or some other, more benign profession.

At that, Ilie mentally checked-out for a few seconds, which was quite evident to me. Her eyes opened wide, tears still rolling down her cheeks, and her hand suspended in mid-air. Her lips were parted slightly as if she were about to say something, but instead the thought became trapped in her memories. What I would give to be inside people's minds for a moment at a time like this...

Ilie remained silent for a time before touching her cheek with her hand. Her eyes seemed to labor, and then produced wave after wave of tears. She then looked at me. She was suddenly back in the moment with me. She simply nodded my way, and it was enough for us to begin.

My name is Ilie and I'm 32 years old. My parents are Romanian, but I was born and raised in a small town in Russia. The Russian way of life is harsh, conservative, and very strict. I didn't deal with it very well; my parents were quite stern with me, and my siblings and I complied with their every expectation out of fear of punishment. I became a little rebellious as I grew into my teenage years and by the time I turned 19 I decided to move out of my parent's home. They hated it, but I couldn't be there any longer. I enrolled in college and rented an apartment with two friends who were students like me.

I met my first husband, Javok, while I went to school. We fell in love quickly and although we were busy with a strict school regimen, we managed to make time for one another and to make things work. We got married within a year and found a small apartment of our own. My parents were happy; I was going to school and even found a husband—I didn't turn out to be that much of a screw-up after all.

We were happy for months before our problems began. Like many Russian men, Javok liked to drink heavily and party with his friends. He would go out just about every night of the week and would come home late, drunk and reeking of cigarettes. He would plop on the bed next to me and pass out like there was nothing wrong. I tried talking to him about it but he would usually just get angry and yell at me. He thought I was trying to control him, but I just wanted us to spend some time together like we used to.

I hung onto our relationship thinking that we could get through this—we had been through so much more than this in the past. About a year later when I was 25 years old I became pregnant, and right around that time is when everything took a turn for the worst.

I gained weight and had some complications with my pregnancy. I became sensitive to foods and smells and the wrong combinations of things could easily send me vomiting. Cigarettes were one of those things. It made me so ill that I seldom wanted to leave the house since just about everyone smoked in the streets. My biggest problem however, was that Javok never quit smoking, going out, or coming home drunk. Here I was completely ill roughly 80% of the time, and he was hardly anywhere to be seen.

I got tired of feeling abandoned and alone and I began to feel angry instead. I tried to talk to Javok and in my frustration I even yelled at him a few times—but it didn't work. He yelled back and even slapped me in the face once. I felt lost, hopeless, and powerless to change my situation, so I allowed my anger to finally take over. Javok left me about three months before I was due to give birth to our daughter. I never saw him again.

Being a single mother in Russia is not a job for the faint of heart, and in my small town it's not something that is looked upon approvingly. I more or less fell into the same status as a prostitute, and I struggled to find work. I was forced to move back in with my parents who helped me somewhat reluctantly and took almost every chance they had to point out to me my failure as a wife.

A few years went by and I began to grow desperate. I managed to hang onto my job, but it barely paid anything to support me and my daughter Anastasia. I was lucky that I had a roof over my head living with my parents, but they made life for us very difficult. They often told Anastasia how "her daddy was a mean drunk," and then blamed me for the way things turned out. "A good wife knows how to hang on to her husband and turn around his vices," they would tell me. I was just too different for them to understand. I was spoiled fruit.

I held hope that someday I would meet a man that would love me and treat Anastasia and me right, but most men usually fled as soon as they learned I had a daughter. The ones who didn't care about that also didn't really care about children at all, and that sent chills down my spine. I didn't want to get involved with a variation of Javok.

I decided to join an international marriage agency. I had come to believe that Russian men would not understand my situation or accept my daughter. Perhaps my journey toward happiness involved meeting a man outside of my own culture.

I became friends with an American by the name of Frank about a month after joining the agency. He was warm, caring, and friendly, and he wrote to me regularly. We exchanged pictures and he even sent me a few small presents. My heart was zooming across cloud nine. Could I have possibly met such a caring and responsible man who was apparently so very interested in me?

Frank came to visit me in Russia after two months of getting to know one another through email. He stayed in my town for about three weeks and we spent every minute of it together. Anastasia loved him and he connected with her right away. I felt so hopeful; it felt so refreshing to feel hope again after my marriage to Javok and the grim years after that. I thought that maybe life had decided to reward me after so many years of struggle.

Frank flew back to my town again almost three months after his first visit and asked me to marry him. I was elated. I felt like a princess being rescued by a knight in shining armor... once and for all.

Paperwork needed to be completed and arrangements made. Frank asked me to move to the United States to be with him and I accepted. I was fearful of taking on such a big move with merely a tourist visa, so he worked with the agency where we met in trying to find the best way for me and Anastasia. He also bought a house and made school arrangements for Anastasia. He found a list of places that offered ESL classes for both of us. "I want you and Anastasia to be comfortable and have a good life here," he would tell me. I couldn't believe my good luck.

Anastasia and I were finally able to move to Frank's house in the United States after several months of waiting for all the legalities to take place. He introduced us to his family and friends and I'll admit they seemed a little suspicious of me at first. They looked at me as if they were worried, even scared. I would later find out they were afraid for me and my daughter. At the time however, Frank simply explained that they were adjusting to the idea of how we met.

It didn't take long for Frank's true colors to come out, maybe three months total. It was as if all of the sudden his patience with Anastasia and I had run out and he would become easily exasperated with us for any small matter. He often accused me of being "bad," and would shut down and completely stop talking to me. He would suddenly turn totally cold, and I couldn't understand why. I didn't think I was doing anything wrong or disrespectful, so I began to pay closer attention to him and his moods. I learned that he simply didn't want me to disagree, question, or inconvenience him in any way. I cared about Frank and didn't like when he punished me with being cold and distant. I didn't want any disharmony between us, so I decided to acquiesce to his temper in order to have a peaceful life.

Yet there was just no pleasing Frank. Once I stopped disagreeing with him and asking him questions, he would begin to turn his attention to me and to all of my imperfections. He didn't like the way I cleaned and he often snapped at me for not learning to cook American food fast enough. He started calling me "stupid" for not making mac-and-cheese to his liking, and soon after that he began snapping and throwing his plate or his drinks to the floor.

I grew afraid of Frank's volatility, so I tried to keep me and Anastasia out of his way. I rarely asked him any questions, and if I needed anything for me or my daughter I would find a way to get it myself—but that didn't make him happy either. He began to follow me whenever I went out of the house to see where I would go and what I would do. The first time it happened I thought to myself that he had decided to come along too, but he never walked up to me. He simply parked far away from me and kept his distance, his eyes always on me.

Once Anastasia began school, I found a part-time job while she attended kindergarten. I felt some relief in being productive and contributing to our living expenses, and also in not being in the house all the time. But my fear of Frank kept growing and growing as the days went by. He worked during the day, and I was afraid of being in the house by myself. I was afraid to break something or even move something that might make him angry. I had a disturbing feeling in the back of my head that I was growing to fear Frank just as much or more than I did my parents when I was a kid.

I thought Frank would be proud of me for finding work, but he never said anything about it. I wanted to help pay for our living expenses, but he would just take my paychecks as if I owed him. At first he only did this here and there, but one day he told me he didn't trust me with money and then began to take every one of my paychecks. He told me that if I needed anything, I would have to ask him for it.

Frank became progressively more exasperated with Anastasia and me. It would take as little as asking to change the channel to set him off, and when he did, he'd begin to yell and threaten me. He never cared that Anastasia was in the room with us. I remember the first time he yelled at me; I had worked up the courage to ask him for some money to buy more comfortable shoes and he snapped. He told me that if I continued to inconvenience him he would make my life miserable, and then kick us out of his house and the country.

He left the room angry and slammed the door behind him. Anastasia was staring at me and I had to keep my eyes open wide to try and prevent tears from falling. Frank was not the man he had initially portrayed himself to be.

I still had some hope that the man I had been emailing with for months was still in there somewhere, and I continued to try to make things work. Anastasia and I kept completely out of his way and I tried to keep the house exactly the way he wanted it. I even followed directions "to a T" when cooking so that it would taste like the American food he loved so much. I thought if Anastasia and I could keep this up for a while, Frank would eventually calm down and be more open to having a good relationship with us. Sadly, that wasn't the case.

Yelling turned into insults, which eventually turned into physical violence. Whenever Frank was angry he would grab me by the throat and shake me, then throw me to the side. I often slipped or tripped and I had bruises all over my body, but he showed little compassion. In fact, he would shrug it off afterwards and tell me that the bruises would eventually go away.

It happened numerous times. His temper escalated quickly and before I knew it, he had me by the arm, the hair, or the neck, and was yelling at me for something "bad" that I did. He then began to "discipline" Anastasia without my permission and would spank her whenever she did something that he didn't agree with. I remember begging him to stop beating her and even put my hands and arms between them as he spanked her, but he wouldn't stop. He said he would teach us a lesson. Clearly he was determined to punish us. But it was a losing battle, because no matter what we did or didn't do, we could never please him and thereby avoid his brutal beatings.

The last straw in our relationship happened one day when we were returning from a fast-food restaurant. We had gone through the drive-thru and I was reviewing the order as he drove away when I realized they had put hot chilies in Anastasia's food when we had asked them not to because she was allergic to them. I told Frank about this and asked him if we could turn around and fix it so Anastasia could have something to eat and he became enraged. He began to scream about my audacity and that I only demanded things from him. He yelled other insults at me, and then grabbed me by the hair and pulled me towards him. Anastasia tried to stop him, but he pushed her back into her seat and she hit her head against the back passenger window.

Frank continued to yell at me and hurl insults while he had me by the hair. He then grabbed the food and began to shove it in my mouth and smear it all over my face. I started to cry when he decided to let me go. He then pushed me hard over to my side of the car. He didn't say another word until we got home. Once we were inside he told me that he would kill me next time I was "bad" and tried to be a nuisance to him. He then took the telephone receiver off of the phone and took it with him so that I wouldn't contact anyone.

I missed work the next day, but I didn't tell Frank—he had left for work earlier than normal anyway. I grabbed Anastasia and we went over to my neighbor's house, a woman who had become a friend. I told her about everything. She called the police to report the incident and Frank was arrested and taken to jail for assault. I didn't know how long he was going to be gone and I didn't know what was going to happen next. I began regretting having told my neighbor about what had happened because I feared what Frank would do to us upon his return. I was afraid that this time he would beat us even harder and send us back to Russia. I felt like I needed to run away, but I didn't know where to go. I had made some friends at work, but I was still so new there and I really didn't know anyone all that well.

After the incident, we went back and forth between my neighbor's house, women's shelters, and other friend's homes. Frank was released from jail and he was livid with me. I was deathly afraid of what he would do if he got a hold of me. I was so afraid of what he'd do anyway in order to punish us for calling the police on him. I was so very afraid that he'd send us back to Russia.

I tried to talk to my parents about this, but they told me they were no longer in a financial position to help support me or my daughter upon our return to Russia. They also didn't care to understand everything that had happened here over the past year, and were simply looking at it as another failed marriage by their failure daughter. In fact, my mom told me my only accomplishment in this situation had been not getting pregnant again. "Women can't go on having bastard children over and over," is what she actually said.

My two siblings have left Russia. They struggle to make a living in nearby countries and I cannot rely on them for help if I had to return. I would be virtually alone there and I wouldn't know how to make things work. At least here I have some friends who are willing to give me support and point me in the right direction. In Russia, even if my parents agreed to let us stay with them, life would be similar to the last year with Frank. Not that my parents would hit us, but they would certainly yell and insult me all the same. The only reason why they spared Anastasia while we lived there is because she was only five years old at the time.

I don't know what I would do if I were forced to return to Russia. I gave up everything in order to be with Frank. I put all of my peas in that pot, all of my hopes and dreams. There is no going back. I have no place to live or a job to help me provide for my daughter. I have no one there that cares about me or is willing to give me a hand. Even though it's my native country, I have absolutely no idea how I would be able to survive there. In fact, I feel more at home here in the US, despite my fear of Frank. At least here people care about me and I have access to shelters and help should I need it. In Russia there is no one and nothing awaiting Anastasia and me. What kind of future could I give my daughter there with grandparents that consider her a bastard-child and consider us to be worthless and a burden on them? I don't know how I will make it here. I just know that we have a better chance in the United States than in Russia. Surely we could find some way to survive over there, but that wouldn't be living. We'd be no different than filth in the alleyways, and our lives just as dark.

. . .

As I often find with other cruelty victims, Ilie's background "primed" her for what would later unfold in her life. The way in which she was forced during childhood and beyond to obey and acquiesce to her parent's demands set the stage. Her over-familiarity with neglectful relationships and fear of punishment was a pattern laid out for Ilie to accept and follow. She never consciously entered into these toxic relationships, yet once she discovered herself embroiled in their abusive dynamics, it felt normal to her and she remained enmeshed and trapped. Her parents' behaviors and actions inoculated her to enduring cruelty and abuse, and her subsequent partners endorsed and validated these early experiences. Living in this way blinded any instincts she may have had to protect herself and her daughter and to flee right away. After all, she lived with her parents for many years and survived. In that she had little else going for her and no apparent via of escape to a better place, why not stick around and hope to resolve the conflict?

For many people from a similar background, their minds tell them that there is no conflict; it is simply the way it is. Both of Ilie's husbands were abusive, with overt anger issues. Anger can at times become a positive force and can drive one to preserve oneself. It can serve to motivate one to remove obstacles in the way, or protect one on life's journey. However, the way in which anger is expressed and handled can turn events from a potential into a living nightmare.

Ilie's fear having turned to anger propelled her into doing the right thing and calling the police, notwithstanding her later reservations, which is common in such cases. I commend Ilie for summoning the courage to go speak with her neighbor and ask for help. Countless people in similar circumstances suffer in silence for the entirety of their lives, particularly those who find themselves alone in a strange country and are dependent on their abusive spouses.

I believe that Ilie had been damaged by the circumstances inherent in her upbringing as well as her first marriage. I am certain however, that her traumatic background and subsequent conditioning almost entirely escaped her awareness until Frank assaulted her in the car that day. Her abusive and neglectful relationship with him severely exacerbated her existing symptoms and sent her reeling. The only way now was out.

I was right in that her story would leave me wanting to box his ears off. Part of me truly wanted to give Frank a left-cross down a flight of stairs. I'm only human after all, and I absolutely abhor bullying and abuse of any kind. I oftentimes feel like leaving this office to go round up half of the men on the planet and put them in a re-education camp of some type. It sickened me to hear of how an already traumatized human being fell into another exceedingly humiliating and abusive relationship, in a foreign country no less where she was virtually alone.

Ilie admitted that she currently attends counseling sessions through the women's shelter in which she stayed so often in the waning days of her marriage to Frank. I find her efforts to endure commendable. In her own words; "We just can't go back to Russia, we won't survive there. We have to stay here and I have to be strong for Anastasia and me to find a way to have a good life. For that, I need to make myself stronger and patch up the cuts and bruises in my soul." She couldn't have been more correct, and her words softened my heart that has been hardened by hundreds of such stories.

After two continuances with her legal case, the judge finally allowed Ilie to remain in the United States and become a permanent legal resident. She will now start the legal proceedings for Anastasia to be able to remain in the country as well. Hopefully that process won't be as grueling and difficult as it was for Ilie.

Ilie appeared convinced of her need for counseling, and I felt confident that she will follow through with long-term psychotherapy. I also spoke to her about a seeking out a medication evaluation for her depression and post-traumatic stress symptoms. She explained to me that she was quite strained financially and could barely support herself and her daughter on her minimum-wage, part-time job. Yet she appeared open and interested in the option of counseling and medication later on down the line when she is able to pay for it. "Once we get out of the shelter and I can afford our rent and food, I will definitely consider finding a doctor for all of that," she said. Somehow I have no doubt that she will accomplish all of these things.

LANA

The Lana I saw walk into my office looked like the shell of what was at one time an optimistic and hopeful girl. I wondered if she had ever gotten to experience that brightness and wonder, or if the struggles that brought her to me had snuffed out all that potential before it even got a chance to blossom. I knew I would find out quickly.

Lana walked timidly, yet desperately. She clung to the small child in her arms, almost as if wrapping him with her body as sort of a protective armor. Looking at them together, I knew there was no one safer in the office than this little boy. Even when simply walking with him, she protected him fiercely.

Lana was shy, and unwilling to speak of her past. She simply did not want to remember—"it hurt too much," she told me at one point. It took two full cups of tea before I was able to ease the conversation into her life with her ex-husband. Until then, I learned quite a lot about her. She was born and raised in a conventional home in Russia, where she led a rather insipid life until she decided to join a marriage agency and met an American, Ronald.

"I don't want to cry in front of my child," she told me as she shut her eyes tightly.

I asked my assistant to lead little Marlon to the play room to watch a movie and instructed her to keep the young boy company. Lana shot up in the chair and reached for her son the minute my assistant lifted him from her lap.

"We'll just be in the next room, don't worry," my assistant told her as she smiled. Lana apologized. "I'm sorry, it's just habit. I don't like people taking him from me," she said. To this statement I frowned and wondered who had tried to take Marlon from Lana in the past, and by what means? They had certainly left their mark on this woman.

As Marlon and my assistant disappeared out the door, I turned to face Lana and tears immediately began to roll down her cheeks. She covered her face with her hands, and then ran them through her hair. She closed her hands into a fist as she reached the base of her skull. There had been a lot of damage done here.

"Lana, the sooner you tell me about him, the sooner I can start helping you," I told her.

And so it began.

The change was almost immediate. I noticed things were different between Ronald and I just days after I arrived to the United States. I thought it was me, or that perhaps we were both shocked—I had moved all the way here from Russia after all. I was his new wife, forever—that seemed like a big deal and a reasonable reason to be in shock. I held onto hope. Things would get better.

Russian and American cultures are very different, all the way down to how we clean and what we eat. I tried my best to adjust; I thought I could mix the best of both cultures and improve our lives in a million ways, but Ronald was not impressed. In fact, the more I tried, the more distant he became, and the more he complained about my failures as a housewife. It broke my heart, but I never cried in front of him. I would smile and try harder—he had shown me he was a good man and I wanted to make this work.

Ronald and his family weren't very welcoming to me. On top of that, he didn't allow me to socialize very much with others, which made it impossible for me to make any friends. I felt completely alone in the world, and in my forced solitude I think I began to feel very depressed. I stopped eating and sleeping altogether; I remember trying to talk to Ronald about it, but he would get angry at me and yell at me to get used to it, or go back to Moscow. If he ever found me crying he would grab me by the elbow and shake me as he yelled. It was always the same thing; "If you don't like it here with me you can crawl back to the hole you came from, whore."

Where was the man I had come to know and love?

Not only did he keep any knowledge of bills and finances from me, but after a while he also stopped providing for me. He didn't want me to work, but wanted me to buy my own food, pay for my half of the utilities, and anything I might need. He wanted to eat dinner together every night "like a real couple," but it couldn't have been further from a real relationship. He would have me cook steak and mashed potatoes for him and then force me to sit next to him as he feasted on his dinner and I ate a cup of ramen noodles.

I began to lose hope that things were going to change, but I didn't know what to do. To make matters worse, I became pregnant about two months into my life with Ronald. He wouldn't let me take birth control pills and hated to use any type of protection himself. I tried talking to him about it, but as usual, he would become enraged and yell. He'd tell me that a real couple had no fear of becoming pregnant and that if I was concerned about it, then I was nothing but a Green Card-seeking whore. It was a lose-lose game with him, every time.

Although he spoke so highly about couples and pregnancies, once I became pregnant Ronald couldn't have given me any less support. He even told me I would have to find a job so I could pay for the doctor's visits. I couldn't believe it.

I began to fear that this was truly the way reality was going to be from now on and in my desperation to save myself, I went out as far as I could walk and applied to every place of business I found. About a week later I began to work as a waitress at a pizza restaurant and bar. I thought Ronald would be outraged, but he couldn't care any less. In fact, even though I was pregnant and worked on my feet all day, he never cared to make any accommodations for me at home. He still expected me to have the house clean and his dinner ready by the time he got home from work—whether I was there or not.

Summer came and my pregnancy was well underway. It was impossibly hot, but Ronald wouldn't let me use the air conditioning at home. He wouldn't even agree to give me a ride to work and sent me out there to walk the nine blocks with my ever growing belly, in all that heat from hell. I asked if he could at least help me by loaning me $50 so I could complete the amount I was saving to buy a bicycle, but he called me a "spoiled Russian princess" and warned me to never ask him for money again.

I'll never forget; It was a Saturday, I was seven months pregnant, and it was 90 degrees. I found a shaded spot in the backyard and sat there in the hopes to cool myself down with the slight breeze blowing around. I couldn't help it; I felt so uncomfortable and so heartbroken about what my life had been these past few months that I began to weep. Ronald found me and to my amazement, instead of yelling at me, he promised we would go to the mountains the next day so I could relax and cool myself down. Then he hugged me. I couldn't believe it. I must have looked truly pitiful.

I woke up feeling happy and excited the next day, but Ronald never spoke a word. He went on about his business, puttering around the house for most of the morning. I gave him space thinking he may want to get a few things done before our trip to the mountains, but he never spoke a word. In retrospect, he hadn't even said good morning to me.

I went into the backyard to find him and asked him if we were going to go to the mountains like he had told me. He threw a handful of weeds he had pulled against the wall and yelled at me to leave him alone. "Just go where you want," he told me. The glimpse I had caught from the old Ronald was gone. There was no hope.

I left the house and began to walk. I didn't know where I was going, but I aimed myself towards the mountains—at least I had a direction. A woman pulled by the side of the road and asked me if I needed a ride anywhere; I began to cry instantly and she took me to her home where we spoke for a long time. It was the first time I felt someone cared about me in a long, long time. I didn't want to go back home, but eventually I did. Ronald grabbed me by the elbow and questioned me as to where I had been, and pulled me in the house. Back to reality again, I thought.

Our son was born two months after that incident and luckily, everything went according to schedule. Marlon was a healthy baby boy and I came to feel truly thankful of that fact as time went by, because Ronald would not lift a finger to help with our baby. He wouldn't even buy him diapers or food. The only thing Ronald did was take pictures of me looking tired or disheveled and make fun of me, telling me, "Welcome to motherhood."

Ronald's behavior became even more unpredictable and volatile as weeks went by. I thought our baby would help soothe whatever was bothering him, but it was actually the exact opposite. He didn't know how to treat Marlon and would roughly snatch him from the bed, holding him as if he was made of rubber. I'd become scared and try to take him from Ronald, but he would become livid and begin to yell and push me. Eventually he would just drop Marlon back in the bed and storm out of the house. The next day, he would act as if nothing had happened. He did that all the time.

I began to wonder if Marlon and I should go back to Russia, but I knew there was no future for us there. The violence and corruption at that time was a far worse enemy than Ronald and his volley of insults and mistreatments.

I had made a friend through work by this time, and she secretly took me to a clinic to speak to a psychiatrist. I learned then about abuse and depression and I was told to come back when I was no longer breastfeeding so they could prescribe me with an antidepressant. I told them I had to stop breastfeeding after a month because I simply stopped producing milk. I began to cry because I thought it was my fault and I was just a bad mother, but they explained to me that stress will sometimes cause this to happen. Since I was no longer breastfeeding, they prescribed me with Zoloft.

I never told Ronald, but he found the pills in my purse one day. I had never seen him so angry and scary before. He snatched Marlon away from me and told me he would get me deported and keep the baby; that I was nothing but a "sick, illegal rat." I feared him and I feared he would follow up on his threats. I begged him not to take Marlon away and that I would do anything to make everything alright again. He made me flush my medicine down the toilet.

Nothing improved. I lived in fear every day that Ronald would take the baby away at any moment. I didn't know what to do, so I ran away. My friend took me to a battered women's shelter and I stayed there for a month before a slip and fall where I pinched a nerve in my back and was unable to move for a while. I didn't know who to call for help, so I called Ronald who came to pick us up. He was very gentle and loving about the whole situation. We spoke and he told me that he wanted to make things in our marriage work. I wanted that as well—I just didn't know how to go about it anymore, but I was still willing to give it a try.

Things went well between us for a month or two and I began to feel hope again. Ronald didn't change overnight, but he seemed sincere in wanting to be a better husband and dad, so I decided to overlook his outbursts.

That lasted up until my family came to visit us from Russia. He was initially nice to them, but quickly became bothered by their presence and told me to let them know that they needed to help pay for utilities and buy their own food. I was so embarrassed. To make matters worse, I complimented my brother-in-law one night on how good a father he was, and Ronald lost it right then and there, in front of everyone. He began to yell and insult me in front of my sister, my nephew, my mom and my brother-in-law. He called me a "dirty Russian whore," "worthless," and a "gold-digger." My family was outraged. They left right then and there and went to stay at a hotel. I sat on the floor in shock for a long time. Had that just happened?

Everything ended not long after that. I knew I wouldn't be able to go back to the way things were after Ronald picked me up from the shelter, and just before my family came to visit. Those were memories, blurry, like a dream. I feared him now and I resented him. And I felt pain. I felt so much pain.

We were a few days away from Marlon's first birthday. Ronald had agreed to throw a small birthday party for him and I was busy with the arrangements. Marlon was beginning to walk on his own and he was a handful, but I kept an eye on him as best I could. Later on that day, after Ronald had volunteered to watch Marlon for a while, he caught him trying to get down the stairs on his own. Ronald snatched Marlon up and began to shake him and yell at him, calling him a "little son of a bitch." Terror washed over me like a wave. I knew Ronald was impulsive and violent and I didn't know what he would do to our baby next. I rushed to his side and took Marlon from him. Ronald pushed me against the wall with our baby still in my arms and glared at me. I had never seen so much hate in anyone's eyes. He then told me I disgusted him, that he wanted to divorce me, and for me to make arrangements. The he stormed out of the house, slamming the door behind him.

I called my friend in a flash of desperation—I didn't have anyone else to help, I didn't know what to do. She rushed over to the house and helped me pack a few things, then took me to a women's shelter.

I've been living in the shelter for six weeks now, struggling to make sense of the last 15 months of my life. Ronald hasn't tried to contact me, but I still fear him. Most of all, I fear what he is capable of doing out of spite, just to get back at me. I'm afraid he will take Marlon away and that my son will then be in great danger. I'm afraid of being deported, but more so than anything in the world, I'm afraid of being deported without my son. I fear for my Marlon's life if Ronald were to have custody of him. I fear for what would become of us if we are both sent to Russia. I live in fear now. It is all I know.

. . .

Sadly, Lana's story is another example of these "mail-order bride" arrangements gone wrong. It is still shocking to this day, however, to see how in relationships such as this, the dynamics and ways of relating degenerate into something so twisted and nearly always pathological.

Lana came from neither a notably healthy nor unhealthy upbringing. Her parents were exceptionally average, as was her life growing up. No family history of substance abuse, or any other history of abuse, really. I've continue to wonder how her background primed her for tolerating Ronald's cruelty and abuse. The only reasonable explanation I've been able to tease out so far is that her innocuous upbringing helped raise a rather naïve Lana. She presented well—the sort of image many have of the educated, pretty blonde Russian woman. During our interview I didn't really notice the naiveté in those sad eyes, but it was there, behind the shock, pain and fear.

Yet this quality must have been what Ronald saw in her. Many men who match the spousal-abuser profile have an uncanny ability to pick out the vulnerable ones, women they can easily manipulate and dominate. I have not met the man—but I'd be hard pressed to rule out any psychopathy. He clearly matches the profile of a spousal abuser with all of his anger and control issues.

I don't know what would have become of Lana had she not been able to make any friends; these same friends advised that her situation was not normal and helped her escape to a shelter.

I am convinced that in her naiveté, Lana simply didn't see the outcome of her relationship coming. To this day she isn't really able to come to terms with everything that transpired. I wondered if she ever would avail herself to professional help to work on these issues. I became instantly worried, as I knew her condition would not improve unless she was willing to deal with the ghosts and monsters in that particular dark corner of her life.

Lana was allowed to remain in the country and become a legal resident of the United States. I know the news brought great relief to her, as she worried of what could become of her and her son if sent back to Russia. She mentioned to me that she remained in touch with some of the friends that were here, and I hoped to God this was true, as they could very well be her only lifeline. I tried to tell Lana about the importance of counseling for her, and she seemed to think that the weekly group session at the women's shelter was more than enough—perhaps more than she could ever handle. She simply did not want to discuss her past with anyone. She did not feel she was ready. I continued to worry for her.

I know the best thing that could have happened to Lana was to be allowed to remain in the United States. I hope she takes advantage of this opportunity beyond the fact of simply living a safer and more stable life than what she would've had in Russia. She deserved as much after the horrors visited on her by an American. Yet I truly hope for her sake and that of her young son that she eventually finds herself ready to pursue intensive counseling and can finally begin her healing journey.

TATIANA

Tatiana stepped through the front door hesitantly, looking around as she walked up the steps. There was something of a dual nature about her; on the one hand she seemed smart and capable of handling herself, but on the other, she presented as fearful, erratic, and shy.

"Come on in," I told her. I had surprised her; she jolted back, her eyes opening wide in surprise. She had appeared to be ready to run out the door and I knew it, but I wanted—I needed to find out why.

Tatiana calmed down after a few moments, and as she did, she relaxed her grip on her jacket and lowered the arm holding her purse. She smiled apologetically and gave me a half-truth: "I didn't know you were there." I had been fully aware of that, but her reaction was so exaggerated that I felt something else must be going on. Tatiana had been ready to run for her life.

Tatiana told me of how she lived in a small apartment with her Russian roommate and that it was "so nice" to have someone of a similar background with her. When I asked if they engaged in social activities together, Tatiana's demeanor changed in a split second. She pushed herself further back into the seat of her chair as she gazed downward. She suddenly appeared quite somber and sullen. I had hit a nerve.

"I don't really go out, only for work," she said, "I don't like being outside." She lifted her gaze and looked at me nervously and somewhat imploringly, almost as if she was begging me to not ask any more questions.

I let out a deep sigh. "You know why you're here?" I asked. She nodded "Yes," and began to weep uncontrollably.

"He is always there. He always finds me. He hates me, he doesn't want me back—I don't know why he's still watching me. I think he wants to hurt me," she blurted out amidst a cascade of tears.

I frowned thoughtfully. That's all I could bring myself to do at that moment. Then I got up, locked the front door and handed her a box of tissues.

"If there was ever a time and a place to remember everything that's making you cry right now, this is it. You're safe here and your attorney is working on keeping you safe from now on. I need to know what happened. I need you to tell me everything," I said.

Her crying worsened and became an audible sob. I felt so much compassion for her and yet I knew I needed to remain neutral for everyone's sake. I needed to be the evaluator. I poured her a glass of water from the pitcher and she calmed down somewhat as she took a few sips. She then looked at me, fear oozing from her eyes.

She was ready to talk.

My name is Tatiana and I'm 27 years old. I met Tom through a marriage agency. We emailed back and forth and exchanged pictures for a couple of months before Tom travelled to my home in Latvia to meet me in person. It was love at first sight. We stayed in touch over the phone, email, and video chat for about five more months. Then Tom asked me to marry him, and I moved to the United States in order to be with him.

We had a big wedding with lots and lots of people—friends and acquaintances of Tom. No one in my family attended the wedding and I didn't have any friends in the United States. It was beautiful anyway and one of the best days of my life. I was so happy to marry someone I was so madly in love with and that loved me too.

But then… things changed. I never saw again any of the people who attended the wedding. Tom was always alone. He never had any friends come over, and never spoke to anyone but me. I began to suspect that he had arranged for all of those people to come to our wedding in order to make himself look good. I wondered why he would do such a thing, but it wasn't a big deal to me anyway. I chalked it up to him simply trying to impress me. What mattered was that we were together and we were happy.

After about a month, Tom began to make horrible subtle comments of how he was working so hard but it wasn't enough because he now had to support me. I felt like a burden. After a two or three weeks of hearing him complain and making me feel like a freeloader, I decided to look for a job so I could help with the costs of living.

One day Tom came home from work to find me on the computer looking for work. He told me I wasn't ready to begin working because I didn't speak enough English and that I should take responsibility for the house instead. I tried to explain my feelings and thoughts to him, but he wouldn't have it. He wanted me in the house at all times.

I didn't stop trying, though. Tom never stopped complaining about money and hinting at how much of a burden I was, so I began to look for ways to save him money. Even though it was almost wintertime, I kept the heat off until he came home from work. I showered with almost cold water and I only washed my hair once a week. I tried to make meals out of cheap ingredients and most days I'd only have one meal a day until he got home so I wouldn't use up the food. He never noticed though; he kept complaining about money and I felt more like a burden with each passing day.

310

I didn't have any friends since I never left the house, but I was familiar with my neighbor; every once in a while we would run into one another outside and say hello to one another. It was during one of those days that I told her everything; I don't know what came over me—I think I needed someone to talk to and she sensed it.

A few days later she came knocking at my door to tell me that there was a job opening at the art supply store five blocks from our neighborhood. She said she spent a lot of time there and took me to the store and introduced me to one of the managers. I was offered a part-time job stocking shelves at the store and I took it in a heartbeat. I told Tom that very night, not knowing if he would be angry or pleased with me, but he took little notice of my news.

I began to work at the store the following week and I got to know the girls that worked with me. I began to do clothing alterations for them while I was at home. I didn't make a lot of money, but I was no longer a burden; especially since I gave Tom every cent I made. I didn't know how much he made or what our monthly expenses were. He made it a point to keep me out of our finances even when I asked him. But I trusted that his consternation regarding our money problems was true. Tom had been a good man from the moment I met him; it never once crossed my mind that what he said was anything but the truth.

When Tom saw that I was doing well at my job at the store, he agreed to let me look for another job, and I began to work at a department store at the mall. I also entered a couple of art contests and I won a few hundred dollars each time. Every cent that came into my hands I gave to Tom so he could take care of our home. He never once said thank you or told me that I was doing good.

Six months of marriage went by before he and I began to argue pretty badly. Up to that point he was mostly just neglectful, and would refrain from disrespectful behaviors such as hinting mean things or muttering insults under his breath. One day though, everything changed.

He began to argue with me for even made-up reasons. He didn't like the way I made the table, how I cleaned, how I dressed, or how I spoke to him. He would get mad at me for coiling the garden hose a certain way on the side of the house, and he would yell at me in front of the neighbors and any passersby. In my humiliation I would try to get away from him and go back in the house, but he would follow me, yelling that if I didn't like it I could go back to Latvia. He would even offer to buy me the ticket.

One time I let the dog out by accident and Tom lost it; he threw a glass against the wall, the shattered pieces falling all over me. I found the dog—he had just gone out to the back yard, but Tom didn't speak to me for days.

He continued to grow tired of the way I did things and one evening he exploded. He didn't like the potato stew I had made for dinner and began yelling, "This is America!" and, "What does it take to get some fucking American food in this fucking house!" The mere tone in his voice startled and scared me and I began to cry. Tom slammed his chair on the floor as he got up and went to the fridge, where he got some hot dogs and warmed them up in the microwave. He then came back to the dining room with his plate stacked with a small mountain of hot dogs and bottles of mayo, mustard and ketchup. He opened the bottles and squirted them all out onto the plate, splattering the sauces all over me. He then forced me to eat every single one of the 18 hot dogs. "You are in America, you will learn to eat like an American," he screamed at me. I cried as he forced me to eat everything on the plate, but he didn't care; he held me by the hair until the plate was clean.

The fear and tension were too much for me to bear. I became jumpy at any noise and began to scurry away from Tom anytime he was near. All I knew is that I didn't want to make him upset. I didn't want him to yell, or throw things at me, or force me to eat. Just the thought of it made me cry. I began crying a lot every day. As time went by things got really bad and the mere presence of Tom would make me incredibly nervous. I unknowingly began to twist and pull at my hair, and later began to pull my eyelashes and eyebrows as well. I couldn't handle things anymore, but I had no way of freeing myself from Tom. I had no one here in the United States and I couldn't go back to my small town in Latvia and hope for any kind of future there. In my village divorced women are ostracized from the community and I would be seen as a pariah.

I didn't know what I would do, but I couldn't be with Tom any more either. Between my hair falling out from stress, and me pulling it out, I had a big, bald patch on my head and hardly any eyebrows left. I couldn't sleep, I couldn't eat, and I couldn't stop trembling. One day I mustered up the courage and asked Tom for a divorce; something bad was going to happen to me if I stayed with him any longer, I just knew it. He was outraged. That was the angriest I had ever seen him in my life. He threw his computer against the wall in which I was reclining and it broke half of the plates. He yelled and screamed so loud that my neighbors actually called the police. He was taken to jail and released two days later.

I felt terrible for Tom going to jail. I did love him still, I just feared him terribly. When he came back home he stopped talking to me altogether; it was as if I no longer existed to him. I felt terrible about what had happened to him and I apologized and asked him to work on things with me; that maybe we still had a chance. He looked at me and offered me $8000 to start a new life "somewhere else in the United States." It felt like a knife to the heart. I stood there frozen, staring at him, not knowing what to say. I could see the anger building up inside of him like white-hot coals; he clenched his fists and tightened his lips in an attempt not to grab me. I told him maybe we could attend counseling sessions or anything else he thought would be good for us, but he wouldn't listen. He grabbed me by the arm and threw me against the wall, then he told me that this is the way things were, and they were not to change, and that if I wanted him to be any different or wanted a divorce I could go straight back to Latvia.

He then grabbed two bottles of whiskey and some pills and locked himself in the basement. I froze in panic—he was going to try to kill himself. I ran over to my neighbor's home and she told me to call 911. The paramedics came and busted down the basement door in order to get to Tom. The painkiller bottles were already open and pills were scattered across the floor; the paramedics found him drinking whiskey straight from the bottle. He became enraged when the paramedics came in and began to yell and call me a worthless whore and a backstabbing bitch, among other things. The paramedics attempted to treat him, but he refused. He even signed a form refusing treatment against medical advice.

It was a nightmare, and there was nowhere for me to escape. I remained in the house while our divorce was being processed, but we never spoke again. He acted as if I didn't exist, except for when he wanted to show me that I was unwanted in his home. He bumped into me, dumped food and drinks on me and constantly walked by whichever room I was in and turned off the light. He threw my clothes out of our bedroom and into the snowy backyard, and then installed locks on all the kitchen cabinets, pantry, washer and drier so I couldn't eat or clean my clothes.

Not long after that, Tom left the house and told me he wasn't coming back until the divorce was done so that he didn't have to see me anymore. I felt a mix of relief and another stab in the heart. I couldn't believe that someone who at one point loved me so much now loathed the very sight of me. I didn't respond to his notice. I didn't know what to say. I just bowed my head and let him leave.

About two days later Tom began to send me threatening emails on what he expected of me until the divorce was final, or else he would make sure I got deported back to Latvia. He told me he still expected me to give him money for the cost of the house, and demanded a sum that totaled about 90% of my earnings. He told me that if I didn't pay him he would send people to throw me and my things into the street. He then threatened that he would make sure I'd regret it if I ever brought any men into the house. He told me that even though he didn't live in the house anymore, he had people watching me and he would know of all my comings and goings.

I no longer felt safe and I didn't want to be in that house anymore. I spent my time holed up in one room with a book or watching television. I couldn't bring myself to go outside unless I absolutely had to—I was afraid that whomever Tom had watching me would hurt me. I even asked for an escort to and from my car while at work. I couldn't shake the feeling that someone was watching me.

After the divorce was final, I moved in with a Russian girl from work. Tom stopped asking me for money, but he hasn't stopped following or threatening me. I see him from time to time far away in the parking lot by where I work, standing next to his car. He still sends me emails about once or twice a week telling me what a terrible wife I was and how he would make sure I'd regret ever leaving him. He threatened me to be very careful about what I did. He'd insult me, call me a whore, and threaten me not to get involved with any men as he would surely find out and make me pay. He then went on to tell me details of my life, such as the clothes I was wearing on a particular day, or the times that I went in and out of work—making his point that he was watching me.

If I were able to have a decent life in Latvia, I would absolutely go back to live there.

But the people in my town are very conservative and they shut out single mothers or divorced women from the community—especially someone like me, who left her family and "ran away" to another country with a strange man. I'm not welcome there. One would imagine I could keep my personal life secret and find work and forge a life in my town again, but it's too small of a place. Everyone already knows my story and whatever missing gaps they've already filled in with their own versions. I already feel like nothing, but at least I could maybe do something here, make something out of myself somehow. I can't go back to Latvia feeling like nothing only to be nothing. I couldn't bear my life to continue on in that way; I would likely just want to end it.

...

We generally understand the definitions of violence and aggression as crossing another person's boundaries against their will. The aggression can break through physical, emotional, or psychological boundaries, or, as in Tatiana's case, all three at once. Her story about her life with Tom is a perfect example of emotional and psychological manipulation to the point of creating severe trauma.

Tom continually pressured Tatiana for money. He never cared to communicate with her his financial concerns, let alone allow her to help. His passive/aggressive approach had a subliminal effect on Tatiana, and over time, the damage inflicted was considerable. This effect, compounded with the emotional manipulation and physical abuse, nearly destroyed Tatiana. Was it real or a massive manipulation when Tom locked himself in the basement with pain pills and whiskey? While she has so far managed to survive her ordeal with Tom, the severity of her trauma has pushed her to the edge of her own cliff.

Tatiana is in dire need of psychological help, but feels unable to reach out to anyone for fear of being away from home and falling prey to Tom who still stalks her. Even though Tatiana showed exceptional courage by taking the steps to leave her abusive ex-husband, his continuing presence in her life exacerbates her already severe symptoms and prevents her from moving on. It is impossibly discouraging to see her bravest efforts failing to save her from the fear of her worst nightmares. As I reminded Tatiana however, her fight isn't over and she hadn't lost yet. She simply needed more tools and a different approach to things.

The way Tatiana that explained everything, it appeared that life as a divorced woman would be impossibly difficult for her in her small town. This compounded with the already existing damage and trauma would be too large a burden to attempt to carry on a normal life without any kind of professional support; my prognosis for her isn't favorable unless she is able to connect with medical *professionals, and my concern is that she will not be able to afford such services in her native country.*

Luckily for Tatiana, the judge allowed her to remain in the country and become a legal resident. This means the start of a brand new and more stable life for Tatiana, who, to my surprise, is open to the idea of counseling. She is still severely afraid of falling prey to her husband and is reticent to leave her home, but is open to finding a therapist willing to do counseling session over the phone, at least to start.

I feel hopeful about Tatiana's future. Not simply because she was allowed to remain in the United States, but because she has a certain opportunity now to heal the trauma from her brutally scarring past. I didn't know what would become of her in Latvia, even with her best intentions of seeking out help. At least I know now that she has a real chance of fighting to get her life back.

Political Asylum

ABELINO

Abelino walked into my office sporting the traditional small-town Hispanic manners. He shook my hand and then proceeded to pull out a chair for his wife. "Quite the gentleman," I said, looking over to his wife. Abelino blushed; he didn't say a word.

Abelino struck me as exceptionally demure at first glance, and I soon learned why. In order to ease into the interview process I started the session by asking Abelino some basic background questions. However, he couldn't even tell me his age. Not only did he become confused with simple questions, but he lacked any confidence in his answers. He'd look over to his wife without fail— either to confirm information or to ask her for the proper response. I was surprised that this story already had a twist. How many more would there be?

I quickly realized Abelino needed his wife to keep in track with virtually everything in his life; the current challenge being this evaluation. In a very rudimentary manner, Abelino was able to describe his job duties at the meat packing plant. However, for the life of him he could not figure out his age, or how long he had been residing in the United States. I prevented his wife from assisting him with these answers. A half a minute later he looked at me imploringly and then turned to his wife.

"You've been here since 1990," she told him.

"So... ten years. I've been here ten years?" he asked me. I shrugged, then looked to his wife.

"It's 2006, Abelino. You've been here 16 years," his wife said.

Abelino turned to look at me. He didn't appear to be embarrassed—rather, he seemed to have long since been resigned to accept his cognitive limitations. This is the way daily life unfolded for Abelino; he spoke logically and coherently, yet had great difficulty understanding others. He appeared to become quickly and exceptionally confused with even basic information. Peace and routine were essential in Abelino's world. Even a tiny change in his daily routine would emerge as a virtual cataclysm. For basic daily survival, Abelino's wife had to create a virtual bubble-universe for him. Burst that bubble and Abelino's smidge of functional ability would likely rupture along with it.

I suddenly became aware of the much larger and very dangerous picture if he were ever forced to return to his home country. My eyes widened without me even realizing it.

My name is Abelino and I am from El Salvador. I was born and raised in a small village of about twenty families. Our town was too small for services or luxuries of any kind, so we had to journey out to the neighboring villages for things like supplies and medical care.

School was a complicated matter as well. Our settlement was too small to have one of our own. We were forced to walk several miles each day to the nearest village. It was a long walk on an otherwise deserted path. Many of us got by without going to school or ever even learning to read or write. The times were just too dangerous for us to venture that far on a regular basis; one never knew when the guerrilleros would appear.

My father had been part of the military for a few years. I think something must have happened to him during that time, because the very first thing he did upon his release was move to our village to get away from it all. "People are trouble and their surroundings are trouble. Best keep as far away from them as possible," he would tell me, but he never explained why.

My childhood was exceptionally simple. The other kids and I worked hard in the fields with our parents, and once all our chores were done, we were allowed to play for a while outside while our mothers finished washing clothes or making tortillas. Even though we were in a remote area compared to other villages, our parents always seemed quite wary and never allowed us to wander off on our own or be outside unsupervised. I could hear noises far in the mountains at night, the hustle and bustle of men, donkeys, and trucks. At times I could make out voices and even gun shots. I figured that was the reason the adults seemed to be on edge most of the time, although I didn't realize exactly why. To me it was just noise—I never thought much of it.

One day everything changed and our lives were uprooted. Late that night the guerrilleros swept through town. Like a nightmare, they swept down over our village. It was so unexpected; they demanded our attention and then ripped away our peace. The guerrilleros descended from the mountain with torches lighting their way and firing shots into the air. A few people tried to escape, terrified at the sight of these men flying into the village. But they were way ahead of all of us—the guerrilleros had placed some of their men by the two access roads to our village; no one was meant to leave. We were all so very poor, but they ransacked our town anyway and took everything we had, even the grocery baskets.

We were all huddled into our small house, hoping against hope they would not come. Three big men suddenly barged in through the door—I will never forget. They were just flesh-and-blood men, but they seemed as if right out of a horror dream. All three of them had huge grins and a cruel stare; something very bad was about to happen and

I knew it. I hid inside one of the floor cabinets and I braced against my knees as I watched it all happen. I was in complete shock and disbelief of what my life had so very quickly turned into.

They were looking for my father. They said they "caught word" that Dad had been in the military, and that that was enough to make them dislike him. The men grabbed him by the collar of his shirt and threw him on the floor. He fell on his knees first, then the men began to kick and punch him all over. He quickly fell to the floor. Then one of the men pointed his gun at my dad's head—and he fired! I blacked out.

I woke up to screams and laughs. I don't know how long I had been out cold, but the first thing I noticed was by some miracle I was still in the cabinet—they hadn't found me yet. I looked through the crack and saw that they had a hold of my two sisters and my mom. The men looked crazed and devoid of any human quality. They beat my mother and my sisters, and then piled them up over my dad's body. The men began to drag them by their hair to different corners of the living room where they raped the three of them; I don't know how many times.

This is where I began to scream and they found me. One of the men dragged me out of the cabinet and beat me with the butt of his rifle "for trying to fool them." I heard pops and cracks all over my body as he laid blows wherever he could.

Eventually I fell to the floor. I couldn't move—I couldn't even close my eyes. I watched how the men continued to beat and rape my mom and sisters as I laid in the pool of blood next to my father.

I knew we were all going to die that night; it was only a matter of when and I hoped it came soon—I couldn't stand my watching my mom and sisters suffer any longer. I thought they were going to shoot us like they did my dad, but instead they simply walked out and left us all half-dead on the floor.

The next few minutes felt like a horrifying eternity. None of us could move; we didn't know where they were or if they were coming back to kill us. Then I saw a warm, orange light coming through the window—the guerrilleros had set fire to our fields and some of the houses; they were going to burn it all to the ground and us along with it!

I closed my eyes and waited. I didn't know how long it would take or what it would feel like, but I resigned myself to my fate. Then I felt myself being flipped onto my back and I screamed in pain—some of my ribs were broken. It was my mom. She was still alive and had mustered the strength to get me and my sisters out of the house. They had beat them all quite brutally, but hadn't broken any of their bones—what they actually did to them was far, far worse.

We watched our town and our whole lives burn down as we sat on the side of the dirt road. Everything was gone, including my dad. Now there was just the four of us, and no family nearby could take us all in. My mom had to scatter me and my sisters among family members in other towns. War was everywhere and everyone had been scarred by it in one way or another. Everyone had fathers, sons, or brothers involved in the war, and some had lost family members to the fighting.

Life became a replica of hell, at least what I imagine hell looks like. Everyone lived each moment terrified and panicked; there were no warnings and never any chances to run. If your number was up with the guerrilleros, or if you happened to be in the wrong place at the wrong time, death was coming for you—swiftly.

And the rest of us who were spared to live another day were witnesses to the guerrilleros' brutality. We would find new bodies dumped on the streets every day. They were often burned beyond identification. Children like me were often kidnapped by the guerrilleros and forced to become gun-runners under the threat of harm coming to them or their families—and these men were good about delivering harm.

I was 12 when they kidnapped me. They took me to one of their camps far up in the mountains and forced me to run guns to other camps and do their errands for them so that they could remain undetected by the army.

There were a few other children there with me and they treated us all like rats. They would feed us, but for sport, as we ate they would kick the food off of our plates. These men didn't beat us often, but they made sure we knew of the unspeakable horrors that would befall us and our families if we disobeyed them. I had already seen their threats, first-hand. They weren't just trying to scare us.

I also came to realize that if we stayed here we could never escape that reality and it didn't matter how obedient we were. Sooner or later they were going to kill us and our families, and there was nothing we could do about it.

Except for one thing. I could try to run.

I was there for a month before I made my attempt. I couldn't speak to my mom or sisters and I didn't know the best way to go about it, but I had to try. I figured that I was going to die soon anyway, so I may as well try.

I was good the entire month. I did what they told me and acted much like their dog so I could win their trust. One day they sent me on an errand to a town a few miles away. Whenever we went far, to ensure we wouldn't run away, they often had men follow us at least part of the way down the road. This time though, there were no extra men available and they needed ammunition. That was my chance––the only one I would have.

They beat me up a little before they sent me off; I think they wanted to make sure I feared them enough so I wouldn't try to leave. They made me travel with two men part of the way, but then they went off on their own assignment and I continued on the road to the village of La Libertad (Freedom). Odd how little things line up like that.

I remained on my way to that village for a long time—I was afraid one of those men were actually watching me. Then just as suddenly as I had been kidnapped, I turned and I began to run down the mountain in the opposite direction.

I ran all the way home and I went to get my mom. It took everything I had to convince her that sooner or later they would come for us, especially now that I had run away. I pleaded with her that we needed to flee at that very moment. She hesitated, and I saw in her eyes the automatic fear of a lifetime of terror, as well as submission. Now for the second time in my life, I experienced how a few minutes seemed to last an eternity. Once again, I found myself thinking we would all soon be dead.

Suddenly and quite surprisingly for me, my mom agreed to flee. I don't know which one of us was more terrified. We put everything we had into two backpacks and our relatives gave us a small amount of money. We hitched a ride to a neighboring town to find my sisters. Then away we all went—the four of us, unknowing of where we were headed, but sure that we could never return to that place.

As we journeyed across El Salvador and the rest of Central America, we learned that life and war was very much the same everywhere. Our hopes began to deflate as we ran out of options for our survival. We barely had any money left.

Then our plan fell into place. We had been journeying on foot for most of the way as we had such limited funds. We relied on people's kindness for food and shelter, though more often than not we slept in parks, always hungry.

It was one of those nights on which we met Haroldo and his wife. They were from Honduras and also running away from war—they told us their children had been murdered. Like us, they had no one to rely on and hardly any money to survive, so we decided to travel together and look out for one another.

Haroldo and his wife were headed to New Mexico since both of them had family there. To our great fortune, when they learned that we had no place to go, they invited us to come along with them. Haroldo told us they couldn't promise us anything long-term, but at least we would have a destination and a place to stay until we got on our feet. We accepted his kind offer in a heartbeat.

It took us almost two months to get to the frontier. Each day we had to dodge the thugs and robbers, as well as the Mexican police who were always on the lookout for Central Americans. We had to cross the border three or four times, each time turning back at any sign of danger. Finally one dark night we made it all the way through to the United States. We did it without getting caught! We were so happy.

Haroldo's family was very nice to us and our arrival there was everything we could have hoped for. They took us in as their own and showed us how to find work and get around the city. My sisters and I had never gone to school, so that was out the question for us. I helped out at Haroldo's brother's mechanic shop for a few dollars a week and my mom and sisters began to work cleaning houses. Every Wednesday and Sunday my sisters and I would go to church where they taught us how to read and write and do basic math.

Life was turning into something better and we were safe. Yet everything was so new and different—we knew only of life in our village and it was all just too much. We adjusted to the best of our ability, but it is difficult to adjust to something new when your past is still very much present with you.

I think we all felt quite haunted by the war. I lived each moment as if those men were still right behind me, their grip on my shoulders; ready to beat me and try to burn me alive. Those memories had a life of their own and they played over and over in my mind. They still do. We had been successful in removing ourselves from the place of our trauma, but the place and all its memories remained in us.

Maybe I'm not smart enough to figure out how to do it, but I was never able to get over everything that happened to us in El Salvador. I've always felt limited because I can barely read and write, but my past has truly crippled me. I don't know how to have a normal life despite all of these years of being here in the United States. I don't know how to walk down the street without fearing that someone is going to come at me or mine. I don't know how to go outside at night—I won't. I'm afraid of everything that I see, as well as everything that I can't see that it think is hiding around the corners, ready to pounce on me. Fortunately, because I live here in the United States, it has only been fear that I make up myself and it has never come true.

I know it's been a long time and the war is over in El Salvador, but I can't go back. I still have friends and some family there and they tell me that things have changed very little, if at all. There aren't guerrilleros there anymore, but many of those men have hidden among the gangs and criminal organizations that have sprung up since the end of the war. You don't find bodies on the streets every day anymore, but there are still murders, beatings, and rapes on a regular basis, and for no good reason.

I have a family now—a wife and two kids. She too is from El Salvador and knows what the place is like now. She endured many more years of the war before she and her family fled to the United States. We can't go back. We won't make it down there; we're just too scarred, too afraid, too broken. At least here it is easier to deal with all of that and just pretend it doesn't exist.

Both of my children are developmentally delayed. They have a lot of trouble learning at school and my youngest daughter has even been placed in Special Education full-time. She is like her dad—her brain doesn't work too good for learning. I can't take my babies back to El Salvador; there is no help for kids like them in the schools there. They are still so little—they have a chance to adjust and maybe become something here. If I take them back they'll get pushed aside and considered worthless for being different. I can't put my children through that.

I can't put them in danger either. Those gangs are out there ready to take anyone with even a sign of weakness. What if they take our kids thinking they can get money from us because we come from the United States? What money am I going to give them? What will happen to my children? A couple we knew had to go back to El Salvador last year— within two weeks gangs had kidnapped his oldest son. They killed him—the little boy was only ten years old. I can't let my children die like that.

But how could I protect them in a land that terrifies me to the very core? I don't know what would become of me if I had to go back; the memories from my days there paralyze me to this day. I panic and I become desperate, I want to start screaming and run away and my wife has to remind me that we're here in the United States and we're safe. What kind of a protector would I be to my children in El Salvador if I know there would be nothing left of my sanity if I had to return there?

. . .

No one can go through what Abelino experienced and walk away unscathed. Actually, the mere fact that he was able to survive these experiences at all and still show some degree of functionality, however basic, speaks volumes of his level of resilience—but he is at his very limits.

I think that Abelino's low cognitive functionality has been both a blessing and a curse for him. I have been of the opinion that his ignorance buffered him to some degree, but then again, ignorance is fear. He has long since repressed thoughts about the events in his past and the subsequent wave-like ripples of trauma and fear have defined him to a large degree. His stoic, old-country nature and his obligation to provide for his family has been the very thing that has allowed him to continue to soldier on and survive. On the other hand, it is his very lack of psychological awareness and cognitive sophistication that prevents Abelino now from truly identifying and exploring the roots of the damage inflicted on him, preventing any psychic healing. He continues to live a fear-based existence, and is largely isolated from the rest of the world. He is just marking the days, doing his best to keep out the dark thoughts.

Abelino is correct in that his children need to remain here in the United States. The children are American-born citizens and have been found to have severe learning disabilities. They therefore have the right to the services that can best be provided for them here, in their native country. Should their father have to take them with him to El Salvador, not only would they be targeted as Americans, but also ostracized for being different and having special needs. In my opinion, the already psychologically fragile Abelino would surely not be able to cope with the re-traumatization of going back to El Salvador, and having to care for two developmentally delayed children.

As a clinician, I am certain that Abelino would deteriorate quickly if deported to El Salvador. His memories have been eating away at him throughout the years. While it's true that escaping El Salvador when he did very likely saved his life and that of his family, on a broader perspective it also bought him a slower kind of death. Abelino may have physically left El Salvador, but he took with him the exceptionally vivid memories of his traumatic experiences, which have been playing over and over in his mind for the past sixteen years.

The development of his young brain was greatly affected by the array of dizzyingly distressing and life-threatening experiences during the war. These things are never easily resolved, particularly when the patient does not have the capacity to process higher-level information in a therapeutic setting. Abelino is sitting at the very edge of the abyss at the moment. I figure that given his level of distress and lack of coping skills, without proper assistance he might have another year or so before his mental health deteriorates to a critical level. He is at risk of collapsing into a severe bout of major depression and potential breakdown of his faculties. If that were to happen and he would finally avail himself to counseling and medication, of course there would still be hope for him.

I would lose all hope for Abelino however, if he were forced to return to El Salvador. Not only would a re-introduction to the place of such severe trauma and horror be psychologically devastating for this man, but the level of poverty there would surely prevent any chance for him to procure proper services. Although Abelino has learned to read and write to some degree, he remains largely illiterate. Additionally, he has not been in his home country for the past sixteen years and lacks the social and occupational connections that "the locals" grew up establishing. The chances for Abelino to find work and provide for himself and his *family, as well as procuring services for himself and his children, would be nothing but a pipe dream. These factors alone would sink him, not to mention the guarantee that his prominent symptoms of post-traumatic stress would be certain to put an end his any semblance of functionality or sanity that remains.*

Luckily for Abelino, it turned out that he will not have to return to El Salvador after all. This was yet another surprisingly difficult legal battle that I was part of. I testified in court as an expert witness in Abelino's case. The hearing went on from early in the morning until the first part of the afternoon, but in the end the judge decided in favor of Abelino, and he and his family were allowed to remain in the United States.

The rest of his life can now unfold more calmly, and I can only hope that if Abelino does not heed my advice to seek help, that maybe his much higher-functioning wife got the message and will lead her husband down that road. I have the feeling that sooner or later he will do it; if not for himself, for the sake of his children. Abelino may be a simple-minded man, but he does hold uppermost his duty as a husband and father as his life's priorities. I find that oftentimes the obligation one feels toward those little ones we tow behind is quite enough. In the end they may very well change Abelino's life even more than he initially expected.

ABRAHAM

Abraham came to my office in the company of his father and his partner Raul. I was pleasantly surprised by how well connected the three of them were to one another. I figured it would be wise to try keeping all of them in the room with me during the interview in that I had the feeling it would add some layers to my awareness on this case.

Abraham and his family lived a rather uneventful life here in the United States, which mostly revolved around work, school, and caring for Raul's medical problems. As noted by their chosen sitting arrangement (Raul in the middle, Abraham and his dad on either side of him), Raul appeared to be the weakest member of their family and they very much presented as his protectors and providers. Abraham indicated that his father was often away working in the oil fields, so the financial responsibility of their living arrangement fell heavily on him.

Abraham informed me that his father and mother had divorced when he was only a boy and the family split apart. Abraham and two of his brothers went to live with his dad, while his remaining, older siblings stayed with his mom. "I don't know how she picked who went where," he told me and then went onto say that he never heard from his mother or siblings again. His father interjected at this time and added that they had they moved to the country and basically vanished. They did not leave any contact information and never attempted to contact the other family members again.

I asked Abraham to explain how difficult his mother's absence was for him, but he simply shrugged and shook his head from side to side. "We had other things to worry about," he answered.

I wondered, "What other things can a little boy worry about when his mother abandons him? What else could have had the same magnitude as a parent suddenly taking off for good?" I could not fathom how Abraham could look at me in the eye and simply shrug it off as non-consequential.

His very life, it turns out.

My name is Abraham and I grew up in Guatemala City. My father worked at the power plant and my mom worked from home as a seamstress. I have eight siblings, so my mom couldn't afford to have a regular job since we took up most of her time. It seemed like we did fine though, at least for a while. Then my dad lost his job at the power plant and everything went pretty much to hell.

I was about six years old. There were suddenly too many of us and not enough to go around. Life at home became tense. My dad had to take a job doing labor because he couldn't find anything else, but even then we couldn't afford to live. My mom had to go looking for work and since my dad worked during the day, she had to find a place to work at night. She ended up working in a bar as a waitress. Even though she wasn't doing anything wrong, we lived in a very conservative culture and her job wasn't looked upon favorably. My siblings and I often found ourselves fighting other kids who taunted us and insulted our mom.

At first we would take a beating every time. But those kids ridiculed us so often that guess what? Practice does make perfect. We learned how to defend ourselves and fast. At first I thought the other kids would get scared and stop bothering us, but that never happened. At least we weren't the ones walking back home bloodied up.

My parents separated permanently when I was eight years old. At first, my siblings and I would spend some time with each of my parents, but eventually they split us up between them. My oldest brothers and sisters remained with my mom while two of my brothers and I went to live with my dad.

I don't know how the arrangement was made or why. All I know is that even though I had two of my brothers with me I felt isolated from the world, from my own family. I didn't understand why my parents had separated and I really couldn't understand why they separated us kids. I had a roof over my head, but I felt as though I had no home and no family to come home to.

My dad's work was hit and miss, and he couldn't find anything else. Even though there were only four of us there was never enough to buy food for us all. My dad taught us how to go looking for discarded food in the dumpsters. Whatever we could find is what we had to eat for the next meal, or maybe two.

It was a scary thing, diving in the dumpsters looking for food. Our dad would take us out at night so no one would chase us off. We usually found enough food for a meal or two, which meant that by the time we went out the following night we were already starving. Dumpsters were in dark, filthy alleys, which often smelled like dirty bathrooms. It is not a place you want to go looking or food. We always ran into homeless men taking shelter in the dark and often they tried to fight us for "stealing their food." I felt a lot like one of the dirty rats we competed against for scraps—scurrying in the night, fighting one another for spoiled morsels of rotting food.

About four years went by like this. My dad sent us to school every day; we may not have had food to eat, but he did his best to not let us go without an education. Our clothes were often worn out and my siblings and I had to share a notepad, but he bent over backwards to at least get that for us. I often wondered why my dad kept sending us to school instead of putting us to work like other poor families did with their children. Most of those kids couldn't even count change, but they never went without a meal. Us... well, some weeks we ate nothing but stale bread and half-rotten apples, but my dad would be damned if he was going to let us miss a day of school.

In the afternoons after school, we would come home to do our homework and our chores, and at night we would go scavenge for food. I wanted to quit school. I was tired of fighting kids making fun of us for our dirty clothes or ragged shoes; for not having notebooks in which to write, or for eating brown apples at lunch. It seemed like I'd been fighting for a very long time and I was sick of it. I wanted it to stop. I didn't want to deal with these kids anymore and I wanted to go find a job so I could help my dad, so we could stop eating from dumpsters.

He wouldn't let me, though. Every time I tried to reason with him he would tell me that school was the one thing that would save me, the key to getting me out of the life we lived. He was patient with me, but he would remain unwavering in his decision. I knew that he understood the life he asked me and my brothers to live was insurmountably difficult. I knew that he realized that everything would be so much easier for us if I got out there and began to work. Every time though, he would stare into my eyes as if weighing the options; the far-reaching consequences, and then without fail he would tell me that I was never to give up school no matter who we had to fight, however many times. "Abraham, we are strong like warriors. We don't quit, we survive and one day everything will be all right." It sounded a lot nicer in speech than it was in real life.

Don't ask me how he did it, but my dad put my brothers and I through high school and kept pushing until all three of us graduated. I didn't know what would happen next, but I had the feeling that my dad's "biggest job" was finished. It was our time now to turn this life around and take care of one another.

I always felt different from the other boys, ever since I was a kid. It seemed like I had more in common with girls; I just got along better with them. As if life wasn't difficult enough already as I grew up, me not fitting in with the other boys up really made me feel… inadequate, as if there was something wrong with me.

Other children already ostracized us for being poor, yet my brothers managed to make a friend or two along the way. I just didn't look at boys that way. I didn't want to play cars with them; I didn't know what I wanted to do with them. It made me feel so alone and confused. As I grew up I began to make sense of this secret love/hate relationship I had with boys: I was attracted to them. I refused to believe it, let alone tell anyone about it—they were all so different from me. My father was the true warrior and survivor and he would try to get us to become like him. My brothers... well, they were boys; they wouldn't understand.

Since I didn't know what to do about it and I sure as hell wasn't going to tell anyone, I shoved this predicament as far back in my mind as I could; life was just too difficult as it was anyway. The years went by and although I became adept at ignoring the ever-present fact that I liked men, I began to feel inexplicably sad and unsatisfied with life. Back then I attributed it to the brutal life we lived. Now though... I think that was only part of it.

After I graduated I worked odd jobs for a few years and helped my dad support us. Life was difficult, but it was definitely better. Ironically, I was offered a job at the power plant when I was 21 years old—the same power plant that had laid off my father years prior and was a catalyst to the poorest and most brutal years of our lives. I took the job in a heartbeat and promised myself I would work there until it gave us back everything it took away from us.

My adult years were a convoluted mix between guilt and need. I got involved with a girl to prove to myself and everyone else that I was not gay. Yet about eight months into our relationship I fell in love with a man named Raul. I couldn't believe it; I don't even know how it happened.

Raul worked with me at the power plant. We sat next to each other one day at the cafeteria and we quickly became friends. It was so very instantly special—I guess that should have been my first clue. We understood and complemented one another perfectly. For the first time in a long time I found myself laughing regularly and feeling upbeat. I had a friend, a best friend, and it felt like I had won the lottery.

Raul and I went everywhere together; we were inseparable. I had never had a real friendship in my life and I was too infatuated with the idea to notice at first that this was much, much more than just that.

I didn't know Raul was gay; I'm not sure he knew it either. It all happened so quickly.

Raul lived in a room he rented from an old lady. We didn't make enough money to afford going out places during the weekend, so we often "wasted time" in his room, drinking cheap rum and watching television. I didn't mind.

We were watching a boxing match one particular night when Raul turned around and stared at me for a while. I didn't know what was wrong with him; he looked so troubled—confused. Then suddenly he blurted out, "I love you," and then kissed me.

It was as if someone had removed a thick velvet curtain off my eyes; everything suddenly became so clear. I loved Raul too. I was in love with a man— the best and worst thing that could have ever happened to me.

But at that very moment nothing mattered. My brain and all my prejudices about sexuality shut down and my body and my heart took over. We kissed and kissed and hugged; it felt as if I finally had come home. We stared at each other in awe. We had been side-by-side, best of friends for months, and it had taken us this long to put two and two together. It seemed like a dream come true.

Suddenly it hit me like a bucket of freezing cold water. I was right; I couldn't believe it. I had spent my entire life shoving away any and all homosexual thoughts, brainwashing myself into liking women. I didn't want to be this, I couldn't be this. No one would accept it, no one would understand. What would my dad think of me? What kind of life could I hope for with Raul? Homosexuality is not accepted among my people—call them old fashioned, but it's true. Gay men and women are considered a shame and put in the same category as drug addicts and prostitutes. A dirty, worthless human being—ask anybody around my block.

I freaked out. I pushed him off of me and ran out his room. This couldn't be happening to me—I didn't like men; that had just been some stupid confusion as a kid. I was straight, I liked women—I had a girlfriend! I wasn't gay. I refused to be gay!

But I was. The following six weeks were easily the most miserable of my life, and coming from someone like me, that means quite a lot. I didn't speak to Raul; I didn't know what to think or what to do. I couldn't sleep, I couldn't eat, and I sure didn't amount to much at work or anywhere else during that time. I tried to keep myself from thinking about Raul; I kept telling myself that it was a mistake, that it couldn't be—but it was too late for that.

After six weeks of complete misery I resigned myself to my wonderful, terrible fate. I was in love with Raul and nothing, I tried to tell myself, was going to change that. Despite my remaining disbelief, I secretly hoped that I hadn't lost him.

Raul and I kept a secret relationship for three years—only my dad knew. As much as I feared his reaction, I couldn't keep it secret from him. I will never forget that day; after I told him the truth about Raul, he looked at me with eyes full of confusion. I could tell my dad felt conflicted about the whole situation and was well aware that the next words to come out of his mouth would direct the course of our relationship. He stared at me for what seemed like an eternity before he grabbed me by the shoulders and pulled me in to hug me. "You will never give me grandchildren," he said. "I'm okay with that."

Life wasn't perfect after this, but my dad's acceptance gave me a priceless kind of peace. Unfortunately, our charade could only go on for so long before people began suspecting and speculating. It had been three years, after all.

"Those two are always together, even when they go to the bars—you never see them with girlfriends." I thought we could fool them forever, but I was only fooling myself. It had only been a matter of time before people caught onto us.

I wasn't paranoid. People really did begin to treat us differently. We began to get a lot of cold shoulders and acquaintances of ours suddenly were too busy to spend time with us anymore. My production at work became "not good enough," and my boss suddenly ran out of anything to tell me except for complaints about my work. Our time was running out. I knew things were about to go downhill.

Raul and I always daydreamed about moving away somewhere where we could be open about our relationship and have a happy, movie-like life; but that's all it ever was, a daydream. Our town was all we had ever known and all the people we had ever met lived there. Whether we liked it or not, it was our home; we would have to make it work.

Things truly went downhill. Even though we hadn't "come out" to anyone other than my dad, suspicions were enough to ostracize us from the community. No one wanted to be associated with us and risk being put into the same category. We lost most of our friends, slowly but consistently. Work became progressively more difficult, too. Raul's boss even found reasons to cut back his pay. Luckily that did not happen to me; my boss simply took out all his frustrations on me. It was an exceedingly toxic environment, but I needed the money. I had goals and plans and I had promised myself and my dad that I would carry them out. "You're a warrior Abraham, a survivor." If I wasn't born one, life was sure making one out of me.

Then one day, as it often happens, everything changed. Raul had been walking home from the convenience store one night when a truck full of men began to follow him. He said at one point the truck sped ahead, cutting the way in front of him. Three men jumped out of the truck and beat him within an inch of his life for being gay, for being "a waste of a man." After they were done kicking and breaking his ribs, they left him lying in a pool of blood on the street. The police came to our house to let us know that Raul was in the hospital—his parents had long ago died and he had been an only child.

My dad and I went to see Raul; he was barely recognizable. His face was a swollen mess of purple and blue to the point where his eyes were almost completely shut. He had bandages on every visible part of his body and a cast on one of his legs. Rage and sadness overcame me and I began to shake almost uncontrollably. My dad had to hold me back from bolting out of the room and going to find whoever had done that to Raul.

I was allowed to stay the night with Raul and I called in sick to work the next day—trouble or not, I didn't care. Later that afternoon when my dad came by the hospital he simply looked at me and blurted, "We have to talk." He told me some thuggish looking men had stopped by the house looking for me and when he told them I was not there they made it look like they were leaving, but remained outside for a while in their car.

"If you're never going to give me grandchildren, then you're all I've got. I want you safe," he told me with an awkward smile.

I knew what my dad meant. My brothers had found work of their own, moved in with their girlfriends, and begun their own lives. We all loved one another and got along well, but they didn't come around a lot. For some reason my dad and I had stuck together and I truly felt like we were all we had.

It was decided. We would move away—far away. While we waited for two months for Raul to recover, we saved every penny and sold whatever we had that was worth anything. By the time Raul was released from the hospital, we had nothing but three backpacks and the clothes on our backs.

We set our destination for Greeley, Colorado, where my father had some friends. It took us almost four weeks to get there, since Raul was still recovering and couldn't push himself as hard. It didn't matter; we were due for a new, safer life and we would get there—all of us.

My dad's friends turned out to be two very caring men. They and their families helped us find work and allowed us to stay with them until we got on our feet. Eventually Raul and I rented an apartment of our own. My dad lived with us as well, but he worked in the oil fields with his friends, so he was usually gone for three weeks and would return home for one week.

Almost two years have gone by since we arrived. We don't enjoy any luxuries, but life is quiet and safe and that is all we asked for. I work full-time at a car wash and Raul works part-time at a restaurant. Because we left as soon as he was able to walk, his recovery was rushed and had resulted in damage to his back—he can't stand or walk for very long or even lift too much weight. We've recently been to the doctor because of his back pain and because he continues to have nightmares and wakes up screaming in the middle of the night. The doctor prescribed him with some pain medication and recommended therapy and counseling.

We can't afford all of that, but I make sure he at least has his medications. Raul is dependent on me now, and I'm okay with that. He saved my life back in Guatemala when he made me see who I really was.

We can't go back to Guatemala. I've kept in touch with my brothers throughout these two years and they've told me that things have become progressively more violent back there, particularly where homosexual people are involved. It's true. I've read it in the online newspapers; there is always at least one gruesome article about a gay man or woman tortured and killed by gangs or mobs of crazed, drunken men. It doesn't seem to me like a case of being in the wrong place at the wrong time when it happens so regularly. It's dangerous out there, especially for people like me.

One of my brothers also told me that Pedro, one of my gay friends, was murdered a few months after we left. He said that people had found out Pedro was homosexual and apparently one night some drunken men broke into his home and dragged him outside. My brother wouldn't tell me what all they had apparently done to Pedro; he couldn't bring himself to speak of it, but he told me they found him in a landfill dressed in women's clothes.

I don't want to go back to Guatemala. I don't want to take my chances on whether those men will come for me or not. I just can't—I won't. I'd rather cross the border with Raul on my back as many times as I have to. I can't let us die.

I don't even know where I would live if I had to return to Guatemala. I couldn't put my brothers in that kind of danger—I don't even know if they would invite me to live with them. What would I become, a bum on the streets? Considered scum not only for being homosexual but also for not having a place to live? They will kill me. People back home are ignorant and think all homosexual men and women have HIV and that you can become infected simply by touching or being too close. So whenever they get riled up about it enough they go and kill one of us. Whenever—for no good reason. I may have grown up with nothing, but I know my life is worth something. We don't deserve that kind of death. No one does.

• • •

I had hypothesized that Abraham would develop into a beaten, fragile man, but he in fact grew up to be exactly like his father—a "warrior." Although Raul and Abraham's persecution in Guatemala was short-lived, the threats were so real that Abraham's father was well aware that his son and his boyfriend would not be safe there, even in a different city. They ran for their lives as far away as they were able.

I find Abraham to be a very interesting young man. His very nature is caring and kind, yet he has been severely damaged by an entire lifetime of clinical depression stemming from the persecution and fear that it generated. This, compounded by being pushed away by friends and acquaintances back home and nearly losing his partner at the hands of their abusers was enough to send Abraham spiraling down the metaphorical drain.

356

His survivor spirit has been his salvation and his curse. Abraham was only able to soldier on through life because of the strength that his father instilled in him. Yet this very same quality has kept him blinded for years, unable to recognize the devastation within himself and the dire need for healing—particularly when he carried the responsibility to protect and save Raul.

As his attorney told me, Abraham's case was quite difficult and took quite a lot of litigation and continuances. In the end he was allowed to remain in the United States. I felt relieved for him, considering the alternative he would've had to return to. Yet I continued to feel uneasy about what would become of him.

I tried to make him see that it was not only Raul who had a need for help, but also Abraham himself——even though he tried so very hard to keep himself together. As much as I admired their unity, I grew frustrated with their collective blindness about this matter. I have met few people as strong and resilient as Abraham. It seemed to me that if he would only become open to the idea of getting help for himself, the world would open up to him and he would be unstoppable. It is in times like this that I sometimes wish I could force people to avail themselves to supportive therapy; sort of like when a mother forces their kids to eat their vegetables. Unfortunately I can't. I can only hope for the best for this brave young man.

ALEJANDRO

Alejandro is a man with a good heart and a damaged soul. He has been working for the same construction company for the past seven years and puts in twelve-hour shifts, six days a week, in order to provide for his family and save money for his children's college fund.

He is responsible and well-liked by his coworkers and supervisor. I suspected, however, that this was likely due to the fact that Alejandro prefers to keep to himself and turn off his mind through means of physical labor—the perfect employee. It wasn't hard to see that Alejandro had devised different ways to keep the nightmares inside him fenced off, but that the smallest of cracks in his wall would send the waves crashing down on him.

The effects of his inner struggle were staggering. Alejandro looked and carried himself with the exhaustion of an 80-year-old man. His eyes sunken and rimmed by dark circles from poor sleep were only accentuated by his greasy and tousled hair. This was a man on the verge of being taken over by a darkness that had clearly been with him for a long time. I was quite surprised actually, at the massive amount of energy this man put in fighting it back and in maintaining the mask of quiet, diligent calmness that he hid behind daily.

359

My name is Alejandro. I'm 49 years old and I was born in Honduras. My story begins a little different than most Central Americans. My family and I lived in a small city and although we weren't rich we were able to get by. My dad worked as a security guard and my mom had a small tortilla making business. I am the oldest of seven kids, and because my parents were often away working, my younger brothers and sisters were entirely my responsibility.

Most people wouldn't want to live a life like that, but I actually did quite all right. I still got to play like the rest of the kids, I had friends, and my grades in school weren't bad. I had many responsibilities, but life was mostly uneventful around that time. It wasn't until I was 15 years old that I began to see the effects of the war going on around me—it dawned on me all at once.

People were getting beat up on the streets by government soldiers. I knew many of the victims and they hadn't done a thing, but that didn't matter. All they needed was to suspect you had anything to do with the guerrilleros and they would come find you. It was common to watch soldiers knock people onto the floor and trample on their heads. Sadly, it was also common to see dead bodies in the streets. Shock is the best way to describe my initial reaction to all this. I saw all these horrible things happening around me but inside I felt nothing. I felt as if I was asleep; I hoped to be asleep and wake up from that nightmare any minute.

"Death Squads" is what we called them. They were particular groups of soldiers who would go into towns looking for guerrilleros or anyone linked to guerrilleros in order to "eradicate the threat." In my mind though, they were the monsters. They killed students, adults, and sometimes even children, but they weren't satisfied by just that. Death Squads were made of vicious men who liked to make a statement. Sometimes they would leave bodies in the streets, sometimes they would hang them on doors, and sometimes they would cut them into pieces and throw them in the river. Rapes, beatings, and murders were an everyday thing around this time.

It was like in the horror movies when people go to hell and all you see is gore and tortured bodies. It isn't something you can put in words—the effect of regularly seeing mangled, bloody corpses nailed fresh to doors, hearing of your friends gone missing, of their sisters having been raped. No one deserves to live in a reality like that—no one can survive a reality like that for very long. I remember closing my eyes and my fists really tight whenever I saw dead bodies, trying to will myself back to the days before that nightmare began.

I will never forget the day—November 18, 1979. A Death Squad arrived at my neighborhood and surrounded my house. They barged in our house and forced us to lay face down on the floor while they pinned us down with rifle barrels. We knew we were all going to die; there was no question about that. My mom offered them everything in the house for them to let us live, to let us flee. They didn't let us go.

I was pulled to my feet by the hair, beat and then thrown in a bus—they were taking me to an old field that had been repurposed as an execution field. I don't remember how I got away from them once we arrived, but I do remember that I got away and I ran for my life while they fired shots at me. Planes wouldn't have been able to catch up to me—this was every little boy's nightmare come true; the monster coming to eat you alive. I don't know if I ran so fast to save my life or to just escape from them; they inspired the deepest and darkest kind of fear in me. And because I was barely wearing any clothes, the dry bushes around me cut me pretty badly.

I ran for what seemed like miles before I felt that I was out of the Death Squad's reach. I didn't have any money and I didn't know where I was, but I knew I had to flee somehow. I sneaked around in the shadows and looked for any clothes left outside the small huts nearby. I took what I could find and I disguised myself as best as I could, hoping to become invisible.

I was a college student before that night and I wanted nothing to do with the war—it terrified me.

I thought that regardless of the side they were on people always ended up dead. Government soldiers had been pressuring me for some time to join the military and I had so far been able to weasel out that situation, until the Death Squad barged into my home and took me away.

It changed my life and the way I looked at things forever that night. My brothers were killed, my sisters were raped. The same thing happened to my neighbor and his family. It became very clear to me that I wasn't going to be allowed to avoid war any longer, but I wasn't going to bow my head as the ax fell either. I developed such hatred for the government and its soldiers and its Deaths Squads that I decided to join the revolution and fight them. If I died, it was not going to be on the Death Squad's side.

I was young, full of fear and hate. A lot of time went by before I realized what I was doing to myself and the danger in which I was putting the remainder of my family. I had to leave the war, but it was all around me. I left our town and headed northwest without a destination. I became a labor worker; I worked in construction in different cities for however long they had work for me. I lived hand to mouth, without a home, without a plan—I just kept moving. I worked in Guatemala for some time before I continued moving along and made my way to Mexico.

I met Graciela in Mexico. She had been alone for quite some time too, and after we got to know each other, she never left my side. We struggled to survive in Mexico; we were barely able to find any work and couldn't even afford to rent a room for long. We slept in shacks or stayed in shelters, sometimes we struggled to even afford tortillas to eat. There wasn't a raging war across Mexico like there was in my country, but it sure had its very own, crude, violent and brutal reality.

Graciela and I understood that if we wanted any chance to stay alive we were going to have to leave, so we made our way north into the United States and arrived at La Jolla, California. It took us a little while, but Graciela found a kitchen job in a restaurant and I began to work as a carpenter's helper. We lived there for six years and had four kids together; we were finally able to stop running away and have a decent life like other people. We rented an apartment and although we spent a lot of time working, we always found the time to take our kids to the park, cook and eat dinner together... it wasn't anything fancy by anyone's standards, but to us it was like a dream.

I didn't want my children to be robbed of an education and a good future like I was, so Graciela and I decided that when the time came we would put them through college no matter what. With this plan we knew that we needed to work harder, and we decided to move to Colorado in search of better work opportunities so we could start saving money.

Life has been better and we are safer here in the United States. My children can have a good education and grow up in a normal place away from drug lords and Death Squads. Luckily they will never know war and violence the way I did and will never know what it's like to have a twisted mind full of horrible memories like I do.

It has been many years since I left my country, but I am still who I am, a product of war. I've never been able to heal or forget; too many bodies, too many beatings, too many deaths. It made me who I am—I trust no one, I don't really have friends. I spend my time between work and my family and I depend on them to remain stable and not get lost in the bad dreams of my past. I still have nightmares every day; I wake up not knowing where I am, sweating cold. I get panic attacks from time to time for no particular reason; I become paranoid and believe that people are coming to get me, to hurt my family. If Graciela wasn't there to calm me down and I didn't have my children to pull me through this, I would've gotten lost in my own very dark reality. Who knows what would have become of me?

If I had to return to Honduras, my family would disintegrate. My wife couldn't come with me to Honduras because she is Mexican and my children couldn't live in either Mexico or Honduras because they're American—they would have a target on their backs within two weeks of living anywhere in Central America.

The only option would be for my wife and children to remain in the United States for as long as possible, but they wouldn't survive on Graciela's salary and I wouldn't be able to support them from Honduras. Perhaps my oldest son would have to quit school and find work... how could I do that to my son?

I know the war has long been over in my country, but gangs and organized crime have taken its place. It's the same reality under a different name and I'm terrified of what will happen to me if I'm forced back in there. I feel that my mind will snap and I will literally go crazy. I can't even handle thinking of that place, living with a sword dangling over my head... I just can't. I know I have family here but I wouldn't be any good to them in Honduras. All the memories I've worked so hard to shove to the back of my brain would come crashing over me. I know they would kill me, or drive me to kill myself.

. . .

Everyone becomes damaged by war. Some people can bounce back and live a close approximation to a normal life, while others like Alejandro are haunted by these experiences forever. Alejandro was so critically traumatized by the events of his life in Honduras that his symptoms of post-traumatic stress disorder quickly generated into a variety of other debilitating maladies and met the criteria for generalized anxiety disorder and major depression. Additionally, he presented with many features of schizoid personality disorder, something he likely has suffered from since his youth in which it interferes with all desire for any close, interpersonal relationships with others.

If deported, Alejandro would not be in Honduras long before his memories of terror and desperation began to take over and cause him to lose all control of himself and perhaps even his sense of reality. Although this is also a possibility for Alejandro even while living in the United States, this is not the environment in which all the terror from his life occurred. For Alejandro, the United States is in fact the environment in which he first felt safe in his life, and was able to build a family and seek out help.

Alejandro has been receiving intensive outpatient therapy to help him deal with all the trauma of his past. He is also currently heavily medicated with anxiety medication as he cannot cope with the current stress of his legal situation, not to mention his ever-present fear of dying a violent death. Alejandro reminds me of a thin piece of glass that needs very careful handling in order to remain stable and intact. Indeed, although without him even being aware of it, his seeking out help through counseling and medication was likely the one thing that saved his life. Yet I have no doubt in my mind that if any small part of his personal universe was to become destabilized, this man would be lost to us for good.

ANDRES

Andrés worked in a restaurant as a waiter and lived with his boyfriend in a small apartment in the north part of town. He was just 23 years old when we met, but it was apparent that his excessive worrying had aged him well beyond his years. At first I could not understand why Andrés was so visibly and desperately scared, until he told me in a very matter-of-fact way that he was afraid he was going to die.

Andres' curiosity and intelligence shone through his eyes throughout the entire interview process, but his uncontrollable nervous affect had degraded his ability to keep himself composed. By nature, Andres, from Mayan lineage, was stoic and controlled; yet he sat in front of me a mess of nerves, constantly shaking his legs, and biting his while he told me his story.

"I don't want to die," he told me. "I don't want to be burned alive." I couldn't understand who would want to do such thing to this seemingly good-natured young man, and I proceeded to tell him how many times our fears go wild and create stories that go beyond reality. Andrés then proceeded to tell me that people in his native country are quite conservative and that he knew a man who had been burned alive a few years ago simply for being found to be homosexual.

369

The ambience in my office became somewhat tense yet somber after his confession, and I saw that Andrés was beginning to doubt if I would be able to understand his predicament at all. I stared at him for a few seconds to accept his reality, then relaxed and told him, "I understand; there is nothing I haven't heard here in my office. I am not young anymore and I have heard it, seen it, or done it myself. Let's begin."

My name is Andrés, and I am gay. I was born in Mexico City, but moved to the United States when I was five years old. My dad immigrated to the United States many years ahead of us in order to work and send money back to Mexico so we could eat and go to school. I didn't get to see my dad very often—I don't really have any memories of him actually, until my mom, siblings, and I came to live with him in the United States.

We lived in North Carolina for the first two years after our arrival. My dad worked as a gardener and life was rather uneventful. I went to kindergarten and part of first grade while we lived there. My dad then decided to look for better work opportunities and heard that there was a lot of work in Colorado, so we moved to Fort Morgan. Like many immigrants, he found work at a slaughterhouse and kept his job there for many years.

I kept going to school and actually did really well. I learned English quickly and I was a good student; I even took accelerated classes and made the honor roll. I remember being the only Mexican in the accelerated classes in high school; it's funny how little kids notice things like that. I loved every second of it, though. So many smart kids, so many things to learn—I had never been around something like that before. It made my head spin and I began to have dreams of going to college and having a big job someday, and I actually did—I signed up for college after completing high school.

I struggle a great deal to pay for college since I have to pay out-of-state tuition because I'm undocumented, and I don't qualify for financial aid for the same reason. It makes life very complicated and my school progress is so slow; sometimes I can only take one class each semester, but I'm still trying. I'm the only one in my family to even accomplish that much. But at this rate I'll probably never be able to finish. It's so hard to see the other students who I grew up with merrily going along their way in college without any of the same financial issues that I have. It doesn't seem fair. Just because I was born on the wrong side of a line, and came here before I can even remember, somehow that makes me a second-class citizen who isn't supposed to get educated. I guess they want people like me to have to clean bathrooms, or work in the slaughterhouse and cut meat for other people's dinner.

My parents don't work at the slaughterhouse anymore; they now help out at my uncle's grocery store—same thing though. My brother works with livestock; he got married and has a little girl. My little sister lives with her boyfriend and they have a little girl too—she's two years old.

My brother and sister know that I'm gay and even though they accept me, things were never the same between me and my brother after I told him. My sister and I became closer, but my brother keeps me at arm's length. It's a weird kind of sadness to feel rejected by your own brother; even though I went off to college and he didn't, he has been a great dad to his kid and I've always looked up to him. My dad doesn't know I'm gay—he would be livid. We have a distant relationship anyway; we talk but not really about anything meaningful and we don't even look at each other while we talk. It isn't right. He doesn't approve of homosexuality either; he gets so offended when he sees something related to that on television and begins to make outrageous comments as to "what the world is degenerating into!"

My mom knows who I really am; I'm very close with her. She approached me once while I was still in high school and told me, "Your dad thinks you're gay." I told her that my dad was right and she told me I had to change. We both cried; she told me I needed help from a psychologist and to get close to God so I could "fix" my problem. She feared what my dad would think about it and told me she didn't want him to hate me—that told me a lot about my dad… and about my mom. I grew up a few years that day.

My dad's younger brother is gay, but not openly. He lives in Mexico City and has a boyfriend there, secretly. I keep in touch with him through email, especially because he's the only one in my family who I feel really understands me. My mom told me once she has known he was gay for years and told me that people used to make fun of him because his friends were very effeminate, but that he always managed to keep the lid on it. Can it run in the family? I don't know.

I've always felt different than the other boys, but when I was younger I didn't know what "gay" was. Little kids that age don't know much about those things and I remember them treating me the same as the rest. There was nothing out of the ordinary in our eyes, because no one knew any different. I think my teacher knew right away that I was different, though—I was the one little boy who liked to hang around the girls and play their games.

I always felt okay with being different, but the saying is true—kids can be mean. They started teasing me around the time I was in second grade. The Spanish speaking kids were the meanest, and would even try to beat me up—we were seven years old! I felt safer around white kids, so I was usually with them or with girls. I couldn't understand why the Mexican kids hated me so much; whenever they had a chance to hurt me, they would take it in a heartbeat.

The teasing got worse in middle school—kids made me the focus of their practical jokes. I felt like an outsider; I kept telling myself that I had to be strong, and I managed to never give them the satisfaction of seeing that they hurt me. Going to school felt like going into battle all by myself every day; I couldn't even go to the bathroom without someone cracking a joke in the hallway or pushing me against the stalls in the bathroom. I couldn't understand what the big deal was about me not acting like the rest of the boys—it wasn't like I was trying to start a trend. I just wanted to be left alone.

I was never ashamed to be Mexican, but I think Mexican boys were ashamed of me. Hispanic girls didn't seem to have a problem and I was usually friends with a few of them. The problem was that as soon as they got a Hispanic boyfriend they would pull the girls away and I would lose them. In the end, I surrounded myself with white girls, since their white boyfriends tolerated me. Tolerate is a good word; their boyfriends would invite me to their parties and other outings, but I never really felt that they cared about me. I knew I was safest when I was with white girls though, and that is where I tried to spend most of my time.

All of my romantic boyfriends have been white. But I had a friend named Marco who was from a Mexican family like me, and he was gay too. He was born here, so he was lucky and he even got a scholarship to go to college here in Denver. He lived with his older boyfriend in an apartment. One day a girl from our school who was like his best friend was going around crying and telling everyone that Marco killed himself. She was blaming his family and saying that they were always mean to him because he was gay and telling him that he was going to hell and things like that. She gave me and a bunch of other people notes that he wrote before he died. The note he wrote me said, "Stay strong mi amigo. I love you."

My first relationship lasted a whole year—I was 14 years old. I smile when I remember it because I was confused through the entirety of it; I didn't know what I was doing and I wasn't really sure if I liked boys. I began to notice that my interest in boys grew stronger around the time I was in high school, but I still wasn't willing to accept it. Actually, it wasn't until my junior year in high school that I was able to admit to myself that I am gay. After this, I had another boyfriend and our relationship lasted for two years. I am gay, and I have accepted this part of me without shame.

Whenever I go back to Fort Morgan to see my family, people gawk at me because I'm openly gay. I just don't feel the need to hide myself to fit in—I am who I am. All in all I feel safe here in the United States—most people tolerate differences. Even though growing up was really difficult, I am still here and for the most part I'm safe.

375

Because we were brought when we were children rather than being born here, my siblings and I are not legal residents of the United States. It was never much of a problem until I got older and needed to work. I tried to use a fake Social Security Number to get a job some time ago, and I got caught. The police arrested me for forgery and I spent eight days in jail. They put me on probation for two years, but the real problem is that now I may be deported to Mexico.

Living in Mexico to me would be like being thrown back to the days when all the little Mexican kids wanted to beat me up for being different. I know it's not safe for me there. It's still a very conservative place and I've heard and read on the internet that there is regular violence against homosexual people, even hate crimes. I'm not like my uncle; I don't know how he has been able to hide who he is for so long. I know people would be able to tell I'm gay right away—I'm afraid to live there. Even though same-sex marriage is allowed in some places, it only makes people angrier. Living in areas that seem tolerant of gay people only puts gay people in more trouble.

Homosexual people are harassed in Mexico and it's even hard for them to find work. I wonder what they'd do to me since they probably wouldn't even consider me Mexican. Although I speak and read Spanish, I haven't lived in Mexico since I was five years old. Their culture is alien to me, and I would be an outsider for them; I'm not even sure where I could live. My mom's family does not support my sexual orientation, and my dad's grandmother lives in a remote town disconnected from the city.

My uncle gets by in Mexico, but only because people don't know he's gay. I really don't know how he has kept it secret for so long—people like to gossip. He says that life in Mexico is especially hard for homosexual people, and he feels that he has no choice but to hide his true face so he can avoid being targeted. He told me that at the very least he would be fired from his job. He also told me that for his safety and mine I could not stay with him if I had to go back to Mexico. He knows they will figure me out, and he would get thrown in the bag if I lived with him.

My uncle told me that life is hard in Mexico, and it would be easy to for me to become a target there. He told me that he really worries about me going back there and that he is afraid I'd eventually end up dead like his two friends. He told me that one man was kidnapped and beaten to death before he was thrown in a stream and another man was raped with the stick of a broom. Then they bound him in wire, poured gasoline all over him, and lit him on fire. My uncle said that his friends were really nice men who helped the community and didn't have problems with anybody. He also told me that it broke his heart to pretend that he didn't know them so he could keep himself safe. He didn't even go to the funeral. How could he pretend he doesn't know me? I can't put a death sentence on my uncle; where else would I go? I really have no one there.

I'm horrified of the things I've learned about life for people like me in Mexico; I don't want to die like that. I don't even have memories of that place; I grew up here, this is my language, my culture, my home. I just want to live here like I always have and be able to make something of myself regardless of who I like.

. . .

It was obvious to me that Andres' very life was saved by the judge's rule of allowing him to remain in the United States. While it is true that his life would have been in great danger by being forced to return to Mexico (hate crimes had increased by 100% there around the time Andres' evaluation was done), the waiting period of not knowing what would become of him and what could he possibly do if he were not allowed to stay in the US was eating him alive and worsening his anxiety disorder, try as he might to minimize his symptoms.

Andres' life while he was growing up was not easy. He lacked any true support and understanding from his family and spent much of his time isolated from others or engaged in superficial relationships. I believe that although he was greatly damaged by the humiliation he suffered at the hands of others, Andrés was able to maintain a moderate threshold of functioning due to the fact that he was never exposed to any extreme acts of violence due to his sexual preference.

All of this changed however, when he learned about the reality for many homosexual people in Mexico and that he could possibly be forced to relocate there. The intensity of terror and desperation visible in Andrés was only the first sign of the true inner turmoil that had been eating at him with dangerously increasing velocity.

Andrés will likely go back to being a moderately well-functioning individual now that he feels that his life is safe and he can remain in his home. I can only hope that this experience has opened his eyes to the very real damage he carries within him from his life experiences and follows through with my recommendation for seeking counseling. Andrés has very big plans and dreams for his future—I just wish that he soon begins his healing process so he can thoroughly enjoy all the good things coming his way.

BIJAL

Bijal is probably one of the most tender-hearted men I've met in my entire life. A true Sikh gentleman, I could instantly sense that behind his calm and polite exterior he fiercely battled with depression and suffered with a great deal of desperation from his plight.

Bijal had left his country many years ago in order to escape the brutal religious persecution and police corruption that oppressed him and his family. Such was his desperation that he picked up and walked away from his family to come to the United States after his travel agent pointed out to him "that everyone had equal rights there." After years of being subjected to violence and brutality by the police, that's all it took for Bijal to make the decision and jump on the plane, not knowing what would be waiting for him upon arrival here.

Even though his travel agent's promise was true and Bijal has been living a life free of persecution, he continues to have to live in hiding as his tourist visa has expired. Bijal's brave determination throughout these years is something I cannot describe. What I can describe, however, is the great toll that his whole story has taken on him—which is only becoming worse due to his forced separation

*from his family, and the uncertainty of his future in
this country, his safe house.*

My name in Bijal, and I was born in India in the
mid-1950s. I grew up in a Sikh family in a small
village in the Punjab region. My father worked as a
farmer and my mom took care of my four siblings
and me—I am the youngest of them all.

My family loved and cared for one another very
much, and my village was a good place to grow up;
everyone was kind and knew one another. Most of
the people in the Punjab region were of the Sikh
religion, so there was very little conflict among us. I
very clearly remember not knowing what it was to
fear people when I was a child. Those were good
years.

My oldest brother moved to West Bengal in the
mid-70s and my family and I followed a few years
later. My father had recently passed away recently
and as the oldest, my brother took up many of the
family responsibilities. He even tried his best to
guide me like a father would—he and I grew very
close to each other.

Even though the people in West Bengal are
primarily Hindus, they welcomed and respected us
as Sikhs. The people in our religion were
considered a buffer for all the conflict between the
Muslims and the Hindus. Hindi people even saw us

as their protectors and often referred to us as "Sadarji," the word for "leader."

Life changed for us very quickly when Prime Minister Indira Ghandi was assassinated by two bodyguards. The media reported that Sikh separatists instigated the assassination and chaos was given loose reigns. Hindi people rioted and destroyed Sikh property and businesses. Many Sikhs were even killed during this time. This is when I learned to be afraid of people.

I became a target because of my religion. The riot lasted for many days and the police would not do anything about it; several days went by before they even stopped the looting and destruction. I was beat up by a group of Hindus who then set fire to my car and flipped it upside down. It was a horrifying time to be a Sikh, and our persecution lasted for many years.

From being the respected Sadarjis, we Sikhs quickly became close to scum; it only took walking down the street for the Hindus to give us dirty looks and insult us. They even assaulted many of us and tried to take away our identity by forcibly cutting our hair and beards, which is against our religion. It took several years for the direct violence and harassment to stop, but they never gave us back the respect any human being deserves.

My family and I nonetheless lived as best and peacefully as we could, but trouble soon found us again. I used to drive to another town in order to pray at their Sikh temple and on one occasion I found a man on the side of the road who I thought was Sikh. It looked to me like he was stranded, so I decided to give him a ride even though I did not know him.

It was common for the police to stop vehicles for any reason and that day the police pulled us over on our way back to West Bengal. To this day I don't know why the man in my vehicle ran away; he just opened the door and disappeared into the side of the mountain.

I can only imagine how suspicious that must have looked. The people in this area are very poor and the government corrupt. The police assumed I was affiliated with the man who fled and held me for questioning. Then they decided to arrest me; I denied knowing this man and I explained to them that I had picked him up on the side of the road, but they took me away anyway. I didn't know what would happen to me, but I was afraid because I was a Sikh. I had learned long ago that people would hurt me simply for who I am.

They locked me in a cell for two weeks and would hit and kick me constantly. When I couldn't stand up, the police would beat my legs and feet with a stick to where they would swell up and didn't look like legs or feet anymore. They didn't have a reason to keep me in jail, but they weren't planning on releasing me either. My brother had to bribe them so they would let me go. Many days went by before I could leave my home because of my injuries and even more days went by before I could muster enough courage to go outside and face these people again. I could not rest. I felt persecuted and in danger at all times. My dreams came to match my reality as well—I had no peace whether awake or asleep.

We were targeted again not long after that. My brother had started a trucking firm a few years prior to all of this. It was a rather monotonous and uneventful business, but it gave our family some financial stability and this motivated us to keep the business going. Not long after my release from jail, however, someone tipped the police that my brother and I were terrorists disguised as truckers.

The police didn't really investigate the matter. They came to arrest my brother and me for distributing firearms and ammunition to a militant separatist movement that wanted to create a separate Sikh state. It was a lie; we didn't even know those people, but they wouldn't believe us. They tortured me to try to get information; they beat my back and feet so badly that I began to consider making up information just so they would stop. They refused to release me despite the fact that I didn't have any information to give them, and my family had to bribe them again so they would let me go.

I began to feel that this is how the rest of my life was going to be, and I wanted to dunk my head in a bucket of water to wake myself up. We lived a good, honest life, but it made no difference because we were Sikh, and in the corrupt policemen's eyes, we were just as corrupt as they. I told myself that I wouldn't let them crush my spirit and I found it in myself to get out there every day and do my job, yet deep inside I couldn't help but compare myself to one of those alley dogs that people harass and beat.

It was spring of the following year when my brother decided to run for one of the main positions in the trucking union, even though he would be running against two Hindu candidates. I loved my brother very much and I supported his decision—I even became involved in his campaign and did whatever I could to help him. I wanted to see him succeed. The police, however, thought that it was all very suspicious and decided to bring me in for questioning. I was held in a cell for two days and I was beat and tortured for information once again. I knew nothing! We weren't doing anything! We weren't even associated with any activists out there. I never thought I would break from desperation and frustration and I almost did. To add to my shame, my family had to bribe the police once again so I could be released.

I found later that my brother had also been arrested and was still being held. After his release he had to spend two months in the hospital and became mentally disturbed. They ruined his life.

We didn't even get a chance to speak to him and find out what had happened—he vanished as soon as he was released from the hospital. To this day we don't know where he is or if he is dead or alive. He was like a father to me—look at what they did to him, and thereby to our whole family.

Our family continued to be harassed for our religious beliefs and political opinions on a regular basis. Without my brother, I lost any purpose for living in West Bengal, and I had also grown tired and afraid for our safety. My family and I tried to escape persecution by moving to different jurisdictions, but the authorities would be informed no matter where we moved and it wasn't long before they would begin to oppress us. No matter where we lived the police would constantly show up at our house or at my work, always questioning, always accusing and always trying to take me in for questioning—for torture. They were set on their belief that I was part of the separatist movement and no matter how many years went by and how many times I told them I didn't know anything, even when they had beaten me raw, they would not believe me.

I decided to move my family to Punjab, away from West Bengal and its corrupt jurisdictions. I heard that the police raided the truckers and took some of them in for questioning. They then told the police that I had moved away to Punjab with my family. I thought I would be safe in Punjab, the former land of the Sikh people, but I wasn't. The police arrested me again and accused me of violent acts towards the creation of the separatist Sikh state. My heart sank to my feet; I could not escape, no matter where I went.

The Punjab police beat me with sticks and punched and slapped me. The torture was far worse than in West Bengal. They pulled me by the hair to the interrogation site where they questioned me about militants hiding in West Bengal. This went on for three days before they accepted my family's bribe of 25,000 Rupees to free me from jail. The police told me to inform them if I travelled anywhere, and warned me that they would arrest me again for any transgression. As much as I had lived a good, honest life, I wanted to crawl out of my skin and become someone else. I don't know why they were fixated on me and my family; they had already driven my brother mad and into hiding. The rest of us just wanted to cut our losses, patch ourselves up and be allowed to live, but no matter where we went, they would not even allow us that.

A few months later the police came to my house looking for me. When they couldn't find me they threatened my wife and tried to scare her into telling them where I was. That was the last straw for me; I couldn't let them put their hands on my wife and children—it was the last thing I had for them to take away from me, and I wasn't going to let them harm my family. I decided to stay away from our home after that thinking that if they were keeping an eye out for my whereabouts they would see that I wasn't going home and they would leave my family alone. I hid on a farm not too far away and would go visit my wife late at night, when I could hide in the shadows and between the huts. It was a difficult arrangement and it didn't make things any better. In the end I had to say goodbye to my family and stopped going to the house altogether so I could keep them safe. I had nothing left, and my heart was ripped to shreds.

I came to the conclusion that the only way to escape persecution was to leave India. It was the least I could do for my family. I travelled to Delhi and met with a travel agent who told me that I would be safe in the United States and have the same rights as everyone else. Honestly, I didn't have a preference—I just needed this persecution to end once and for all. I arrived in Chicago and stayed with a nephew for a while. I then moved to Denver, because someone from the same village as me lived there and told me he could help me find work. It was true; I began working in an Indian restaurant. Nine years later I continue to work there and I've even been offered a partnership.

It was difficult to adjust to a life without having to look over my shoulder and anticipating danger. I didn't know how at first—it had been years since I walked down the street alongside people different than me without anticipating some form of danger. What a wild feeling! Years went by without entanglements with the law, without imprisonment or torture. Years. Years with my life intact, but without my family as well.

I saved every penny for several years and I was able to buy a house. I want my wife and daughters to come to the United States and live with me. I want my family together, and to provide them with the safety and opportunities we don't have in India. I miss them—there isn't one day I don't feel my heart ripped to shreds for not being able to be with them, for not knowing if I will ever be able to see them again, but I work hard to support them and I try my best to hold onto hope.

The police continue to harass my family about my whereabouts, so I limit my contact with them in my attempts to keep them safe. They've had to bribe the police in order to stop the harassment. I can't speak to anyone back home because I'm afraid that they will be pressured into telling the police where I am; then they would just demand more money to leave my family alone. Things haven't changed and they haven't forgotten about me. I can't go back to India and put my family in danger.

I don't know if other individuals have been persecuted the way I was. Sikhs are a persecuted minority in India. Some Sikhs have been beaten, burned, or stoned to death. Sikh children used to be thrown off high rise buildings. If I go back to Punjab, I believe the police will beat me to death this time in their efforts to get answers. My wife tells me I am still wanted by the police, and I am sure they will arrest me and torture me as soon as they are able to do so. Or they would kill me in a fake encounter and be done with it. The corrupt police officers of India are most at fault for my problems; it is a vicious circle—we have to bribe them to stop harassing us, and they continue to harass and terrify us so we keep giving them money. It will never end.

I would like to continue living in Denver, but I worry about my family. Even though I cook food at work, I never eat much—I have no appetite. I hurt because my family is not with me. If I had three wishes every one of them would be to be with my family here in the US. Even though we are far apart, my wife and I are still happy together. We are one, and if asked, we would marry each other again. My daughters are wonderful, smart, strong women and all they want, despite the fact that they are already adults, is that the family be reunited.

It has been one week since my final court date. The judge decided that I could not stay in the United States because there wasn't enough evidence of my persecution and the possible danger for me if I were to return to India. My attorney says he will appeal the decision and advised me to keep fighting it, but I'm not really sure I want to do that. I'm just so tired.

The United States is a wonderful country; I feel so safe here and have so many opportunities… my family would have so many opportunities. I can't go back to live in India, but I can't keep living away from them anymore—I am missing my daughters' lives, my elderly years with my wife. I need my family. I know I will die if I go back to India, but I cannot remain here any longer without them. In London I have friends from my village and they have been able to stay there legally and bring their families. I think I will now just sell my house and forget everything I worked for here. It's time.

. . .

Sadly for Bijal, his legal case was presented in front of "The Hanging Judge," as he is known by the local immigration attorneys. I was nonetheless surprised that a man with Bijal's history of trauma and persecution was required to return to his home country. This was particularly troubling to me considering the heightened level of psychological distress that he suffered upon evaluation. Bijal never even had a speeding ticket while living in the United States, and had actually been under consistent anti-depressant treatment as prescribed by his physician. I reviewed every single one of his medical records.

I don't know what will become of Bijal, but part of me thinks he made the right choice in trying to reunite with his family elsewhere. Even though I am aware that starting over his legal case could take months or even years, Bijal no longer had the strength to prolong matters and continue to fight his case here—I would've been afraid for his sanity if he had chosen to stay. His unwavering faith is likely the one thing that kept him from becoming severely mentally ill and non-functional while he lived in India. It surely was what kept him sane while living in the United States for nine years away from his family. I can only hope he can be safely reunited with his family soon; it will be the one thing to heal him.

DARIO

The very first thing apparent about Dario was just how quiet he was—I almost didn't notice him at all sitting in the waiting room. I couldn't even get a good look at his face as his baseball hat covered it almost completely while he stared at the floor.

"Dario?" I called as I beckoned him into my office. As if ejected by a spring-loaded seat, Dario jumped out of his chair, his expression bewildered, eyes wide open. I had clearly caught him in mid-thought, or as is often the case here, in mid-memory.

Dario walked into my office appearing a bit uneasily. He kept his arms close to his body and his hands in his pockets. He took a seat in the chair across from me and gave a half-smile. I tried to make small talk in order to put him at ease, but it was difficult. It's not that he was visibly frightened or nervous, but more that he seemed spaced out. He looked to be lost in his own mind and was becoming increasingly tense and shut-down.

While asking him about his life, I learned that he and his siblings lived in a small rented house in Kansas. He told me how he and five brothers and sisters live in a three bedroom rented home where his sisters work in housekeeping and his brothers have jobs in a milk factory alongside Dario. "Some people see it as the bottom of the chain, but we see opportunity," he told me. I instantly felt respect for him.

I noticed that as Dario spoke of his family and his life, he constantly touched the same side of his head. He wouldn't stop—he never switched to the other side either. I began to suspect there was a reason for the baseball cap he was wearing.

I interrupted him in mid-sentence and asked him, "Dario, what's under your baseball cap?" He looked at me almost pleadingly, as if I was about to open a great big can of worms. Slowly and somewhat reluctantly, he took off his hat to reveal a long, thick scar across the side of his head.

I looked at it for a silent moment, then sighed and nodded to myself. "I think it's time we get to work," I told him.

My name is Dario. I'm 35 years old and I was born in a small town in the province of Yoro, Honduras. As with any small town in a Third-World country, most of the people worked in the fields, including my dad. My mom took care of the house and all ten of us. She was a strong woman; she had to be—she had to keep us all in line.

I lived much of my young years unaware of everything that was happening around me. I often heard my parents walk about the house nervously or discuss things happening around us, but the severity of these events never sank into me. There was a war going on around me and I had no idea. My older brothers were well aware of it; apparently I was the only one with the problem. While they were planning their time and route to get water in the morning, I was pestering them to go play ball outside.

My awareness grew as I became older. There was really no way to escape the reality around me; everything was very much in your face—gangs, beatings, even murder.

I remember the very first time I felt scared. I was seven years old and I had sneaked out of my house to go buy candy with a few coins I had found. I wish I could explain why I thought it would be okay to go out for a half-mile walk on my own, but I can't. I was aware that the streets were dangerous, but that knowledge never fully sank into my brain—it seems like nothing ever did.

I wasn't far from the store when I saw a group of young men beating a man near a dumpster. The man was screaming, but no one would come help him, not even me. Transfixed and terrified by the scene, all I could manage to do was hide behind the dumpsters across the street. They stood in a circle and ripped off the man's clothes as they pushed him from one gang member to another, pummeling him. They then looked through his pockets and, being unhappy with what little money they found, one man hit the poor guy on the head with the back of a gun, and then another kicked him in the ribs while he lay on the ground. Then they peed on him and one of the gang members even tried to light the guy's clothes on fire. When they grew bored of him they left him immobile where he lay.

As they made their way down the street one of them noticed me staring. He told his three other friends and they all began to walk in my direction. I panicked. I thought I'd have the same fate as the guy I thought they had just killed.

Buying candy seemed the most stupid, childish idea at that moment. I ran. I ran with every bit of strength that I had and I cut in and out of streets in the hopes to confuse them and lose them. I must've run three times the distance from my house to the store and I aged a year in every step. Reality had never hit me so quickly.

I never left my home alone again. Not for a single thing. My mom and her beatings could not make me go out of the house alone for anything. Nothing was worth my life—that became clear to me on that day.

I began to help my mom sell meat in the market after I finished fifth grade. It was terrifying, but we had to try and make a living. We were robbed by gangs about twice a week without fail; my mom was too afraid they would hurt her or take me away, so she never put up a fight. I think that's why they kept coming to take from us, but really, no one could have fought them and won.

It was years of this—years. In the end, the anticipation of these savages coming to jump us at any moment took a toll on me. I gave up—I couldn't see the point of feeling deathly afraid every day working at the market when in the end we barely ever had enough left over to even buy eggs. I resolved to travel to the United States like many others in order to support my mom and siblings. My dad couldn't support us on his own—we were just too many.

I tried but couldn't come up with the money to cover the trip and the cost of hiring a coyote, so I had to stay put in Honduras. I decided to join the military instead; I thought I could do something more positive with my life—perhaps even keep my family safe.

Boot camp was fast and rather brutal, but it was nothing compared to what I saw on the streets once they put me to work. If I finally realized the world was a dangerous place that day on my way to the candy store, it was during my years with the military that I truly witnessed the ravages of the war raging all around us, all the time.

I was in the military for ten years and travelled all over the country and took part in different missions. War was everywhere and it hit every single place with all its might. If towns weren't

399

plagued by guerrillas, they were plagued by gangsters who treated people like disposable bags. So much violence… so much death. I had no choice but to become numb to it all, otherwise I wouldn't have made it through. I know now that all the brutality, all the fights and shootouts and bombs did take a toll and even killed part of me—I just wasn't aware of it at the time.

It was too much. I was lucky to come out of those ten years alive. When I did, I returned to my parent's town and I decided to open a little convenience store as a way to help my parents not to have to work so hard, and also afford to have a life of my own as well.

I never forgot the incident from when I was a child, even though I had seen far worse horrors during my time with the military. That memory has chased me every single year of my life and I remember it as if it were yesterday. It was for this reason that I was reluctant to open the store in the busier neighboring town, but my parents convinced me that it would be best for my investment to do so.

Before I had the store open for even a month I began to regret having followed my parents' advice. Bigger, busier towns were even more brutally violent. As I stood behind the little counter on my store I saw people being chased, beaten, robbed, women assaulted and dragged away to some awful fate. It was like having the television permanently dialed into the horror channel. I tried to tune it out

like I had in the military, but there had been too
many years of it. I couldn't take it anymore.

When the drug traffickers moved into this part of
the country, things went wild. Every day there were
bullets, screams, and dead bodies on the streets—
the drug traffickers fought whatever gangs didn't
join in their ranks and both sides were merciless
with each other. I guess someone had to pay for
their war, so both sides began to walk into local
businesses and demand protection money. We had
to pay both the drug traffickers and the gangsters,
even if we had not made any money that day.
Refusals or "bravery" were met by beatings, and
many times, death. I was ex-military (though no one
knew), but I couldn't stand up to these men
anymore. I was too afraid, too scarred, and too
ripped to pieces emotionally from fighting them and
seeing what they were capable of for so many years.

Every other day they would come in asking for
money and each time I would hand it to them. Then
my mom fell ill with a tumor on her hip, which then
resulted in complications and she remained in the
hospital for a long time.

My brothers were barely making any money, but
we all contributed to our mom's treatment as much
as we could. The doctor put it in simple words for
us, "She needs her medicines or she will die." I
couldn't let my mom die.

But I had no other way of helping her either. Those drug lord gangster bastards were taking whatever little money I made. They watched the stores to assess their traffic so they could come hit you after they thought you had made some money. Every time I handed them their money I thought of my mom in her hospital bed and I went a little madder.

One day, a small group of these thugs came into my store. I couldn't stand them; they were nothing but scum, yet they behaved as if they were the lords of the town. They walked in as if they owned my place and demanded that I give them their share for the day. I guess it was a wrong-day and wrong-time kind of thing; not only did I refuse to give them money—I also beat them for all they were worth. I just didn't realize what I was doing and I definitely wasn't thinking of any possible consequences. I was just so sick of them taking my money even while my mom was on her deathbed, when sometimes I barely had enough to eat myself.

I took the money that was still in my hand and ran. I ran away with "their" money and I didn't stop until I got to the hospital. It wasn't much, but it was the most I had been able to give my mom in a long time. I didn't know what would happen next, but in that moment everything was good.

I would prefer to say that the gangsters became afraid of me and left me alone until the end of my days, but of course they retaliated—and more than once. There was no safe time of the day for me; they would come get me wherever they happened to find me. One time I went to buy supplies for the store early in the morning and they saw me; they followed me for a few blocks silently. No insults, no threats—then one of them approached me and shot me in the head.

I was sent to the hospital and luckily, they were able to take the bullet out of my skull. I was alive, but my recovery took months. I regained the mobility I had lost on the left side of my body, but my memory was gone forever.

I still was able to remember bits of my life. I remembered everyone in my family very clearly; some things from my childhood, some parts from my years in the military, and I had scattered memories of my life after I was released from duty. But none of it made sense, and I struggled to connect whatever information I still remembered about my life. I still struggle to this day.

The one thing that never left me and in fact became worse was the fear. I returned to the store once I fully recovered and I tried to keep running my business, but I couldn't do it alone anymore. I needed help remembering things and handling the more involved physical tasks. I had survived a shot in the head, but somehow I felt defeated.

The gangs began to make their appearance again not long after I re-opened the store. They continued to demand "protection money," and oftentimes just stopped by to threaten me for sport. It was a hellish life. I tried to make it work; I wanted to be tougher than them, but I couldn't do it. Every day that went by I felt a little closer to death; they had shot me once, why not again? These guys shot alley cats for fun. I had to leave. I knew I had to leave if I wanted to stay alive.

I moved to the United States with two of my brothers. We lived in New Mexico for a while and then made our way to Kansas where we found work in a milk plant. We don't have a luxurious life, but it's peaceful. We are saving money in the hopes of bringing our whole family here before our parents get much older. We have been able to bring three of my sisters thus far. They say things are getting very dangerous in Honduras, so we are working as much as possible to save money fast and bring everyone to safety. I just hope we are not too late.

Even though I've had a peaceful life in the United States, I've never been able to get over my life in Honduras. I know I don't remember over half of it, but the fear and the terror never went away. Sometimes I wake up screaming in the middle of the night and I don't know why. I don't even know where I am at times like that. I'm always nervous, jumping at any sound, getting caught in my head and losing any sense of what's happening around me. That shot in my head made me forget a lot of things, but the entirety of the damage is still very much present in me.

We can't go back to Honduras. It would be dangerous for my brothers and sisters, and it would be certain death for me. The gangs already have it in for me. It would be icing on the cake for them to know I came back from the United States–they'll assume I have money and they will come for it. What will they do to me when they find out I don't have any money?

. . .

I'm not sure if Dario's brothers and sisters would survive a return to Honduras, but I know Dario certainly could not. He had already lost a great deal of his capacity to deal with his environment during the time that he still lived there. In fact, I believe he would have spiraled into a nervous breakdown had he remained in that environment much longer.

Dario is a special man. Not only does his trauma stem from witnessing the effects of war (as is the case for so many people from that place), but he was also directly involved with it during his time in the military. To make matters worse, he was later specifically targeted by criminal organizations that were just as violent and ruthless as the groups he fought against while in the army.

The damage caused by his post-traumatic stress disorder is astounding. During the day he lives in a permanent state of hyper-vigilance, programmed by his circumstances to expect someone to harm him. At night he is not even able to recover from the stress of the day, as his memories regularly bring about nightmares from which he wakes up screaming, unaware that he is in his own bed, in a safe place.

I believe Dario would have died had he stayed in Honduras. It was only sheer luck that he didn't suffer more a more extreme form of traumatic brain injury from that shot in the head. Knowing the patterns of criminal types, it would have only been a matter of time before they made another attempt on his life. Whether they succeeded or not in killing him, the damage to his mental and emotional well-being would have been terminal.

Dario's past is not one that can be healed with a few months of counseling, perhaps not even a few years, if ever. Even though he now resides in the United States and he is no longer at the mercy of criminal individuals, he is very much at the mercy of his own mind as the result of a lifetime of severe trauma. Dario simply cannot tolerate going through life in this manner; he will simply run out of whatever little mettle he has left in him and spiral down into a state of deterioration, and even more complex mental disorders.

In speaking to Dario's attorney, I learned that his case went well and he was allowed to remain in the United States as a legal resident. I can only imagine what kind of relief that must have felt for *someone like Dario, yet as is the case for so many others, this is only the beginning of a new journey for him. I can only hope that he follows my advice and sees the importance of seeking treatment for his trauma. For someone with such demonstrable strength and character, it would open up the world to him. Certainly lesser men have succumbed and perished as the result of similar forms of trauma and abuse.*

ESTEBAN

Esteban was the kind of guy that the mere sight of would intimidate anyone. He was of average height, but of solid build with big, wide shoulders. His eyes were dark and squinty and his forehead bore the marks of years of frowning. His bushy, oversized mustache only added to the overall severity of his look.

To my surprise, Esteban turned out to have one of the most gentle and agreeable personalities I've ever encountered. He was pleasant, polite... and suspiciously acquiescent.

It wasn't his good nature that I doubted; it was the fear that I sensed underlying most of his actions in my office that day, and his personal history. Esteban displayed what appeared to be a near-phobia about upsetting anyone or getting on their wrong side—I just couldn't figure out why. While I could understand that one's nature is typically to avoid conflict, Esteban's exceedingly submissive disposition almost made me feel sad for him. I desperately wanted to know what had beaten this man down to nearly his breaking point.

As have countless others in the past, Esteban sat down in the chair across from me to begin the interview process. We stared at one another as a

*silent moment went by. I could tell from his
presentation and disposition that he was an
inherently good person, and yet hanging right over
that persona appeared to be a dense, dark cloud of
anxiety, fear, and what I suspected to be a deep
depression.*

"Tell me about your life in Mexico," I told him.

*That was the trigger. Esteban began to shake
and cover his head with the palms of his hands,
shaking his head "no," probably without even
realizing it. "My life in Mexico is done," he told
me, tears rolling down his cheeks as he looked
away. "If I go back I die and then they'll go after
my family. If I stay here..." he began to weep.*

*"If you stay here, what?" I asked, growing more
concerned as the clock ticked.*

*"They'll just reverse the order," he told me. My
mouth fell open for a moment.*

My name is Esteban. I was part of the 52nd
Battalion of the Mexican Army for eight years. I
served in many parts of Mexico and was part of one
of the units on the front lines against the Zapatista
Liberation Army (ELZ.) We fought against the
Zapatistas day in and out amidst showers of bullets
and cocktail bombs. Our goal was to prevent them
from abusing and subjugating the citizens, as well

as keeping their movement under control, and eventually eradicate them.

After my time in the army there really wasn't anything for us to do. The police didn't have enough spots to accept all of us and we suddenly found ourselves without the means to earn a living. Many of the men who retired with me banded themselves together to form a cartel called The Zetas. Our fight was done, but they were still hungry for control and power. They went around recruiting as many of my army brothers as they could with promises of money and power. Eventually they made their way to me, but I refused to join them. I didn't want to become a variation of the very thing I spent the last eight years fighting.

I feared, however, just what my choice actually meant. The Zetas had just recently formed, but they were already quite strong and organized. Part of the key to their power was the secrecy of their identities—no one knew who The Zetas were—and they intended to keep it that way. Copycats rose from time to time claiming to be Zetas, but it would turn out to be false. I don't think it was orchestrated by them, but it worked in their favor nonetheless—more mystery around their identities and whereabouts.

The Zetas then, as you can imagine, were very particular about picking their members, and once this happened there were only two possible outcomes; they would either walk away with a new member, or leave a man dead on the streets.

I was slightly luckier. It seemed like they really wanted me to join them, since they didn't kill me on the spot or shortly thereafter. Yet they continued to pressure me and the more I refused the more aggressive they became. They must have felt secure that I knew better than to reveal their identities. But even if I kept my mouth shut, I still feared what would become of me and my family. The Zetas were quickly becoming as corrupt and violent as any of the major drug lords and cartels around Mexico. They followed my family around town and would pop out unexpectedly to meet me whenever I was out alone. They roughed me up a few times and advised me to choose wisely. If I wasn't with them, they said they would consider that I was against them—and that I would pay for it.

My oldest brother worked in the Special Operations unit for the military around this time and had first-hand experience fighting the Zetas and other drug trafficking cartels. His life was constantly in danger, but he was too committed to the cause to simply "up and leave." He often said that he'd rather it be him in danger than anyone else in the family. He knew The Zetas were after me and he was well aware of the macabre endings of similar stories—he had witnessed them in person.

He told me to flee. My own brother, a fighter like me, told me to run for my life. Our last

412

conversation still burns in my mind. He told me, "If they want you, they will get you—dead or alive," and he was right.

I knew it well. These men had been trained the same way as I had back in our military days. Hell, many of us were part of the same unit at one point, and we were ruthless. We had to be. We knew nothing except to accomplish our mission—no fear, no regret. We were trained to shut down all emotion and become machine-like in order to survive and win the fight. The Zetas took all that training and even took it a step further—they shut down all emotion, any sense of a conscience, all of the time. All basic human qualities were gone from them, really. They had not so much become machine-like, but animal-like, and anything that stood in their way quickly became a casualty.

I fled. For my sake and my family's sake, I had to leave. I've been living in the United States for the past six years and I haven't been able to go back to Mexico, even to visit my family. My brother told me that his unit had a run-in with some Zetas and as they fled they yelled at him to advise me to never return to Mexico—or I'd be put in a body bag as soon as I arrived. I don't remember the last time I cried before that night. I would not be able to see my family or have a normal life again. Even worse, The Zetas knew I had left and they knew my family was aware of my whereabouts. Nothing could be done that was ever going to keep them safe.

I initially thought I could hide in the United States for a few years and then resume my life in Mexico with my family. Knowing that I could never return to my home shattered something inside of me, because not only was I not able to see my family—I couldn't even speak to them often either. The Zetas had zeroed in on me and mine and kept an eye on our comings and goings. My brother then told me that most of the family phones had been tapped and that it would be safer for everyone if I called sparingly, and even then, only to contact him directly.

I know it's been six years, but they haven't stopped harassing us. My youngest brother was killed about two years ago. Apparently he had been working on someone's roof and was later found on the ground, dead. It first looked as if he had slipped and fell, except he had bruises on his face and his jaw was broken as if it had been kicked sideways. Someone was up there with him, but the police won't investigate any further because of the potential repercussions. The Zetas have no issues going after anyone at all, and of course, they have people everywhere.

My own wife and three children have to constantly move around in the hopes to remain under the radar. I thought when I left that The Zetas would have no reason to target them anymore, but I was wrong. Now there's no safe way to bring them here, since I don't know if the coyotes will sell them out to The Zetas. Back home we all know that a coyote will do anything for the right amount of money… or with the right amount of persuasion.

I haven't heard my mom's voice even once since I left Mexico. I speak to my wife and children about twice a month and with my brother a little more frequently. As much as my heart yearns to hear my family's voices and speak to them, they are already in enough danger simply because The Zetas want me. The least I can do is keep them safe by severing all contact with them.

I know I'm a big guy and I look mean and I was part of this special unit in the military, but I am terrified of going back to Mexico. They're after me and my family. Every time I speak to my brother he tries to downplay the situation, but then tells me over and over to not return to Mexico. "Esteban, you can't come back here—they will kill you." I think they've killed me already.

I don't know if I could even work in Mexico with the big X The Zetas have put on my back; I understand, who would hire me and put their families in danger? I doubt the military would even take me back—I'd jeopardize their operations. I'd have no money and no job; instead of helping my family, I'd be putting them further in danger and then becoming a burden to them. I'm supposed to protect them—I can't go back.

The threat of The Zetas is still very much alive for us. My nephew was kidnapped only two weeks ago and his whereabouts are unknown. People saw two men take my nephew and throw him in their truck with a hood over his head. No one has seen him since then. The kidnappers haven't even attempted to contact any of us for money or to give us a message. He could be dead by now, we don't know.

There is nothing I can do for them here and it drives me crazy. Not only that, but my brother told me we could no longer speak over the phone because someone is listening in on the conversations. He said that the family is being followed by people who seem to know where to find them and when. He also told me that there have been strange men watching my nephew's home and are following the visitors around town. We don't know what to expect next; if they'll take someone else or if they'll begin to attack my family to scare them—to keep us isolated, to make them pay for not giving me up, for being on the side opposite to theirs.

I can't sleep. I've been away from The Zetas for six years and I live every day as if they are right behind me, about to jump out of any corner. The anguish of the impending danger on my family has been driving me positively insane and I can't keep it together anymore. As mean as I look, I break down and cry all the time; my thoughts become too much to handle.

Ex-soldiers who aren't part of one cartel or another don't last long in Mexico. Those animals come for you and your family along with anything you ever cared about, and they shred it all to pieces. I don't know what to do. I don't know how to keep my family safe. I don't know if I should stay in the United States and protect them with my absence or return to Mexico and fight to protect them—fight to my certain death.

. . .

Esteban. The man who ran away to fight another day. While I do believe that he has been greatly traumatized by his years fighting for the Army, I am certain that it is his present, helpless situation that has taken a toll on him, demolishing whatever little resilience and well-being was left in him.

Esteban was programmed to be a fighter, a protector. After fighting for so many years defending the people in his country, it was simply unconceivable to him to entertain the idea of fleeing, however dangerous his situation may be. But when he was made aware this was the only way in which he could save his family, Esteban knew he had no choice but to leave them—"it was his duty to them." To his ongoing horror however, his family was targeted anyway and persecuted—only now he was not there to defend them.

The anxiety, worry, and sheer terror that Esteban presently feels is nearly unbearable for

417

him. He is trapped in his own mind, worrying about his family and their fate to such a degree that he no longer eats much and rarely sleeps. Consequently, as he puts it, he "has gone mad." He is mentally unfit to deal with everyday life on his own. He has lost all ability to focus on anything other than his family and their precarious situation; it is almost as if he has lost touch with reality, his mind checked out from the present moment to be with his loved ones in Mexico.

This situation has been slowly but savagely eating away at Esteban and his personality structure. For him, the stress of dealing with his current family situation is possibly worse than his time fighting in the army. As Esteban explains it, at least during his service in the military, it was his own life on the line and fully in his hands. Having his family targeted by The Zetas and him being so far away and unable to protect them has been the proverbial straw on the camel's back.

His attorney informed me that Esteban was allowed to remain in the United States and become a legal resident. There was tangible, resonant proof of the imminent threat to his life if he was forced to return to Mexico and he was granted asylum. Although I feel relieved that Esteban was not sent to his sure death, part of me continues to feel concerned about his current psychological state. He still does not have his family with him and they remain under threat. Hopefully he can soon reunite with them here in the United States where they would all be safe. In the meantime, I can only hope that Esteban follows my advice and he gets a hold of professional help before it's too late.

LEON

Leon approached my office hesitantly. He stood in the doorframe for a few seconds looking around my office, weighing his decision to go through with the evaluation. He caught my eye briefly before turning his stare to the floor, absentmindedly smiling to himself. "I don't know if I can do this," he mumbled. "What if it all goes wrong and I'm sent back?"

"What if it doesn't?" I asked him. "Great things require an act of faith sometimes. Anything can go south at any moment; you can go home and resign to the outcome of what you fear, or you can step through this door and give yourself a 50/50 chance."

Whatever it was that Leon connected to at that instant apparently struck a chord with him and he seemed to have a sudden change of affect. He looked up at me, nodded in agreement, and sighed as he walked through the door and sat down.

At 33-years-old, Leon had visibly gone through more than anyone I've ever met. His tall and lean exterior was marked by physical scars. One particularly deep scar that ran across his forehead caught my attention; it looked like the kind of would one would've spent hours getting stitches in the

*emergency room, yet somehow I doubted this had
been the case. Leon raised his hand to feel his
forehead as he said, "I got hit with the butt of a rifle
a while back." I nodded in understanding, my
imagination running wild wondering what could
have precipitated such an event to have happened to
this pleasant young man.*

*Leon remained quiet for a brief moment before
quickly apologizing and explaining that he was
tired—he had been working long hours at a
warehouse. I smiled at him and offered him a cup of
coffee; I knew that whatever Leon had gone through
in his past made the long hours at a warehouse
seem like a walk in the park by comparison. I knew
that he wasn't that tired—that rather, I felt as if he
was gathering his last bits of courage and resolve to
reveal to me the details of his horrific story. He
appeared to be readying himself to stand up and
fight one last time.*

My name is Leon. I was born in Tanzania, but
my family moved to Rwanda right after I was born.
I'm of Rwandese nationality and I grew up as part
of the Hutu Tribe.

I don't remember anything particularly bad
about my childhood. My parents and grandparents
were healthy people; they took good care of me and
I had a good relationship with all of them. Other
kids weren't as lucky; I remember the angry,
drunken dads of some of my friends, and I
remember the couple of kids who always showed up

with bruises on their faces. In comparison, my childhood was by all accounts unremarkable, but to me it was magical. I used to play that I was a king who lived in a fortress where no monster in the world could come hurt me. "My guards" (my parents and grandparents) made sure of that.

My parents sent me to elementary school and high school. I wasn't always the most well-behaved kid, but I meant well. I loved being in a classroom with so many other children, having books and pens and notepads... I was bursting at the seams with excitement. I didn't have the best disposition for sitting still and learning at first, but I caught up quickly. So much so, that after graduating high school my parents sent me to a boarding academy in order to prepare for college.

I met my wife Urimana while I was in college, and we married shortly before I graduated. Her name means "daughter of God," and just like God, she has been good to me. We had a quiet, happy life together and unlike most marriages in our culture, we took our time spending several years together before we decided to have children. Anyone could've looked at our life together and found hardly anything remarkable about it, but to me it was perfect. We lived in a world of our own in peace, away from the rest of the people and their violent ways. We smiled often, we understood one another—when we were home we felt safe. Eventually we even had two children, a boy and a girl—twins.

After I graduated from the National University with a degree in finance, I went to work as a professor for a private university. I worked there for several years before I switched to a different school where I taught economics until I fled Rwanda in 2005.

The problems between Hutus and Tutsis in Rwanda began when it was first colonized by Belgium. Most of the people who lived in the Kingdom of Rwanda were Tutsi back then. Belgium supported the Tutsi monarchy and the conquest of independent groups on the outskirt kingdoms, which were mostly Hutu. The Tutsi were an ethnic minority, but they had political control with the help of Belgium.

After World War II, many European colonies in Africa sought independence, and a revolution in 1959 gave Rwanda independence from Belgium. The majority (which was Hutu population) elected a Hutu as president in 1962. At this time, many Tutsi fled the country and went to Uganda. The Tutsi became organized and elected their own president in Uganda, and Uganda waged a war against Rwanda in 1990. The war ended in 1994, when the Hutu Rwandese president was assassinated.

All of this happened around me; I graduated college the year our president was assassinated. Up to that point, life was tense, but I had always been able to find a way to escape the feeling of impending danger and remain serene, peaceful… strong. Although the reactions to the assassination of the president felt somewhat far away from us, the changes that they triggered soon came to find us all and change our lives for good.

Hutus loyal to the president blamed the Tutsi and began killing Tutsi people. The genocide of the Tutsi people continued for months. When the Tutsi gained control over the Rwanda government, they brought with them a sentiment of revenge. Any opposition to their regime was conveniently linked to the Tutsi genocide and met with crushing retaliation. It was easy to find yourself standing on the wrong side of the tracks in those days, which made being outside the four walls of my home a very dangerous and volatile situation.

Many Hutu fled to other African countries, but they eventually came back to Rwanda. Even though Rwanda became a democracy in 2003, the government tried to put many people in jail, accusing them without proof of being involved in the Tutsi genocide. I sympathized with the Rwandese People's Rights movement, which was in opposition to the Rwandan Patriotic Front. Anyone that expressed opposition to the government was basically considered a terrorist and accused of aiding Hutu fighters hiding in the Congo.

It was the middle of August of 2004, I'll never forget. The army came to my home in the middle of the night and dragged me outside. They charged me with treason, perpetrating genocide, and accused me of conspiring with Hutu fighters in the Congo to kill Tutsis. They were so wrong about me and I was so scared that in my bewilderment I laughed at their accusations. They beat and kicked me to the ground, then they took me to a "safe house" where they tortured me and other prisoners for information.

They would lay us on the ground and pour cold water on us claiming that they were giving us a bath, except no one gets beat up while they're taking a shower. They beat us while we "bathed," and then they beat us while we stood outside to "dry." They didn't give us food and rather made us spend large portions of the day laying down staring at the sun without blinking. Whoever didn't comply with the order was isolated from the others and given a merciless beating.

We were beat with everything, with anything, all day long. Toward the end of my days there I was hit with the butt of a rifle on the forehead, several times. I don't remember what happened next, but my spine was severely damaged after that and I could hardly move. They put me in a cell and left me alone for three days and my condition only got worse. Someone came to examine me on the third day; they must have thought I was beyond all hope because shortly after that, three guards came and threw me out of their safe house and into a gutter.

I never felt more hope in my life. It didn't matter that I couldn't stand and run; I crawled my way to a friend's home. They hid me there and gave me time to recover from my injuries. I feared for my wife and children; I wondered what had they done to them. I knew that being around them would only bring them great danger, so I remained hidden away. No one knew where I was. Most people thought me for dead, probably even my wife.

A few weeks went by before I formulated any viable plan on what to do next. I applied and was granted a visa to travel to the United States, but I was still very much recovering and couldn't leave right away. When I was finally able to sit, stand, and walk for a reasonable amount of time, I began to make my way out of Rwanda. I knew it would be foolish to attempt to leave to the United States from Rwanda, so I travelled to the Tanzanian border. After several tries with different guards, I was able to bribe my way into Tanzania. I stayed there for a few days before I left for the United States.

I had to leave. Most people in Rwanda who got taken by the army didn't live to tell the story; I knew they would come for me as soon as they knew I had survived after all. I couldn't stay hiding at home and become a burden to my family, much less put them in danger. They couldn't even know I was alive—they were safer this way. It was all I had left to offer to my family and in this way I saved them, so they too could later flee to a safer place. As for me, I died the day I separated from them. I haven't been able to speak to my family since then either.

I had always hoped I would be able to return to Rwanda one day and reunite with my family. I thought things would calm down and slowly get better, but they haven't. I am still a marked man and the government is still corrupt. If I go back it won't be long before they come looking for me, pressing more false charges against me. As certain as there is air in my lungs now, I know I will die if I go back— justice does not exist in my land. I know people are still being hunted and killed and I have no doubt they would do the same to me.

I have nothing left in Rwanda. I no longer have a home, a family, or a job there. Many of my friends have died and others have disappeared and their whereabouts are unknown. I learned through the friend that hid me in his house that the Army continued to come by my home after they left me for dead. They questioned my wife many times and wanted to know if I had returned, or if she knew where I was. They never stopped harassing her and making threats. Eventually she and the twins fled, too; I was told that they went into Uganda, but I don't really know where they are.

Adjusting to all of this has been beyond hard— separating from my family has been devastating for me. I'm not the man I used to be and I'm not yet the man I'm supposed to become. I haven't made friends here yet and I feel very alone. I'm tormented day and night by nightmares and fears and they keep me from living like a normal person. Pictures of death plague my mind and the ever-present fear for my family and my own life is holding onto me with clutches of steel. I feel like a madman in the midst of chaos, and I'm fighting for all I'm worth to make sense out of life.

Even though I'm not in the direct path of danger here, life has still been quite difficult for me. Nonetheless, I would rather stay—things will get better in time. I have a work permit and a driver's license. I found a job and I have my own apartment. I would like to bring my family to the United States to live with me if I am allowed to stay. I want my children to be free and grow up in a safe place, and I want to see my wife and have a world of our own and our life together again—this time in a place where we can blend with the community and make a home where we'll spend the rest of our lives.

· · ·

Leon's leap of faith paid off for him in the end. His attorney informed me that they had won the case and Leon was allowed to become a permanent legal resident of the United States.

Leon is now safe. He no longer needs to fear deportation to Rwanda or persecution from his country's army. He has become a free man, able to begin the search for his family in order to reunite with them as he has dreamed of for so long. For years, Leon's only hope had been for something so basic most of us don't even stop to consider the possibility of it ever not being there—freedom, and life itself.

It is amazingly gratifying to me that this young man can now finally move onto bigger and better things, such as building a new life with his family. He is quite right in that he will never be the man he used to be—and he is even more correct in his awareness that he is not yet the man he is supposed to become. But surely he will be able to begin moving in the right direction.

Sometimes it isn't the horrors of one's life that make the lasting impressions, but rather, the scars they leave behind. It is this idea that concerns me the most about my patients. I know that eventually most people will get back up and carry on, but the strength to continue moving forward through the trauma and disfigurement is the true miracle.

Leon went through quite a lot in only a few years—yet he shows the same levels of anxiety and post-traumatic stress disorder as patients who have been tortured and persecuted their entire lives. I was quite surprised to find that he was still a well-functioning young man despite his impactful story, and it gave me a good indication as to the quality of his resilience.

I believe Leon survived not only because he was lucky to be thrown in a gutter, broken and half-dead that night, but because he refused to be crushed by these sadistic circumstances in his homeland. This

*utter refusal to be beaten down and conquered is
what I believe has saved his life over and over
again; not only as he crawled from the gutter that
night, but the agonizing separation from his family,
making his way into Tanzania to try and start a life
in the United States and later fight his legal battle,
alone.*

*It is this very same, ridiculously amazing
tenacity that it will take for Leon to one day find his
family, and will also eventually get him on the road
to healing, helping his to find "the man he's
supposed to become," with the bright future he
deserves.*

MARCO

Marco used to be a hard worker and excellent provider for his family before he was detained by Homeland Security and incarcerated at the Immigration and Customs Enforcement Detention Facility. When I visited him in order to conduct the evaluation, I found the remnants of a fighter, and he was now slowly deteriorating into what appeared to be a deep depression.

He hadn't been able to see or have contact with his family for the past month and had been incarcerated for five months up to that point. Marco had submitted an application for asylum several years prior, and in his ignorance he never found out what occurred with his process. Unbeknownst to him, his application had been rejected and he missed his hearing. He learned about his situation many years later when he was pulled over by a police officer, but by then it was too late. He retained an attorney who filed to re-open his case.

Marco told me that he had grown up to be a brave and outgoing individual, but I could not find traces of either one of those left in him. It seemed as if the months in jail had worn a lifetime of loss on Marco. He avoided looking at me in the eye and spoke in a sad, hopeless monotone. His sadness was contagious. This was a man who was certain he had finally lost the ongoing fight that he had waged his entire life.

Or had he? When he finally lifted his gaze I could still see in him a spark of that will to survive, and I smiled—there might be hope after all. As usual, I steeled myself for the story he was about to tell me while we sat surrounded by the four walls of his solitary confinement cell. I told him he could trust me and to be completely honest. I sheepishly assured him that "I had heard it all," and that nothing he said could possibly surprise me.

Boy, was I wrong about that.

My name is Marco. I'm from a small town in El Salvador. I was born with a medical problem my parents didn't know much about—I am what the doctors call a hermaphrodite. I have breasts, one testicle and a small penis that hangs very close to my body. I feel like a man; I urinate and have sex like a male and I've always thought of myself as a guy. I was confused when I began to grow breasts during puberty, but my mom thought it was just an anomaly. I was shocked as an adult when the doctors told me I also have a woman's vagina and explained my condition to me.

My parents are field workers from a remote village. They never went to school and are very simple in their understanding of the world. My birth certificate says that I am male, but I didn't have a penis you could see at that time; they called me a male because I lacked any visible female genitals. My mom was very confused and didn't know what to do about my gender disparity, so she dressed me in colorful clothes until I was six years old. When I had a say in what I wanted to wear, I began to dress myself like a tomboy, though I have little hands and fine fingers with long fingernails that start way back by my knuckles like a woman. I didn't have a normal childhood, or even one I can feel fond of; other kids teased me a lot and called me "mari-macha" (boy-girl.) No one really understood what I was. I didn't either.

My mom raised me as a girl, but I felt like a boy inside. Even so, I started growing breasts when I was 13—I was horrified. I kept looking at them thinking that I was getting fat, but the rest of my body stayed the same. I was so confused; in my mind I was a boy! When I asked my mom what was happening to me she began to cry and said she didn't know either.

People can be sick sometimes. There was a man in our neighborhood who really zeroed in on me. He would always find an excuse to invite me over to his house or to give me rides if he found me walking on the street. He looked at me as if he was hungry and it gave me a really weird feeling. He made me so uncomfortable that I began to imagine he was always lurking around some corner, spying, waiting on me. When I finally told my mom about him, she simply told me to stay as far away from this man as I could. Luckily it worked. I think that's how I came to learn how to deal with difficult situations. I started to avoid everything, just like I avoided that man.

I had a few friends that accepted me, but I was mostly alone. Kids harassed me so much in school that I finally quit going altogether when I was 13 years old. I didn't care; my parents hadn't gone to school at all. I began to work with my sisters as a street-vendor and I watched their kids whenever they worked at the market.

Even though I acted like a man, people were never sure of what I was. I remember this one boy that approached me one time and flat out reached to grab my chest. I was 16 years old and we were at a party, but I don't think he was drunk. I remember stopping him before he got to touch me and he swung his other arm and punched me in the face. We began to fight and no one stopped us; I was their circus freak. I hated that boy and everyone at the party and I used every bit of that anger to win that fight. After that I became a good fighter. I carried knives with me wherever I went. I accepted that people weren't going to be my friends and I began to live on the defensive. People continued to come at me, rude in their ignorance, trying to grab my breasts—but I was prepared every time, and I stopped them all.

Life in El Salvador is not easy for people who are different than the norm. One of my older cousins is homosexual and told me he had a really hard life. He was raped and beaten several times before he gave up on the possibility of living safely in our town and decided to flee to Texas where his sister lived. If he returned to El Salvador, people would pick up right where they left off and he would be harassed again without a doubt. People in my country are very conservative and just as they drink, cheat, and beat their families, they don't accept people like my cousin or me.

My dad and I began to fight as I grew up; it was the normal kind of friction between a parent and teenager, until he told me one day that I could leave if I didn't like the rules of his house. I left—I moved to San Salvador (the big city) and lived with my cousins. My cousins had a cleaning business and I worked for them, but didn't earn very much. Time went by and I wasn't making any progress with my life, so I felt it wasn't worth the cost and the risk of living in the big city. I decided to move back and work for my sisters again.

I began attending meetings for the National Republican Alliance (ARENA) once I moved back with my sisters. I handed out information and I took people to and from meetings. The paramilitary harassed us a lot. One night, members of the paramilitary pulled me and my friends into a side street; one soldier held me down and I prayed he wouldn't notice my breasts—it would only make matters worse. We were lucky that the town mayor happened to pass by and recognized me. He ordered

437

the soldiers to let us all go and I ran back home as fast as I could.

I instinctively knew that life in El Salvador wouldn't improve and I began longing for a place where I could live in peace. I was often harassed for who I was or for my political inclinations or because I was poor and worked as a vendor on the streets—there was no end to the unrest in my life. I didn't have an education to aspire to any better work opportunities and my political activities and social standing kept me from fitting in the norm. Work was hard to find and I became less and less able to support myself.

I thought I could find a new life in the United States. I thought I could hide away in the big crowds of the city because people wouldn't know anything was wrong with me. I thought that even if people found out I was different they would still accept me, because they accepted everyone. I came to the United States when I was 18 years old. I walked the border with a large group of people I didn't know and arrived in California. I was lucky that I knew some people in the United States and I was invited to live with a friend from my hometown in El Salvador for some time before I moved to my cousin's house.

Friends here helped me file for political asylum because I was a member of ARENA. I paid $300 to a legal form preparation company where the employees helped me fill out the paperwork. They submitted it once everything was ready, but they didn't tell me what to do or expect from that point on. I don't really know anything about paperwork or procedures, so I kept on waiting, thinking that they would eventually contact me, but they never did.

My cousins moved to Colorado in 1993, and I followed them. I thought I should try to do things right and I applied for a work permit and a Social Security number. In the meantime, I began to work in a restaurant. I earned enough in five months to move to my own apartment and then I switched jobs to a warehouse that offered to pay me better. Life was becoming stable and for the first time in my life I found myself looking into the future and making plans. It was a surprisingly great feeling.

I met my wife, Amelia, at a park near her family's home. We began talking and became friends; I didn't know many people here and she didn't really have any friends. The second time I saw her, I noticed that she had a black eye. She trusted me with her personal problems and told me that her father had been abusing her. I was also able to open up and tell her some of my story; it only helped us grow closer together. We continued to get to know one another and eventually decided to be together and marry. After moving to the United States, it was the best decision I ever made.

I worked in construction for one year and did really well for me and Amelia; I was a good worker and did a good job for the company—it made me proud of myself. After a while, one of my female supervisors came onto me—I think she thought I was a lesbian with a male identity. It made me uncomfortable but I didn't know how to handle it; I ignored her at first and hoped that she would go away, but she never did. Eventually I had to face her and tell her that I wasn't a lesbian and that I was actually married and she needed to leave me alone. I don't think she liked me any more after that; she began to skip me for promotions and raises and would give them to people who hadn't been there as long as me. She later began to treat me badly and supervisors began to criticize my work because she would make up stories about my performance. In the end I had to leave; I couldn't take it anymore.

I worked odd jobs from then until I was incarcerated. It turned out that my application for asylum I submitted in California was denied and I never knew. I was even supposed to attend a hearing, but no one had tried to contact me; I knew nothing of it. I'm in trouble because of it and I might get sent back to El Salvador. They have even begun to say I'm a gang member, but I'm not.

I have a record of arrests with the Denver police, but some of these are not true. Perhaps I should've stayed in school and become savvier—I just don't understand how any of these things work. I've never sexually assaulted anyone or been arrested or charged for it. I also never resisted arrest; maybe someone has the same name as me. Some things in my records are true, like the time I missed a traffic court hearing. I was also charged once with carrying a concealed weapon because I carry a knife in my boot out of habit. I didn't know it was illegal here; I never hurt anyone.

Then I did something truly stupid. I told the Denver Police that I was a member of the Mara Salvatrucha, an El Salvador gang. It isn't true—I was hanging out with some acquaintances one night and I was trying to impress them. I was riding in the car with them, and one of them said he was in a South American gang. I always want to look macho when I'm around other men because I feel self-conscious about my chest. I wanted them to respect me, so I told them I was a member of Mara Salvatrucha for eight years.

It was stupid to try to impress them, especially since I didn't have the gang's tattoo. I said I worked for them undercover and I didn't need to have the tattoos. I don't think I've had a more stupid moment in my life. In reality, I've known people in that gang but I've never been a member. There is definitely no such thing as a special member, and you absolutely have to have the tattoos if you are part of their gang.

I do dress like a gang member—the baggy clothes help me hide my breasts. When I was taken to the ICE detention center I was outfitted with clothes that were too tight for me. The men in my ward began to stare at me because they noticed I had breasts. I was terrified; I knew it was a matter of time before something really bad would happen to me. A doctor examined me and put me in a medical isolation unit because of what I am—a hermaphrodite. I was thankful for that; most of the men in that prison were Central American and I knew they would try to hurt me for being different.

I'm devastated by this situation. I was the sole provider for my wife and my two-year-old daughter. Since I was arrested by ICE, my wife has been forced to work and take care of our daughter all on her own. She's had to move a few times because she can't afford a place to live and eventually gets kicked out. She's young and does not earn much money; she gets taken advantage of a lot. I asked my sister in California to take care of the baby for a while, but I don't know how long she will be willing to do that.

If I am deported, I hope that my wife and daughter would come back to El Salvador with me. They are all I have; I couldn't live without them, even though I really don't know how we would survive in El Salvador. We would even have to hide a little, since we couldn't have people figuring out that both of them are US citizens. Gangs are a big problem there; it's almost like a civil war—my wife and daughter wouldn't be safe. My activities with ARENA and my odd sexual appearance would draw attention to us and increase the danger for me and my family. It would also make people discriminate against me for being different and I wouldn't be able to earn enough to provide for my family as I have here in the United States. I don't know how we would survive.

It's been two months since my last immigration hearing. The judge postponed any final decisions on my case for another six months because my criminal record will be investigated. Luckily, I was allowed to return home for the time being—I don't know how much longer I could've been in solitary confinement.

Returning home and being with my family gives me hope and really makes me want to stay in the United States so I can provide a good life for them, especially for my daughter. No one cares about sexual or political orientations here, no one targets me, and no one ridicules me. As safe as I feel being allowed to live in peace, it is my daughter who I think about the most. She deserves to have a normal childhood with a normal dad that is never called "mari-macha" or gets beat simply for being different. She deserves to grow up like a normal kid and not worry about what other children will think of her family—I can give her that here.

. . .

I saw Marco once more after he was released from the detention facility and I was relieved at the improvement I saw in his presentation and countenance. Although he was still suffering from chronic, severe major depression, his time out of jail spent with his family had reminded him of his sense of purpose in life and gave him back some strength to continue his fight.

I told Marco again that he was suffering from a deep depression and that it was of utmost importance that he seeks out a medication evaluation and begin counseling sessions with a professional. It is hard to get this through to most Hispanic men; they seem to see any sort of therapy and medication due to an emotional cause as a sign of weakness and will instinctively brush it off. Marco opened up and told me that he had been entertaining the idea of counseling but had not yet acted on it. I silently hoped that he found the motivation in himself to get this done ASAP—he was going to need it.

Shortly after the second time I saw him, I spoke briefly with the Medical Director at the ICE detention facility who happened to be an old acquaintance. It was a simple follow-up call to ensure I had not forgotten to ask him any questions about Marco. My colleague then proceeded to tell me that Marco had a full check-up (after the time I visited him and before he was released from the detention facility) and was informed that Marco was sterile; he had been sterile his entire life.

I don't know if Marco will ever find out that his wife was unfaithful to him and his daughter is not really his. A softer human part of me hopes that he never does. It isn't that I don't value honesty—I just

*don't know that he will ever recover from his major
depression and I am very concerned of what could
happen to him.*

*Marco has placed his wife and child as his sole
reason to keep going in life. Due to his life-long
struggle with post-traumatic stress disorder, he
never established any meaningful connections with
other individuals and has either spent his time in
isolation or living defensively in order to avoid any
judgment or derision from others. His family unit
means everything to Marco because they are the
only people he perceives to have loved him
unconditionally—the only people he has ever
allowed to get close to him.*

*His chronic post-traumatic stress disorder
helped create many of the character traits in Marco
that would later in his life degenerate into a clinical
depression. If he were separated from his family
due to a forced return to El Salvador or the
dissolution of his marriage due to learning of his
wife's infidelity, Marco would surely fall apart
beyond recognition.*

*The last I heard from his attorney, the judge's
decision in Marco's case was again continued and
Marco had finally taken my advice and began
therapy sessions with an El Salvadorian counselor.
I hope that he continues with this journey so he can
better understand and heal himself.*

NADIA

Nadia is a strong woman, but not by choice. I could tell right away it would be a while before her Eastern European stoicism loosened up and she let me see her true feelings. She began by speaking in general terms about her upbringing and would gloss over entire periods of her life unless I pressed her for more information. It was clear that Nadia did not want to remember. I could see the timid and traumatized part of Nadia fastening herself to the chair as a way to fight the side of her that wanted to flee from the interview.

Nadia spends her time surrounded by broken violins and other musical instruments, consumed with replacing their strings and fine tuning them for their owners. She savors the one good memory of her past when she was happy and in love. Meanwhile, thoughts of her stolen career as a violin prodigy in a symphony orchestra still haunt her. It seems that Nadia's stoic nature is the one thing that helped her maintain her job here in the United States and allowed her to conform to society's basic expectations of her.

No one but Nadia knows about what is really happening behind the brave mask she wears—she won't let anyone see. When her attorney first contacted me I had expected Nadia to have experienced a difficult past, but I was dumbfounded by the ignorance and brutality that exists in this world once she allowed me in and revealed her full story.

I am Nadia. I was born in Eastern Europe back in 1981. Back then my country was still part of the USSR which made life quite different than the norm. As a child though, politics didn't matter and I didn't think our little world was so different. Everyone around me grew up the same way I did, so I never even imagined that things were different elsewhere. I am an only child, but I grew up in a tight-knit community. I was always surrounded by people, but I didn't always enjoy that—I remember trying to get away to spend time alone.

My parents were nothing out of the ordinary— my dad managed a toy store, and my mom took care of our home. You'd think it would be every child's dream come true to have a dad with a toy store, but he didn't ever let me play there. I should remember it as a magical, happy place, but the words "rigid, strict, and dull" come to mind instead. My dad was a very strict man; he should've owned an accounting business or a hardware store, not a toy store.

Where I'm from it is normal for a husband and wife to hit each other and to hit their children, so you could say I had a "normal" childhood living with my parents. My culture is extremely repressed and uptight and strict moral values were harshly enforced. Like I said, beatings were the go-to punishment for any transgression.

My parents thought I had a gift for music, so I attended a music conservatory and learned to play the violin when I was just a kid. They weren't wrong about me—I was very good at it, and it actually made me happy to play the violin. I was even thought to be one of the best in the conservatory, but that somehow wasn't good enough for my parents. I couldn't get anything less than perfect grades; my parents were extremely unforgiving and would beat me for bringing home anything less than the best grades. They held high academic standards and they punished me regularly for any hint of a deficiency.

The community I lived in had very well-cemented modus operandi; it didn't matter if you felt or thought this or that way, people were expected to fit into the norm. All of the independent thinkers, mad geniuses and strong personalities were basically outcasts; they didn't fit in and no one wanted them around—as if they had an infectious disease. There was a certain way in which to go about everything in our lives, almost so that people never even doubted how they were supposed to behave. It was unacceptable for young people to date until well into their teen years, for example. It just didn't happen... publicly.

Homosexuality wasn't even a conversation topic. It was completely out of the question and it was even considered a crime—you could spend up to five years in the hole for it. An openly gay person was simply unheard of. No one accepted it, no one even tolerated it. It was the equivalent of the Bible's account of leprosy in its time... only this you could hide.

I became aware of my interest in women when I was 18 years old. I spent all day daydreaming and had all the curiosity and urges other teenagers had, only mine were directed almost exclusively towards other girls. I really only thought about girls, but I would make myself think of boys from time to time to make myself feel normal. Thinking about boys never felt normal to me though.

I met Liro in the conservatory. She was this gorgeous girl with shiny eyes and really long dark hair. We got along from the minute we met and began spending time together practicing the violin and talking and laughing... I fell in love. I fell in love with her right away, and she fell in love with me.

We didn't tell a soul. No one could ever find out about us or we both knew that hell and all its rage would come for us. We became masters of flying under the radar; to the human eye we were nothing but two giddy girls who spent time doing homework and probably thinking about boys. Truth is that we used everything in our power to get every possible minute alone together. We stayed and practiced violin after school every chance we got, we timed our bathroom breaks. We lied and said we were afraid of walking alone so we could walk to school together. We were predators and time together was our prey—any second away from the eyes of people was a second where no one else in the world existed but Liro and I.

Our plan was working and we couldn't believe it (even though we both felt that it was our right to like whomever we chose). Unfortunately, problems began when a boy in my class began to court me and later asked me to be his girlfriend. I wanted to die. Liro and I came up with the best story possible and I refused him as politely as I could, but it didn't save us. You see, this boy was the son of a professor, which sort of gave him movie star status at school. People were surprised that I didn't just swoon with excitement when he asked me to be his girlfriend, as that would've been the case with any other girl. No one saw my response coming and people were so shocked by it that I became a subject of scrutiny. It wasn't long before rumors began flying about Liro and I and people began to suspect we were lesbians.

The Dean of Students called Liro and me into his office and grilled us about our relationship and the reason why we seemed to spend almost every moment together. We denied everything; we pretended to be as appalled as everyone else and even offended at being thought of as lesbians, but everyone already believed the rumors and nothing we said changed that. The Dean ordered us to end not only our relationship but our friendship as well and then separated us by putting us into different programs. I was removed from the first chair violin position, and they threatened to expel us from the conservatory if we didn't stop seeing each other.

Just like that, the world as I knew it evaporated. I was torn between feeling terrified of what would happen to us and the desperation and sadness of being separated from Liro. My life as I knew it was over and this was just the beginning. It took all my strength to control myself and keep up the appearance of looking appalled at the situation, when in reality my heart was trying to claw its way out of my chest and run away with Liro.

As if things weren't already bad enough, the school called our parents to inform them about "the situation." My dad was waiting for me at the door when I arrived home from school. We didn't get to discuss anything—he started hitting me as soon as I entered the house. He hadn't been able to find the broom, so he picked up a toy racket he brought from his store and hit me with that instead. My mom took away all the pictures of me and Liro and just about started scrubbing the floor with bleach. She wanted to remove any memory that Liro and I ever happened. To them, it was an unbearable disgrace to our family and they couldn't stand it, or me.

But it did happen and none of that stopped us— we were in love. Liro and I began to see each other in secret, away from school and our parents. We had made friends with a lesbian couple a while back, and they agreed to let us come into their apartment and hide for a little while so we could spend time together whenever we could get away. I suddenly found myself needing new books from the library and having to go to the market for new violin strings—anything to be able to see her.

The prospects of a good future in our own culture had just about vanished for both of us. The conservatory had us playing in the lowest ranks and no university would accept us (because of our ranking in the conservatory and the fact that we were lesbians). Even though our grades were the highest in our classes, no one wanted lesbians in their schools, their symphonies, their businesses... we had become the lepers of our time.

We quickly grew to understand that if we were going to have any chance at a decent life, we would have to move far away. We decided to travel to the United States in the hopes of finding work as au pairs and planned for our trip by learning English and saving money. We put away every penny and read every English textbook we could get our hands on for the next two and a half years. Then Liro was murdered and all our plans disintegrated.

Liro and I had agreed to meet at our friend's apartment as usual—except this time, unbeknownst to us, her father and brother had been following us. We were reading books in the guestroom when

Liro's dad and brother kicked the door down and came inside yelling for us. They dragged us out into the living room and began to beat and kick us to the floor. Her dad was yelling at me, telling me how he had called the police and I would go to jail "for being a filthy lesbian and perverting his daughter" and so on. And that is when I heard a scream. The sound pierced my chest and ripped it apart, and suddenly time froze and I felt a thick wave of terror wash over me.

Liro was dead. Her own brother had stabbed her in the chest while he beat her on the floor. I couldn't believe my eyes; I couldn't believe that was Liro lying in a pool of blood on the floor. I felt as if my brain didn't know what emotion, what response to assign to what I had just seen—everything went in slow motion. I saw her brother coming after me next, and I smiled to myself, surprised to realize that I didn't care anymore about what happened next.

In my culture, it's considered an honor to get rid of a family member when they are believed to bring shame to the family. The police barged into the apartment in time to stop him from stabbing me as well. The women who owned the apartment and I were then arrested and taken to jail. The murderer became a hero.

I spent that night in jail and I bribed the police to let me off without charges. I was surprised to see my parents at the police station when I was released. They took me home with them, but neither one spoke to me for a long time. Actually, after all this time only my mom speaks to me–I brought shame to my family and so to the rest of them I'm as good as dead. To the people in our town all the unmarried women in my family are suspected to be lesbians and ostracized from the community. They will never accept them—they might never marry or have families of their own.

I don't know why I stayed there for as long as I did. I guess I didn't care about all the plans and dreams I had now that Liro was dead. One day blended into the next without much meaning anymore—I had become an empty shell. I became an abomination to the people in our community, a freak of nature. They would spit and yell at me on the street for no other reason than being a lesbian. They humiliated me wherever I went. It got to be so bad that my mom had to handle all my affairs because I couldn't leave the house.

The initial shock of losing Liro made it easy for me to feel indifferent to other people and what they thought of me. However, as time went by their hate and the way it extended towards my family wore heavy in my heart. I didn't know if I wanted to live anymore and I struggled between honoring Liro's memory and following our dreams, or just putting everything behind me and joining Liro on the other side. I concluded that even if I chose to live, neither I nor my family deserved the kind of life that was imposed on us… imposed on them… because of me. If I left them they would stop being persecuted and I could find a place where I could live in peace, so I decided to move far away from my city and everyone I knew—forever.

I arrived in New York City as an au pair, but there were complications with my paperwork and in the end I was unable to work. I knew that my only chance to survive and have a decent life would be in the United States, so I felt that I had to find a way to stay. Luckily I had some family friends in the city and they let me stay with them while I got on my feet. Eventually they found out about what had happened with me and Liro back home and gave me two days to leave their apartment. They called me a liar and said I was filth. So much for my brand new life—it was looking very similar to my old one.

I had some more relatives in Oregon and they invited me to live with them. I was surprised when they told me that they had heard rumors of all that happened between Liro and me and yet they still welcomed me into their home. I lived with them for a few years while I adjusted to my new reality.

It was a relief to live in a city where nobody knew who you were and no one cared who you liked. I felt free, and also tremendously alone. I couldn't stop thinking of Liro and the world we could've built together here. I couldn't walk past a mossy tree or a bridge without that stab of pain in my heart because I knew she would love those things and she would never be there to see them with me. I spent most of my time torn between that feeling of relief and safety of my new life, and the grief that was eating away at me. I tried to kill myself twice during that time.

I don't know how I made it through, but as time went by I slowly came to terms with things. Not completely—but enough to get on my feet and try to make a life worth something. I found a job at a small musical instrument repair shop and I was able to rent an apartment of my own. I would like to go to school, but I can't afford it yet.

I've made a few friends, but I spend most of my time by myself—I feel I still have a lot to think about. People are nice to me, but I don't feel very social. I feel different than everyone else, like no one would understand all of what I've gone through. I still have nightmares about the day Liro was killed; I see the whole thing in my dreams every other night. How do you talk to your new friends about something like that?

Perhaps one day it will all get better; I hope for that. I have already gained a lot by moving to the United States—here I'm just one more girl in the crowd. I can safely walk down the street and go to sleep without fear that someone will throw rocks at my windows. Here I could even openly have a girlfriend if I wanted to and no one would hurt me. That just blows my mind.

I'm terrified to be deported. My dad won't take me back in his home or bribe the police the keep us safe—he is done with me. I would have to beg someone else in my family to allow me to live with them, but they all hate me there. Even if any of them accepted me, I've brought so much shame to my family that socially they would be expected to hate me and act the part. I'd have no one to rely on and no place to live.

I could try to live on my own if I could find someone willing to rent me an apartment or a room. The trick to that is that I'd have to find someone willing to give me a job first. The whole town knows my family and sadly, I'm quite the legend. Everyone knows about "filthy Nadia and her lesbian girlfriend." I'd bring a stigma to anyone associated with me, so no one wants me around.

If I had to go back home it's very realistic to assume I'd be living in the streets. Maybe I'd have to become a prostitute to survive, but I fear what men would do to me if they discovered I was a lesbian. My life would be in danger if I had to go back to my country; others would persecute me, humiliate me, abuse me, and ostracize me just for sport. I know that I couldn't endure it even for the short term after people found out about Liro and me. I don't know how I'd endure it for the rest of my life. I wouldn't, I couldn't. I'd join Liro on the other side.

It's been a four months since the judge allowed me to remain in the United States, and for the first time in my life, I feel hope. I've been going to counseling for eight months now, and although I know I won't ever be like a normal person, and the thought of ever feeling peaceful about what my life has been sounds like a dream, it seems as if I've just discovered what it's like to breathe. No more beatings. No more persecution. No more "filthy Nadia." No more hiding. I'm over 30 now and all the years I should've spent in carefree fun are gone, but I'm okay with that. Now is when my life really begins.

. . .

Nadia's life was saved when she was allowed to remain in the United States. The simple fact that she now has hope about her future speaks volumes of this. I cannot say what will become of Nadia, but I do know that she has the will to fight for her life now. When I first met her, I wondered if I had gotten to her a little too late; I wondered if she wouldn't decide to give up on her own life even if she were allowed to stay in the United States—she had been dangling off her personal cliff for far too long.

For the first time in her life, Nadia is truly free. I can only imagine how reviving and overwhelming this must be for her. The healing process for Nadia will be a long and difficult road, but at least now she has the chance to begin that journey. Just like she said, this is when her life really begins.

NICOLAE

Nicolae arrived to my office that day much earlier than expected. He appeared to second-guess himself as he nervously danced between opening the glass door to my office and turning to wait for me to invite him in. He quickly apologized for being 45 minutes early to our appointment and sheepishly admitted that he was quite anxious and wanted to make sure he had plenty of time to arrive "in case something happened."

I could tell right away that Nicolae's overly polite manner and somewhat submissive nature were genuine and inherent parts of his character. At first sight, Nicolae would've fit the bill for any average office worker; he was well-groomed and wore a clean pair of pressed slacks and a button-up shirt. His manners were impeccable and I could tell that he was well-educated.

After the initial four minutes of our introduction, the real Nicolae began to emerge—he appeared as a massive mess of nervousness and desperation. His legs were constantly shaking under the table, his hands continually fidgeting with an old pen. His eyes were rapidly darting from the floor to the door and everywhere around the room—this man literally vibrated with anxiety. I silently wondered what could possibly have happened to Nicolae to have had such scarring and prominent effect on him. I didn't wonder for long.

My name is Nicolae, I'm 36 years old and I was born and raised in a small city in Romania. Back then, Romania was still very much under the control of the communist party; both of my parents worked on the collective farms. Although my siblings and I have fled Romania, my parents still live there. They are unable to leave but also unable to find any work because they left the communist party many years ago. They survive on the money my siblings and I are able to send to them.

I haven't seen my brother in ten years. Every day I wonder what his life might be like, alone. He fled to Spain in order to escape the persecution and political pressures directed at our family. My sister and her husband also fled—they went to live in Germany four years ago. I had no choice but to flee as well, and as much as it pains me to have left my parents, I know that they're actually safer without us there.

My very first memories are of being kept at home in this alternate reality. I laughed and I played imaginary games every day. I wasn't allowed to go outside, but I never thought much of it since life in the house was so normal. I was too young to understand; my parents tried to keep me safe by keeping me in the house as much as possible and pretending that we were just like any other family living an ordinary life. I believed it for a long time… I'd like to think that maybe for a little while it was even true.

Our problems began when my parents decided to leave the communist party in support of the opposition. Of course they didn't announce it; they kept it secret from everyone so we could remain safe, but that kind of information never stays secret—people gossip. It was that time when the proverbial political winds began changing and whoever went against the communist party was oppressed, questioned, and persecuted by any and all authority in Romania.

Right around that time I began noticing that life wasn't all that normal. Even though I was still a kid, I could tell somebody was after us; there would be mysterious phone calls that would make my parents afraid and sometimes men in cars would drive very slowly in front of our home. During these times I wasn't allowed to even go out to the front door and play. They tried to keep me from knowing the danger we were in, but it was almost too late. I began to notice all the little things, and very diligently (and secretly) began putting the pieces together in my mind.

Everyone else seemed to know about our family though. I got beat up pretty badly by some hardcore communist kids when I was 16 years old. It was confusing to be hated not by something you've done but by something you supposedly are. It happened during the first week of school; they hit me until my teeth loosened up—I didn't want to go back. The principal eventually came to my house and personally escorted me back to the school, but I was still terrified—I knew nothing had changed. Kids would taunt and ridicule me and would warn me that they would beat me if they ever saw me anywhere but in the classroom. That room became my prison and my fortress and I became an extremely vigilant, nervous wreck. I never left the classroom for any reason. I used to sprint from the classroom and back just to use the restroom, and my parents had to take me to and from school because I wouldn't walk alone in the streets.

I stopped sleeping. I felt worried all the time and I had constant nightmares. Things snowballed from there; I couldn't pay attention in school because I was sleep-deprived and drained from the anticipation of being attacked at any moment. I remember that used to wake up in a cold sweat every morning and even if I had managed to sleep the night prior, I would automatically begin feeling sick as soon as I awoke. I stopped eating too and I lost a lot of weight. Between the fatigue and the tightness around my chest I didn't even feel like smelling food.

There wasn't a day I didn't feel like quitting school, but my mom kept encouraging me to just endure the two years and then "everything would be over." Right. School eventually (and finally) ended, but the torment was far from over. I enrolled in a

464

university nearby and went to live with my aunt. Even though I spent my time between school and home, I couldn't escape the persecution and the violence. I remember being at the student's lounge once for a friend's birthday party when the police came looking for one of my friends. They said that a girl had gone to report that this guy had raped her. It was a lie, but they took us all away anyway.

They questioned my friend and the rest of us had to give statements. We were terrified to the point of tears while we waited at the police station—that's the last place on earth you want to be if you lived in my city. When my turn came, I was handed a statement that said that I had seen my friend abuse this girl. I refused to sign it and stood up to leave; the policeman punched me in the chest and knocked me to the floor. He insisted that I sign the statements and threatened to have me jailed or beaten further if I refused.

I was then handcuffed and my feet were shackled, then they connected both chains with an iron bar. I felt like I was in the 1800s and I had committed a serious crime. They propped me onto two tables and they began to push down on my back which was hanging in mid-air. They wouldn't stop pushing—I felt my body was going to break in two. I cried in terror and they yelled at me to keep quiet and agree to sign the form. I endured the whole thing as well as the beatings on my arms and legs. I think they got tired of me eventually and decided to let me down to check on me. They released me that night, but not without a warning that there would be consequences for refusing to sign the statement and that they would be calling me in again.

I ran. They released me and I ran and I didn't stop until I got to my grandmother's house outside the city. I changed my phone number and hid in my grandmother's house for two weeks. I feared that the police would go looking for me at school, or find me walking in the streets of my town. No one knew anything about me for that time—I didn't even so much as peek out the door. Things settled down after a while and I was able to calm down enough to return to my aunt's home and go back to school, but I never saw or spoke to my friends again. To this day I don't know what happened to them after that night at the police station.

Life was pleasantly uneventful for a little while, and I felt good enough to go visit my parents. I stepped into a bar one night during my visit and I found the Mayor and his associates celebrating; the Mayor had announced his affiliation to the Democratic Party. I've never been a particularly political person (and with reason) but I had always thought the Mayor was a good man, and decided to stay and support his celebration.

The police were waiting outside. No one knew. When I left the bar to go home I saw about eight or nine police officers posted around the bar. Chills ran down my spine and that's the last thing I remember. I was hit in the back of the head with something hard, and I woke up in jail with a broken nose and a bloody face.

The policemen knew exactly who I was and told me I'd be staying in jail for a while. I had no idea what they meant. I was thrown in a small room with four or five other men. They didn't give us food or medical attention and the cell didn't even have a toilet. It was so small, in fact, that we had to take turns just to sit down and rest. They kept me there for sixteen hours and upon my release they warned me to keep from following in my mother's footsteps. I really had no idea what they were talking about.

I went crazy for weeks after this. I couldn't eat, I couldn't sleep, I couldn't control my mind, my fears, my thoughts. I was a paranoid, agitated mess. I would become progressively more wound up and then I'd explode over any little thing. My mom took care of me as best as she could, but my situation didn't improve—I couldn't take it anymore; I wanted to die but I also didn't want to. People would do drive-bys near our home, throw rocks at the windows, and we began to get a lot of threats on the phone in the middle of the night. My mom was even beaten by some men one day while she was walking down the street.

My mom was a brave woman. She hated the corruption that came with communism and did everything she could to stop it. She didn't care if people threatened her, followed her, or even beat her. She told me she had promised herself she would not stop until she saw some justice and we could all live without being afraid of what we say or do. I couldn't even imagine being as brave as her.

The communist party was successful in oppressing the uprising and came back into full power the following year. The whole city began to make demonstrations on the streets and there was much violence, looting, and destruction. I was traumatized by my previous clashes with the police, so I didn't want to have anything to do with what was happening outside—I stayed home and worked on my thesis.

The streets were empty since all the demonstrations were happening downtown. I walked to the bus stop to pick up a friend when an armored truck drove by and four men wearing masks jumped out to grab us. They handcuffed me and my friend and put hoods over our heads. I was convinced that my luck had run out and I was going to die this time for sure. We drove for what seemed an eternity before they threw us in a room and removed our hoods. When my eyes adjusted to the bright lights I saw that we were in a room full of students, and I suspected we had been taken in for interrogation. My body began to shake violently; there were two guys in the far corner of the room who had been beaten to death. Thoughts began to spin in my head and I blacked out.

Apparently I was of no use to them. They hooded me and my friend the next day and threw us out of their truck in the town's square. They gave me a list of everything I had with me which was now in their possession and told me they would be calling me later.

I was still with my girlfriend Irina around this time and when she found out what happened she told me without a doubt that it was time for us to flee. We had travelled to the United States for a three month work assignment a few years back, and decided that moving there would be the safest and best option for us.

It is true, we are safer here. Things haven't changed much for me however—I can't forget my past. Every moment I feel with every fiber of my being that there's someone waiting for me around a corner, lurking in the dark, ready to pounce on me and Irina and hurt us. We hardly ever go outside. We go to work and we come back to our apartment and we stay in—we haven't really been able to make many friends.

I know we don't have a perfect life here, but we are able to live. I'm far from the corruption that scarred me and my family, and that has lifted a crushing weight off my shoulders. Here in the United States you can have your own opinion (outrageous as it may be) and you're still safe. I know I haven't overcome the trauma from my past and this is why I will never be able to have a normal life anywhere, but at least here I feel that I might live to see tomorrow.

If we are forced to return to Romania we won't live long. My parents are still targeted and persecuted for their political views—my mom was even accused of helping people travel to the border to escape, which is a lie. It served its purpose, though; it segregated my parents from the rest of the community. No one helps them and no one speaks to them, because no one wants to get in trouble with the police.

If Irina and I were forced to return to Romania, not only would it be a matter of time before our lives were in severe danger, but we wouldn't be able to support ourselves to survive in the meantime. People don't want to be exposed to danger; any association with people "in trouble with the law" automatically puts them in peril. It would be hard for us to even find work. My parents don't work, they survive on the money my siblings and I send them. I can't ask my siblings to try to support me; they're barely scraping by. If the police didn't succeed in eliminating us, poverty most certainly will.

It's been two days since my legal case was reviewed in court; I'm finally calming down from all the anxiety and uncertainty of anticipating the outcome these past months. The judge decided to postpone any final decisions on my residency status for another year and that gives me a bittersweet feeling. It's soothing to know that I get to remain in the safety of the United States for another year, and yet it eats me up alive, the anxiety and the uncertainty of not knowing what will eventually become of me and Irina. I don't know how I'll manage to keep myself together while I wait—I can't stop my brain from coming up with these horrible scenarios of what could happen to us. It is like Irina says, though, "Today we live."

· · ·

Nicolae was clear that there was no choice but to escape the traumatic experiences and constant persecution in his native country in order to survive. Nicolae told me that he simply didn't care if this meant spending the rest of his life in a basement apartment of some remote town in the United States working as a cashier in a gas station (even though he has the equivalent of a Master's degree) because even if this translated into a colorless, insipid life, it also meant that he got to be alive.

Nicolae presented with enduring and pervasive signs of a person who has suffered the effects of generalized anxiety disorder throughout his entire life. Of course it is unclear if he was born that way, or if life events and growing up under such stress and fear exacerbated this condition. This disorder later served to amplify the development of his chronic symptoms of post-traumatic stress disorder.

In Nicolae's perception, the brutal political violence and corruption is as great a threat to his safety if he were to return to Romania as the physical and mental abuse he suffered in the past. I agree with Nicolae in that any alternative is better for him than returning to his native country, but I too wonder how he will fare in the coming year while awaiting the outcome of his case. He seemed to take to heart my recommendations for counseling and a medication evaluation, and I can only hope he follows through with it as it will likely be his only hope for survival until he learns the outcome of his case.

Conclusion

It is my hope that the reader will reflect on the stories in this book and the humanity within each individual's struggles. It is always troubling to be made aware of the neglect, abuse, and even violence that enter into people's lives, especially during childhood, and the oftentimes self-destructive ways in which they try to cope. Without professional help, sadly, many such people are doomed to repeat in adulthood the patterns of passivity, submission and acquiescence that they learned as children. The missteps or misperceptions of adults seeking a pathway through their lives, only to encounter unwanted pain and adversity are equally disquieting. The levels of hate, persecution and violence brought about by the stories of the quest for economic, political or social freedom shock the senses. Perhaps these narratives will offer a deeper understanding of the effect of trauma on human psychology, as well as the role that the most shocking aspects of the human condition play in discerning "hardship" in these types of immigration cases.

Conversely, most of the narratives in this book reveal some modicum of hope, if not a degree of contentment and security, that undocumented immigrants find here in the United States. In cases of Americans or legal residents with psychological issues, they have oftentimes benefited from the stabilizing effect on their lives that their immigrant loved-ones provide them –people who risked their freedom and even their lives to immigrate here illegally. Regardless of the nature of the referral of the individual I evaluate, it is impossible not to feel some degree of empathy and compassion for these individuals who are caught up in deportation or removal proceedings. They are people after all, many of whom have been here for many years, and oftentimes the lives of innocent children are involved.

As a psychologist I have a great deal of knowledge and training regarding the issue of counter-transference, or a therapist's emotional entanglement with a client. I have to constantly be on guard in order to identify it as it appears, and to appropriately and professionally complete my work without allowing such feelings to interfere with the truth of the matter at hand. Nevertheless, in one case in which I testified in the matter of a man who suffered ongoing sexual abuse as a child by a person in authority, I was completely taken by surprise when I broke down on the stand and began to weep. After over 14 years and countless times offering testimony in court, I had never before had this happen to me. I struggled mightily to stifle my sobs and tears, and it took a good five minutes to compose myself before I could continue speaking. Therefore, I am acutely aware that these stories are quite troubling in their intensity, but they are equally inspiring in the perseverance and courage that they express–all despite daunting obstacles.

My work with illegal immigrants and their loved ones over the years has been undeniably challenging. This work has significantly elevated my skills as a mental health professional, and I have become quite adept at perceiving the emotional reality behind the masks that people don to hide their suffering. I feel that I am highly capable at gently, but firmly procuring the truth about their experiences, and in drawing out the underlying causes of mental illness as well as in discerning the true nature of these peoples' afflictions. My own trauma history has, I feel, served to prepare me for this work. I feel that my own particular background allowed me a level of compassion and empathy that helps me to "see" when a patient might be unconsciously covering over the past, and I can then assist them in confronting those dark secrets which they had heretofore neatly evaded and avoided discussing with anyone else. It is a gratifying aspect of my profession to provide assistance to people in need.

While I conduct my evaluations in a professional, unbiased manner, some part of me can't help but hope that many of my patients win their cases. I know that they need help and their lives would be better if they were allowed to stay, and I would like to think that most people reading these narratives would feel the same way. As such, the legal process can at times be disheartening. I have participated in several cases brought before a judge well known for his harsh manner. His inexplicable decisions have often produced unexpectedly shocking results for my patients, and such cases always challenge my faith in the concept of justice in our system. The same judge was involved in a case that was highlighted in a newspaper article several years ago. A young man from Central America said that if he was sent back to his homeland, where he had escaped the gangs a few years prior, he would be dead within two weeks. That is exactly what happened. I have handled many evaluations for Central Americans seeking asylum, and the stories are just as horror-filled as those in this book. Even if such people arrive here without legal documentation, it does not seem just or right to send to them back to near-certain death. I am reminded what the Buddhist monk Thick Nhat Hahn once said: "True justice should have compassion in it."[3]

I have been witness to many legal hearings in which the pursuit of truth and justice appears secondary to the zeal of the government's desire to win its cases. I understand that this is the nature of the adversarial system of justice that we have in place, and that these public servants are only doing their job. However, the resultant lack of humanness is not only disturbing to watch, it serves to re-traumatize my patients. They have already suffered

[3] Nhat Hanh, Thick, *Answers from the Heart: Practical Responses to Life's Burning Questions* (Berkeley: Parallax Press, 2009).

the indignity of violence, neglect, cruelty, persecution and other abuses. The legal process itself then creates an additionally tremendous emotional toll. It is discouraging to see them reach the court of law on the day of the hearing only to be treated as an object, something to be won or lost.

There are other concerns as to the insufficiency of the legal system. Immigration attorneys have told me that for every case that turns out well for the petitioner, ten others are sent back to their home country because the petitioner could not afford an attorney or an expert witness like me. Those who are deported without a whisper have equally compelling stories as those in this book. Surely, many of these individuals would have stood the same chance to qualify for residency, but advocacy typically requires money.

All of the immigration attorneys I work with perform a good deal of pro-bono work, as do I. Yet, obviously, there would never be enough of this type of low-cost or free help for those deserving or in dire need of such legal and psychological services. I can only imagine that tens of thousands of such people each year that are not even aware of effective avenues toward legal documentation. The stories of immigrants abused by spouses who are American citizens or legal permanent residents are prime examples. The immigrants' lack of knowledge provides spouses with a weapon of power and abuse in the threat of deportation. This has a particular manifestation among men who pursue the mail-order bride arrangement. They state a preference for submissive wives who want "traditional" marriages as a wife and homemaker. These men are financially secure but pursue relationships where they have full power and control. This is easily obtained by choosing women who come from impoverished or politically unstable areas where women do not have the same educational and employment opportunities as men, and are disempowered by virtue of their legal status in this country. Additionally, a mail-order bride may be more attractive to some men since the potential mates are often younger and less experienced. These women tend to foolishly envision American men as kinder, better husbands who do not cheat on their wives. They become dependent on the man to provide for them financially, and they often live under the threat of being deported by their husbands. Thankfully, the International Marriage Broker Regulation Act of 2005 added safeguards, such as requiring a criminal background check of the potential husband as well as the provision of information to the bride about her legal rights once she arrives in the United States.

Another concern is that illegal immigrants are often prey to the criminal elements in their communities that take advantage of their undocumented status to torment and victimize them. I have heard countless stories from my Hispanic clients about how they or people they know first approached a "Notario" for assistance in their immigration case, only to pay large sums of money for worthless advice. These people will typically be removed forcibly from the United States forthwith, many quickly returning here once again to live in the shadows. These individuals often feel they have no choice but to return illegally to support their families. They slink about and work using false documents, hoping to avoid future entanglements with the system. While this huge undocumented population can legally request protection from police when a crime is committed against them, they rarely do so for fear of being identified and deported. Such individuals seldom step inside their children's schools for the same reasons.

Of course, most of the individuals with whom I perform immigration-related evaluations have found themselves in removal proceedings because they somehow did not follow the rules. Over the years, the legislature in its wisdom has enacted statutes to protect various classes of individuals and to give them a chance at residency. While criminal-types have immigrated to the United States and cause serious problems here, those are not the cases that are referred to me. In the many hundreds of cases that I have accepted, virtually all have involved honest, hard-working people–of "good moral character"–those who clean our homes and offices, wash our cars, mow our lawns, harvest our fruits and vegetables, and prepare our meals. Many are here because they perform the type of "unskilled" manual labor that appears to be undervalued by the immigration system, but not by the employers or purchasers of goods and services. Nevertheless, they have come to the United States because it is the country that promises freedom and opportunity in the pursuit of happiness.

Each individual narrative has implications for the lives that it touches, and immigration is an issue that affects all citizens directly as well as indirectly. It appears that in many recent elections votes are oftentimes cast for one candidate over another as a direct result of a particular politician's stand on the issue of immigration. Once elected, laws then are enacted that create changes in immigration policy, which then directly affects the lives of these people.

However, attitudes have been changing in the recent past and many Americans appear to want undocumented aliens to be allowed a legal path toward residency and citizenship, if not simply a green card so that they can legally continue on with their lives. The 2012 election seemed to be a watershed year for the issue of illegal immigration as the increasingly powerful Latino electorate swayed the results toward certain politicians and parties, including the office of the Presidency of the United States, in accordance with their support for avenues toward legal residency. In the next few years bipartisan efforts are expected to lead to the enactment of laws to make probationary and legal residency possible for millions of people, as well as to overhaul the entire system of immigration in the United States. Both political parties are acutely aware of the implications of their party platforms regarding immigration policy reform.

Just like most everyone else, I look forward to the day when our elected officials can untangle the confusing and conflicting maze inherent in our current set of immigration laws and policies. Sensible solutions are desperately needed that respect the humanity of those who find themselves caught up in our system. From my perspective, the legal definition of "extreme hardship" or "exceptional and extremely unusual hardship" often seems to be a very high bar to cross as the strain on families and individuals, especially innocent children, makes meeting the criteria a daunting challenge. I hope that procedures one day are developed to address the seemingly unjust system currently in place. The narratives included in this book speak loudly in the stories they tell.

Up to this point I have avoided advocating for any immigration policy, either during the course of my career or in the writing of this book. However, I do have a few strong thoughts and feelings about systemic failures that I regularly witness. In particular, I must state emphatically that in my experience most immigrants need not be incarcerated for multiple months while awaiting their hearing date. From my many years of involvement with these honest and decent working people, I can assure you that they will absolutely appear for their court date. Those that request credit from my office for their evaluations can reliably be counted on to make their payments each and every month.

In my strong opinion, it is a travesty of justice for our country to have to incur the enormous financial cost involved in the prolonged and pointless incarceration of these people, not to mention the damage this action inflicts on their American-born children who suffer in their parents' absence. It is not only totally unnecessary, but quite inhumane. I am not speaking here as to the need to protect the community from the criminal element, which most obviously is a necessary thing. But rather, I am appealing to policymakers to consider the wrongfulness of locking up these hard-working people for months on end for no other reason than the fact that they had entered the country illegally to work and find a better life.

Another thought that I would like to share with the reader is that of the inherent unfairness of the child who is brought into this country while still quite young, and the subsequent nightmare of having to live forever in the shadows in fear and poverty. Through no fault of their own, they live as marginalized people –they didn't choose to be brought here. They grow up here just like others, and in all but the legal reality of their status, they are identical in speech, dress and looks. Early on, even their dreams and aspirations are the same as other children. However, as they get older, they begin to realize that they don't have the same ticket of admission to the important facets of life in

America. These children will soon come to understand that they are somehow quite different from their peers.

Living as illusory Americans, these children will continually be punished by the capriciousness of our system. As a former bilingual middle school and high school teacher, it broke my heart to follow my top students as their dreams of a higher education and a career were crushed because they were born on the wrong side of a line. Having to pay the much higher out-of-state college tuition rates because they are "illegal" is simply not an option for most of these great kids. They are therefore relegated to work in minimum wage jobs, typically in the fast-food industry without any benefits. In their simple desire to work they become forced to break the law by using fake documents, and thereby risk everything in doing so.

Twice this past summer I traveled to Northern Baja, Mexico to conduct research into the school system. I was astounded by how many young men I encountered there who had lived in the United States since they were young children, but were deported to Mexico in their 20s and even 30s. These men were literally "men without a country," as they had no other identity than that of being an American, but found themselves living hand-to-mouth in a foreign land. Many had obviously been forced to separate from their families and the only life they had ever known. They appeared confused and defeated, which was understandable and quite sad. These men are much like anyone that you meet here in the United States each day, yet seemed so out of place in the streets of Mexico. They clearly do not fit in there. They oftentimes have no family or any occupational connections, and although born in Mexico, are simply not accepted by the people there. They also encounter tremendous danger and great risk living in a "foreign land;" extortion, violence, and the punishing life of the streets. The gangs and cartels recruit such men, as they have nothing and nowhere to go. To have spent your entire life here in the United States since a toddler, only to suddenly find yourself plopped down in a strange place they know nothing about is like a scene from a science fiction movie.

I would appeal to all reasonable people and policymakers to consider the inexplicable human tragedy and waste of human resources that are byproducts of our current immigration laws. While I certainly don't believe that I have all the answers, these poignant and heartbreaking problems mentioned above seem a terrible injustice. There simply must be other more sensible and humane solutions to solving our immigration dilemma. The purpose of this book, however, is not to offer any concrete solutions for immigration reform.

This book is a collection of a few of the multitude of stories of immigrants and American citizens who face overwhelming odds in bringing some kind of normality into their lives. "Normal" means people can work without the cloud of fear hanging over their heads that at any moment their lives could be turned upside down, or that they could be torn away from their children for an indefinite period of time. In normal life children freely can dream about their future. While all people contend with day-to-day stresses and might also have financial difficulties, their lives at least possess a semblance of order or rhythm. On the other hand, the folks who find themselves entangled in these kinds of immigration cases channel much of their emotional and financial resources into attorneys and protracted court cases rather than into pursuing their aspirations, acquiring useful skills, learning English, or providing a quality of care that they would like for their loved ones. Instead, they struggle simply to be stable and whole and to live safely with whatever loved ones they may have.

I do know that contact with these strong and courageous individuals inspires me; the immigrants as well as their families, including their American-born children and spouses. I would imagine many readers of these stories also have found a bit of inspiration here as well. If nothing else, the people whose lives are highlighted in this book clearly deserve our compassion, for like us, they are human. I would think that after having learned of their experiences and struggles that most would agree these people truly are –The Unenviable.

Dedication

This book is dedicated to all of the individuals and their families who come to this land of liberty and freedom seeking a better life and adding immeasurably to the fabric of our country. My grandparents, coal miner Simo Mirjacic and his wife Andje came to the United States in the 1920's from Montenegro. Simo worked on the Panama Canal and was a Union organizer during the infamous "Ludlow Massacre" in Southern Colorado. My grandmother, "Baba" was honored with the National Mother of the Year award in 1974.

Of their seven children, all of the men were war veterans who went on to earn their graduate degrees and became leaders in their fields. My father, professor and author Dr. John Mirich served in Okinawa and Iwo Jima and was President of the Faculty at Metropolitan State University of Denver. One daughter, Helen has a doctorate and still works at MIT, and the other, the eldest child Mildred was a highly honored volunteer from the state of Wyoming and state Democratic Party Delegate. Pete has an elementary school named after him in LaSalle, Colorado. Nick was Aide to the Governor in Wyoming for 12 years and a long time County Commissioner. Guy was a Colonel in the Air Force, and Daniel was an All-American Football player and USAF Jet Fighter Pilot. He became a Vice

President for Hewlett Packard and later a successful entrepreneur.

These men and women set a standard for excellence and exemplary citizenship for their children and grandchildren who have all gone on to pursue their own successful paths in life, thanks to having such wonderful role models –the children of illiterate peasants from the "old country."

I would like to thank my former assistant Cecilia Ramirez for her unique skills and support in assembling this book. It would not have been possible without her. Mary Tradii provided superb assistance in content development and the editing process. Jim Salvator and Dr. Roy Aranda provided invaluable support and keen intellect in looking over the final drafts of the book. Finally, I would like to thank my publisher Derek Vasconi for believing in this book and guiding it through to completion.

About The Author

David G. Mirich, PhD, is a psychologist in private practice and has long specialized in assessments used for immigration court proceedings. He is a fully bilingual Spanish speaker and conducts all of his evaluations without the need for an interpreter. Dr. Mirich also performs a variety of other types of forensic evaluations, including those used in criminal court cases, fitness for duty evaluations, and in cases dealing with victims and trauma. Additionally, Dr. Mirich specializes in conducting neuropsychological evaluations on individuals with brain injuries, learning disorders, severe mental illness, and issues of aging or dementia.

To contact Dr. Mirich about his practice or inquire as to his availability for speaking engagements or other services, he may be contacted through his website at www.Pathscenter.com, or by email at Dmirich@pathscenter.com

Made in the USA
Middletown, DE
06 September 2024

60497282R00285